3.15.78

THE RELUCTANT EUROPEANS

The Attitudes of the Nordic Countries towards European Integration

TOIVO MILJAN

McGILL-QUEEN'S UNIVERSITY PRESS
Montreal 1977

First published in the United Kingdom by
C. Hurst & Co. (Publishers) Ltd., London

Published in North America by
McGill-Queen's University Press, Montreal

© 1977 by Toivo Miljan

ISBN 0–7735–0293–9

Legal Deposit 2nd Quarter 1977
Bibliothèque Nationale du Québec

Printed in Great Britain by offset lithography
by Billing & Sons Limited,
Guildford, London and Worcester.

CONTENTS

PREFACE

This book is about the Nordic countries' relations with an integrating Europe during the three decades since the Second World
War. I have attempted to analyze the attitudes that underlie
these relations as they are conditioned by history, politics,
economics and the Cold War. An examination of the data leads me
to conclude that Denmark, Finland, Norway and Sweden have been
reluctant to approach Europe closely and have regarded themselves
as forming a region apart from Europe. It is only during the
1960's that increasing economic independence among themselves
and between themselves and Western Europe led to the realization of the necessity of coming to some form of accomodation
with the European Economic Community. The first to realize
this was Denmark, the last Finland.

There are four different sets of policies in the Nordic
countries on the question of European economic integration and
these are the result of four different sets of circumstances and
perceptions of external demands and internal requirements relating to security and political and economic questions.
Nevertheless, all four countries have placed sovereign independence as the over-riding objective. The demands of eco-
omic interdependence have been recognized, but have been
placed within the primary demands of sovereign independence.
The desire to conserve the nation in the form of independent
sovereign nation-state has produced reluctant Europeans of the
Nordic countries.

For encouraging my interest in the Nordic countries and in
European integration I am grateful to Professor Karl Aun of
Wilfrid Laurier University. The book was originally written
as a dissertation in the Faculty of Laws, University College
London, for the Faculty of Economics, University of London, in
the preparation of which Dr. John W. Burton provided unspa-
ringly of time, patience and valuable criticism. In gathering
the material for the book I received the assistance of scores

of senior diplomats and civil servants in the Nordic countries. Many academics in the Nordic countries generously spent hours in discussing various topics with me. Canadian ambassadors to the Nordic countries arranged for several series of interviews with Nordic politicians and officials. I am indebted to all of them, and to my colleagues Karl Aun and Nicolas Nyiri for their comments and criticisms in the preparation of the manuscript. For what appears in these pages I alone am responsible. Unless otherwise indicated, all quotations from Nordic sources have been translated by me.

I am very grateful to the Canada Council and to my University for their financial assistance for the research leading to this book. For a meticulous job of typing the manuscript through repeated revisions I am most grateful to Arvis Oxland, Doris McPhee, and Angie Sirois, and in particular to Judie DeGuire.

Wilfrid Laurier University
Waterloo, Ontario
December 1976.

CHAPTER 1. INTRODUCTION

1. The Integration of Europe

Among the political, security, economic and cultural considerations which help to explain the erratic progress of integration in Europe during the three decades since the Second World War there is a value attached to globalism, regionalism and subregionalism. Globalism manifests itself in two ways in western Europe. In the core states of the United Kingdom, France and West Germany it is expressed as a desire to continue exerting, or to regain, a dominant role at the global level, either through the continued shouldering of the "white man's burden" in the non-industrialized world -- whether through military, political or economic activity is unimportant -- or through a central role in international world organizations such as the United Nations and its agencies. In the peripheral states of Austria, Finland, Sweden, Norway, Denmark and Switzerland it manifests itself mainly in political and development assistance activity through international organizations -- mainly the United Nations and its agencies -- on behalf of the Third World.

Both versions of globalism, but particularly the latter, contain large doses of idealism, born of the frustrations of the 1930s and the experience of the war years. The idealism of peace through world cooperation was frustrated by the Cold War antagonism between the Soviet Union and the United States. This, however, disrupted the euphoria of the immediate post-war years and brought a measure of realism to world relations. Quite naturally it also reawakened the self-interest of powers both large and small. It is this self-interest that has led the world to move towards greater cooperation, not on a schedule determined by idealistic programming, but on pragmatic considerations necessitated by the inexorable demands of mutual self-interest produced by an ever-growing technological interdependence.

In western Europe the competitive fusion of the ideal with the utilitarian produced a situation where on the one hand there was European cooperation, and on the other hand European nations and groups attempted to compete with each other, and with the overarching region of Europe. Thus we have the appearance of the region of Europe: one of minimal cooperation in the Organization of European Economic Cooperation, and in the Council of Europe. At the same time we have the appearance of the Europe of regions, of the Benelux countries, of the Nordic region, of the Communities and of the British Isles.

The first to recognize the absurdity of sub-regionalism within a region was the Benelux group, but only after the core states of France, Italy and West Germany decided to integrate their coal and steel production in the new European Coal and Steel Community. When the idealistic European Defence Community failed, a compromise organization -- the Western European Union -- attempted to bridge the gap between the three core countries and the fourth natural core member, the United Kingdom, but failed again. When finally in 1961 the United Kingdom realized the absurdity of its position and attempted to take its rightful position within the core, the EEC members had become sufficiently self-centred to exclude it. Hence it was not until the end of the 1960s that the Community members and the United Kingdom, for selfish reasons of economic advantage, decided to enlarge the Community.

The Nordic subregion has adhered to the strangest combination of regionalism of all. On the one hand the Nordic countries have made attempts at closer cooperation among themselves: successfully, in 1953, by means of organizing the Nordic Council, and a Nordic Economic Union, unsuccessfully three times over a period of twenty years, while at the same time they have adhered to the concept of minimal pan-West European regional cooperative activity. The Nordic countries still appear to adhere to this minimialism of Europe as a region, even at the beginning of their necessary and inevitable integration into the region of Europe that is represented by the European Community.

In retrospect, it is clear that once the core states of France, West Germany and Italy had determined to form a region of Europe from the Europe of regions, the United Kingdom would in time have to adhere to the concept. And once all four had accepted the new structure, then it was inevitable that the peripheral states would have to participate. But participation for core countries is always much easier than for peripheral states, because power capacity and geographical location allow them to disregard extra-regional forces in their regional ar-rangements, whereas the peripheral states are much more exposed to extra-regional political demands. This is particularly true of the peripheral states of Austria, Switzerland, Sweden and Finland. Sweden and Finland, as well as Norway and Denmark, have developed during the past quarter-century a global political thrust to provide a platform which their peripheral and exposed position denies them in Europe.

As for particularistic gloablism engaged in by the four core states, the twenty-year period from 1947 to 1968 saw disengage-ment by all of them from their primary overseas activities and a withdrawal into Europe. In contrast, the latter half of the period has seen increasing cooperation among them in utilitarian international extra-European activities. The future, if the operation of the Davignon inspired Political Committee of offi-cials and regional meetings of ministers of the Nine are to be considered as a weather-vane of things to come, will see increas-ing integration of Europe's extra-regional international activity.[1]

The three decades since the end of the Second World War have seen the euphoric intent of world cooperation in the interests of continuing peace move towards utilitarian globalism and a utilitarian regional activity within Europe, which is moving toward a region of Europe that is slowly becoming not a collection of cooperating powers, but a single major world power, though as yet not an integrated and united one.

2. The Nordic Countries and European Integration

The main determinants of the various positions that the four countries have taken on the European question are, first, security and, secondly, economics. Both have external and internal components, but to varying degrees in each of the four states. In the security determinant the external factor is the post-war balance of power condition and the particular state's political position; the internal factor is the particular state's perception of its role in the security system and the attempt to maximize independence. In the economic determinant, the external factor has two components: the first is the restructuring of the conditions of international trade at the instigation of the principal trading nations; and the second consists of the market control activities, either on a regional or unilateral basis, by the main trading partners. Similarly the internal factor may be divided into two component parts: the internal perception of the effects that the external rearrangements may have on the internal economic growth and wellbeing of the particular country; and the constraints that the internal socio-political and economic structures place on the particular Nordic country's ability to adapt to the external changes.

The security determinant has remained relatively constant throughout the period under review, but the factors in the economic determinant have changed considerably and rapidly

---

[1]This can be seen in the "caucusing" of the Nine at the U.N., NATO, CSCE, MBFR and the Tokyo round of GATT meetings.

throughout the period. Indeed, the two sets of factors originated out of phase. The security factors came to a head for all four Nordic countries in 1946-52 during the period of systemic metamorphosis from war-time anti-fascist alliance to antagonistic Cold War bipolarity. The basic positions taken by the four at that time, though changing according to the conditions of the international security system, have remained stable within the locus of the original decision.

In contrast, the factors in the economic determinant have been relatively unstable, having followed a sequence of development largely unrelated to the changing security system. They have gone through four phases. The first post-war reconstruction phase was completed by the beginning of the 1950s; this was followed by a period of internal growth and economic modernization during the 1950s; the trade liberalization phase overlapped both the previous and the following period; the fourth phase involved the development of the European Communities and took place from the late 1950s through to the early 1970s. Though each of the four Nordic countries went through the above phases, each was affected differently both in substantive terms and in terms of time frames, as a result of the differing relationships between the internal and external economic factors and the differing national perceptions of these factors.

The greatest challenges faced by all four have arisen during the latter phases: trade liberalization and the development of the European Economic Community. During this period four categories of variables, which have affected the Nordic countries' internal arguments and external responses to the "European" challenge, may be discerned: The first is the markets variable, which is a purely economic variable, its importance being derived from the fact that, despite changing national and international economic conditions, between one-fifth and one-quarter of the GDPs of the four Nordic countries have been generated by exports. Its importance is further compounded by the fact that the share of foreign markets in the GDP has tended to increase in three of the four countries. The second variable, again basically econ-

omic but with political overtones is that of economic integration: a *de facto* integration of the Nordic economies with their
principal trade partners has been taking place, in particular
during the 1960s. This has occurred primarily as a result of
division of labour and economies of scale in the industrial
sector in all the Nordic countries. The third variable is the
political dependence-independence, or "sovereignty", argument
which has played a role in the politics of the economics of
Europe in three of the four countries, as a result partly of the
economic integration variable and partly of the peculiar political union overtones of the European Economic Community's
teleology. Fourthly, there is the category of national values
and objectives.

Clearly there are many values and objectives in democratic
societies, but for the Nordic countries the overriding one is
that of sovereign independence of the political, social and
economic systems represented by the concept "nation-state". When
the question of sovereignty arises, the question of security is
also inevitably present. In the case of the Nordic countries the
security question may be expressed in a two-dimensional continuum, with one dimension expressing minimum to maximum value
placed on security by the members of the nation, and another
continuum representing the implicit to explicit expression of
that value in political-social debate. The position that a
particular state occupies on the two continua helps to explain
the interpretation placed on the dominant value and objective of
sovereign independence. Denmark, for example, has a minimalist
position on the question of security, which furthermore occupies
an implicit and covert position, rather than a central and public
one, in political discourse. Hence the value and objective of
sovereignty is publicly expressed as "the viability of the Danish
way of life" and is supported by both economic and socio-political values. It should be noted that these values were in
conflict throughout the market debates of the 1960s and early
1970s.

For Norway the security question is located somehwere in the middle of both continua with a tendency to maximize in the first continuum and a tendency to implicitness in the second. The result has been an interpretation of the primary value and objective of sovereignty, perhaps best expressed as "the preservation or conservation of the Norwegian way of life". This attitude has permitted considerable latitude for the different socio-economic groups in Norway to present their particular interpretations of the Norwegian way of life. The two sets of values which conflicted consistently throughout the debate of the challenge of the European Communities were those of economic wellbeing and growth on the one hand, and socio-cultural values on the other.

In the case of Sweden the security question throughout the period under review has been at the maximal and the explicit ends of the continua. The result has been that the Swedish view of the value and purpose of sovereignty, in public debate and in policy position, has been consistently interpreted as "the maximization of political independence". The maximization of political independence has become so "sacred" that all other values are almost automatically subordinated to it. Hence the values of economic wellbeing and growth have in general acted in such a way as to support, rather than conflict with, the social, cultural and political values of independence.

In the case of Finland, the security question is of maximum importance and its public expression is more implicit than explicit -- with the result that the Finnish interpretation of the value and objective of sovereignty may be expressed as "reason of state". In other words, the value of security is so overriding that no other values, however important, are allowed to interfere with the operation of security. Hence, the challenges of trade liberalization and of the European Economic Community came late to Finland and were handled largely by political sleight of hand at the official level, without much public debate taking place.

It is against the background of the European scenario and within the constraints of the four sets of variables outlined above that the "politics of the economics of Europe" have been played in the four Nordic countries during the three decades since the Second World War.

To analyze these developments this study is functionally divided into three parts: chapters 2 and 3 establish the security and trade perimeters of the Nordic countries' relations with Europe; chapters 4-6 outline the various Nordic responses to the economic challenges of Europe up to the first round of EEC negotiations; and, chapters 7-9 trace the four countries' negotiations with the EEC and analyse these within the framework of each country's internal and external needs and policies.

More specifically, chapter 2 outlines the structural components of the Nordic security problem, including the differing geographic positions, historical backgrounds and national perceptions of external security demands and internal requirements to meet them. The chapter describes the calculation of differing perspectives of strategy that the four countries have had to contend with since the formation of NATO in 1949, and analyzes the security policies devised to meet the threat to security. The objective in this chapter is to show why security considerations play the primary role in policy determination in the Nordic countries, whether this is explicitly acknowledged (Sweden and Finland) or not (Denmark and Norway). The objective in chapter 3 is to show the importance of trade to the Nordic countries, and the changes that took place in the structure of direction of their trade with the main trading areas between 1950 and 1970, the period during which the European integration challenge arose and had to be met by each Nordic country.

Chapter 4 traces the parallel development of an inward-looking Scandinavianism culminating in the formation of the Nordic Council, largely as a result of external "Europeanist" influences and challenges. It is suggested that the way in which Nordic solidarity has been maintained despite diverse security and political pressures on the four countries is through the operation of the politics of the Nordic consensus. The initial response of the Nordic countries to the challenge of European integration was to support a free trade arrangement for western Europe. Chapters 5 and 6 trace developments surrounding the Wide Free Trade Area and European Free Trade Association negotiations and analyse the positions taken by the four Nordic countries during the negotiations. It is discovered that Denmark, though anxious to come to an accommodation with Europe, had to contend internally with political cleavages that arose out of the structure of its economy -- a combination of a highly competitive agricultural industry needing no tariff protection and an inefficient manufacturing industry hiding behind non-tariff barriers. In Norway and Sweden there was general agreement among the different sectors of the economy and among the political parties that joining the WFTA was necessary, but that joining the EEC was out of the question. Finland, because of the suspicion with which the Soviet Union regarded the entire European integration process, remained aloof from the WFTA discussions and did not enter the negotiations until the final stages of the formation of EFTA.

In chapter 7 the course of Danish policy on membership of the EEC is traced from the late 1950s to the successful accession to membership in 1972. The interaction of political and economic factors in the development and conduct of this policy is analysed against the background of the framework of Danish foreign policy, the Danish economy and internal interest politics. The latter eventually led to the necessity to hold a constitutionally binding referendum on the ratification of the treaty of accession to membership of the EEC. It is discovered that throughout the decade and a half of the EEC question, while economic considerations dictated ever more insistently the necessity of full membership of the EEC, popular fear of the political and cultural impact of membership also increased. These were the main grounds on which the battle between the pro- and anti-market forces, culminating in the referendum of 2 October 1972, was fought. The analysis of the unsuccessful Norwegian bid to join the EEC, in chapter 8, is similar in structure to that of the Danish bid. The Norwegian economy and polity is, however, structured differently from the Danish. The Norwegian economy has not been as dependent on commodity exports as the Danish; but the persistent imbalance of imports over exports has been covered by the large foreign exchange earnings of the ocean shipping industry. Politically, in contrast to Denmark where there tends to be an integration of interests, the tendency in Norway is for interests to be differentiated on a regional basis. Hence there is an urban-rural split, and an industrial-agricultural cleavage of interests, in addition to the ideological left-right cleavage and the standard socio-economic cleavages. Moreover, nationalism in Norway has a much more xenophobic character than in Denmark or any of the other Nordic countries. In large parts of Norwegian society there is an ingenuous conviction that Norway, because of its moral, democratic, libertarian and egalitarian society, constitutes the world's most pleasant social, economic and political system. The conjunction of these factors produced a decade of debate in which the foreign policy and export-oriented industrial and shipping élites argued in favour of EEC membership along with the United Kingdom, while the "masses" and their leaders argued in favour of national sovereignty. It was the emphasis on sovereignty that led to a parliamentary accord early in the EEC question that a consultative referendum should be held, and eventually to an undertaking by the Government to abide by the decision of the referendum. The referendum was lost as a result of a centre-periphery conflict with cross-cutting cleavages in five socio-economic sectors, including social status, educational level, age and income, between the EEC supporters concentrated in the urban centres and the opponents spread about the non-industrialized parts of the country.

In contrast to the Danish and Norwegian debates about membership of the EEC, which centred on economic and national sovereignty questions, the Swedish debates -- discussed in chapter 9 -- revolved around the question of how to become a full member without the political obligations of full membership. The question for Sweden throughout the decade of the EEC applications was _how_ to react to the impending appearance of a big trade bloc composed of almost all Sweden's trading partners, including the old Six, the United Kingdom and Norway and Denmark, which were expected to join the Community should the British negotiations prove successful; and not whether to react. Over the decade an increasing consensus developed that full membership of the EEC would be incompatible with Sweden's cherished independence based on its policy of neutrality. For the policy of neutrality to have credibility under conditions of increasing functional economic integration -- which has been proceeding apace since the 1960s -- Sweden must consistently make it clear to the outside world that its economic policy decisions are always made independently by Swedish authorities and are never based on any prior external commitments. Though the Government adhered to this policy firmly throughout the decade of negotiations with the EEC, commercial and industrial interests pressed the economic arguments for full -- or at least associate -- membership to the limit. They were able to do this by ignoring the political arguments and in presenting the economic interests in stark and simple terms: because the export sector generates such a large part of the national income and employs such a large proportion of the Swedish labour force, it was imperative that Sweden should associate in some way with the EEC, preferably as a full member, in order to avert the inevitable disaster of economic stagnation, including a falling standard of living, which non-adherence to the Treaty of Rome would eventually bring about. However, the economic pro-EEC drive did little more than underscore the generally recognized fact of life, well understood at the level of partisan political activity, that Sweden is a trading nation dependent for its high standard of living in no small measure on easy access to West European markets. But because politics in Sweden operates on the basis of consensus rather than brokerage, and because decision-making tends to be centralized within Parliament where the different political parties present their views after processing the inputs of their supporting interest groups through a "filter of responsibility", a consensus developed on what was possible to safeguard Sweden's economic interests within the requirements of the policy of neutrality. The opposition political parties did not oppose for the sake of opposing; they tended to argue variations of the national consensus. From this the Government drew a further consensus, which became stated national policy in 1971: Sweden was not going to accede formally to any economic or political integration with the EEC, but would pursue a non-political free trade agreement, and would coordinate its economic policies with those of the EEC insofar as the demands for credibility of the policy of neutrality permitted.

While Swedes think in terms of maximizing independent policy options, Finns think in terms of the preservation of the very existence of the state itself. In the Finnish view this depends on Soviet security perceptions and Soviet goodwill. Neutrality is regarded as a political necessity, the only possible response to Soviet demands for security, and therefore the only possible safeguard of sovereignty. Because the Soviet Union regarded the EEC with mistrust, and because there was uncertainty as to whether the EEC would be expanded, Finland bided its time and did not react at all during the first and second rounds of application. By 1970, however, it had become clear that the EEC was indeed going to be expanded, and that Finland would be faced with two foreign trade problems. On the one hand, two of Finland's leading trade partners, Britain and Denmark, had decided to enter the enlarged EEC; and on the other, two of its leading competitors in trade with the Common Market, Sweden and Norway, were about to either enter or to negotiate an arrangement to penetrate the tariff walls of the Community. During the next two years the Finnish President engaged in extensive discussions with the Soviet Union to convince the latter of the necessity for Finnish accommodation with the EEC. By November 1971 the Soviets had apparently been sufficiently convinced of the necessity of Finland making an approach to the EEC for Finland to be able to put in its application for a free trade agreement. Formal negotiations took slightly over half a year and the free trade agreement between the EEC and Finland was initialled in July

1972. At the same time Finland opened negotiations with the Comecon on an agreement in principle for cooperation which was initialled in the spring of 1973. That Finland was not able to ratify the EEC agreement formally until 5 October 1973 was the result of an internal conflict on an unrelated economic problem in which the free trade agreement became enmeshed to provide partisan political leverage.

The final chapter concludes that the three decades since the Second World War have seen a considerable increase in intra-Nordic interactions and interactions between the Nordic and West European countries -- both conducive to integration. However, the period has not seen any transfer of authority from the national parliaments to a regional authority in the Nordic area, nor has it seen any willing transfer of authority from a national parliament to any international or supranational authority. What has taken place is a minimal transfer, to NATO in the case of Norway and Denmark, and to the EEC in the case of Denmark, given both the desire for retention of optimal sovereign independence, and the increasing functional pressures for interdependence of security and economic interests. The desire to conserve the nation in the form of a sovereign independent state has produced not only reluctant Europeans, but reluctant Nordics of the Nordic countries.

CHAPTER 2. SECURITY

The hallmark of the international system since the seventeenth
century has been the concept of sovereignty. This has always
meant that states do not recognize the authority of any other
state within their own territorial boundaries, and that they have
the right to keep standing military forces to reinforce the
reality of the concept. To this core two circumscriptions have
been added over the years. The first is international law, which
in its normal operation restricts the unfettered exercise of
sovereignty by any given state. The second is the reality of
power, the exercise of which by the larger intrudes on the
sovereignty of the smaller members of the system. It is the
tendency of larger powers to extend their influence and authority
beyond their sovereign territories, and the smaller states' fear
of foreign intrusion into their sovereignties, that constitutes
the problem of security.

1. The Problem of Security

The problem of security arises as soon as one state fears that
another state or other states may intrude into its sovereignty,
regardless of the correctness or incorrectness of the perception,
or of the immediacy of the perceived fact.

The security problem may have a variety of causative factors. In the Nordic region it is possible to identify at least five such determinants: geography, history, technology, international politics, and culture. Of these, history and culture may be regarded as fixed factors while international politics, geography and technology must be considered as independent variables to which the Nordic countries must react. The dominant factor is that of international politics, followed by geography and technology. It is international politics which creates the conditions of fear in the first place; it is geography which determines the direction of fear; and, it is technology which determines the magnitude of the fear. History and culture act in a supportive fashion, either as reinforcements or detractors of the fear. All five factors are out of the direct control of the Nordic countries themselves, for the simple reason that they have had small power status since the end of the Napoleonic wars. This despite the fact that since 1945 Sweden, Norway and Finland have occupied the third, fourth and fifth positions in the physical size of European states after France and Spain but excluding the Soviet Union! The small power status of the four countries of the region may also be shown by a comparison of the population and Gross National Product levels of the area with that of Canada, the western world's largest country in physical size but also a small power: whereas in 1970 the Canadian population numbered 22 million and the Gross National Product reached $100,000 million, the total population of the four Nordic countries reached barely 21 million and the combined GNP was only $37,000 million. In contrast the six EEC countries of western Europe formed a population pool of 150 million with a combined GNP of $400,000 million. Moreover the Soviet Union had a population of 220 million with a GNP of $680,000 million, and the United States a population of 220 million and a GNP of $1,000 million. Such comparisons, besides demonstrating the relative small power status of the Nordic region, also illustrate a basic security problem: the discrepancy between physical size and the relative power weakness, at least as indicated by the two power-indexes of population and GNP.

Considerations of relative power size were of little importance for the Nordic region during the period between 1809, when
Sweden ceded Finland to Russia and made peace with it, and 1940,
when one of the great powers of the day, Germany, invaded Denmark
and Norway. For most of the intervening century and a quarter,
the Nordic countries were left largely undisturbed by the conflicts of the great powers because of their relative weakness and
the small power status of the area. Geographical remoteness,
compounded by technological backwardness in communications and
transportation, added to the relative unimportance of the region
to the great powers. Thus, for example, in the the First World
War, three of the four countries -- Finland remained under
Russian suzerainty until 6 December 1917 -- were able to declare
neutrality and remain largely, though not completely, outside the
conflict.

In the Second World War, however, despite similar declara-
tions of neutrality, all except Sweden became directly involved
in the military conflict between the Allies and Germany because
of their strategic importance to Germany in the fulfilment of its
military objectives. In addition, Finland became embroiled with
the Soviet Union, and with Germany, because of the defensive
needs of the former and the offensive strategy of the latter.
Technological developments in communications and in aerial and
naval warfare had removed the protection of geographical remoteness. Small power status had changed from an asset, in that it
did not provide a threat to large powers, to a liability, in that
it appeared to permit easy conquest.

The Second World War conclusively demonstrated their small
power status to the Nordic countries, the end of the possibility
of isolationism, and their subjection to the international
system. The political and economic activities of the four states
have since 1945 become dominated by the requirements of the
international system to the extent that even internal influences
in their foreign economic and political policy-making have been
reduced to searching for optimal adaptation solutions. Indeed,

the system domination of the external activities of the four
countries has been so strong that it has determined even the
intra-regional arrangements among them.

In the field of security the euphoria of the first two
postwar years was quickly shattered by the antagonism between the
United States and the Soviet Union, the two new great powers of
the system. As this antagonism developed into the Cold War in
1947-9 and resulted in the organization of two security systems
splitting Europe in half, each operating as buffers in the
interests of the two poles, the Nordic countries again felt the
fear of external intrusion into their sovereignties, this time by
powers stronger than Germany had ever been. Their initial
reaction was an attempt to form a neutral but armed alliance. It
was thought that the Nordic countries could isolate themselves
from the concerns of the great power interests through a declaration of non-involvement backed up by the power to make intrusion
into the area very costly. Though the idea was attractive in
1948 and might have been realized had the Nordic countries then
possessed the technological and industrial capability to arm
themselves, by the beginning of the following decade, when the
Soviet Union achieved thermo-nuclear capability, the ability of
the proposed alliance to enforce a position of non-involvement
with the bipolar world would have been drastically reduced.
Nevertheless, the basic idea of non-involvement has persisted in
the region, though in much modified form, as demonstrated by the
Finnish and Swedish policies of neutrality and the Norwegian and
Danish positions of semi-neutrality.

In the event, both the failure of the proposed Nordic
defence union and the arrangements made by Norway and Denmark to
join the Western alliance were dictated from Washington and
Moscow. But it was the differing perceptions of threat, as
conditioned by different geographic, historical and technologi-
cal-industrial positions of the three Scandinavian countries,
that produced the reaction which settled the outcome of the
Nordic alliance-making attempt. Finland was at this time a
virtual prisoner of Soviet foreign policy and was unable to play

any direct role in Nordic politics until 1955. This, however, did not mean that its position was not taken into account, particularly by Sweden and Norway in their policy making.

2. The Calculations of Security: 1949-1975

There is a considerable difference between the political and the strategic perspectives in the Nordic region. Whereas strategic positions are based on 1) calculations of positioning one's military forces during the period of peace in as advantageous a position as possible *vis-à-vis* those of the opponent in preparation for the outbreak of hostilities, and 2) the expansion of one's defensive perimeters as far from the centre as possible and as close to the opponent's centre as possible, political positions are based on calculations of freedom of manoeuvre in peacetime to expand one's authority/influence and to solve problems without encroaching on the perceived vital interests of one's opponent. Hence it is in the interests of both parties to a potential conflict, including the two superpowers in the bipolar strategic and political conflict, to reduce conflict-building tension by either unilaterally or bilaterally withdrawing from positions of direct confrontation and building neutral or at least semi-neutral buffer zones. That both the superpowers have considered political calculations to be at least as important as military strategic calculations within the Nordic region is aptly demonstrated by the Soviet Union's relations with Finland during the thirty years since the Second World War (these relations are political-psychological and economic, and not military-strategic); and by the willingness on the American side to permit both Norway and Denmark -- which occupy nine-tenths of the periphery of its orbit in the northern region -- to remain effectively neutral in peacetime. The Americans have signified this willingness by acquiescing in the two countries' refusal to permit the stationing of foreign troops or nuclear warheads on their soil without an outbreak of hostilities. But it must also be pointed out that political strategy and military strategy are definitely not separable in bipolar systemic calculations.

Indeed it may be argued with some plausibility that in a bipolar
system a continuum exists, not so much between war and peace as
between military and political strategy. In the contemporary
world the superpowers attempt to outwit each other primarily by
political shadowboxing rather than by military deployment, as in
the period up to the Second World War, and use economic and
military power to buttress their political manoeuvres. In the
bipolar system it does not make much sense to concentrate on
either the political or the military, or even the economic,
separately: they must all be looked at concurrently.

Since the security relationships of the Nordic countries are
determined by strategic and political objectives of the two
poles, it is necessary to consider these briefly. A comprehensive listing of specific strategies that the two power blocs need
to take into consideration in evaluating the importance of the
Nordic countries to their particular ends reveals five sets: 1)
nuclear-strategic, 2) nuclear-tactical, 3) conventional, 4) the
grey area, and 5) peace. These, naturally enough, centre on the
two areas where the Western and Eastern orbits of power inter-
sect -- the North Cap, and the Baltic Straits.[1] Of course, the
five do not apply equally to the areas of focus. And the peace
consideration does not apply to either side because neither
consistently thinks of political configurations about the two
foci in which military strategies are absent, though from time to
time strictly political strategies are used. Insofar as the
Baltic Straits are concerned, the strategic nuclear consideration
is absent because both sides agree that strategic nuclear installations in Denmark, the two Germanies and Poland would be indefensible because they could easily be obliterated by accurate

---

[1]The term North Cap is the English version of the Scandina-
vian term *Nordkalotten*. It denotes the area north of the
Arctic Circle and includes the Norwegian province of Finnmark,
Swedish and Finnish Lapland, and the Kola Peninsula in the
Soviet Union. The term Baltic Straits denotes the many narrows
between Sweden, the Danish islands and the Jutland Peninsula.
The three main straits are the Sound (Öresund), shared between
Sweden and Denmark, the Great Belt, separating the Danish
islands of Sjealland and Fyn, and the Little Belt, separating Fyn
and Jutland.

short-range missiles and, in any case, the ICBM and the SLBM make
it unnecessary to take risks which may lead to instability
through the placement of strategic nuclear weapons close to a
belligerent's heartland, as was the case in the Cuban missile
crisis. To some extent similar considerations apply in the North
Cap area, though only on the Western side, since the Soviet Union
has at least two batteries of IRBM missiles south of Murmansk.
Apart from these qualifications the strategies of security in the
two areas of focus are remarkably similar. And we are left with
three sets of strategies, the tactical-nuclear, the conventional
and the so-called grey area. Of these, the grey area, called by
the Danes *grå niveau* -- by which is meant "the condition between
war and peace which is characterized by a period of tensions
where military strategy is used without the actual engagement of
military forces, and where political pressures are supported by
military activities however indirectly" -- is the most important.[2]

An analysis of Warsaw Pact/NATO bloc strategies falls
naturally into two categories, that of aims and that of means.
The aims may be divided into three: the regional, the European
and the systemic. Insofar as any of the aims require Danish,
Swedish or Norwegian territory for their fulfilment, the means
may also be divided into three: naval and air transit, the
opening and closing of the naval door between the Baltic and the
North Seas and the Barents and the Norwegian Seas, and Danish and
Norwegian territory as a beachhead for further attack and/or a
forward base in the defensive perimeter. Hence there are three
levels of aims, three sets of means and three sets of strategies
to consider.

2.1 The Regional Level

Beginning with the lowest level of aims, let us look at the relationship between means and strategies. Should the Warsaw Pact

---

[2]*Problemer Omkring Dansk Sikkerhedspolitik*, Vol. 1 (Copenhagen, 1970), p. 261.

wish to dominate the Nordic area through conventional war, it would be to its advantage to close the Danish Straits and the air corridor over Denmark to NATO aircraft. At the same time, though, the Soviet Union would face the problem of access to the open sea for its own shipping and naval vessels stationed in the Baltic. But in order to close the straits, the Warsaw Pact countries would have not only to control Danish territory but to extend control over the Skagerrak and Kattegat and ensure that the Swedish coastline bordering these seas and the Sound remain free from enemy control. The easiest way to do this would be to invade southern Sweden and southern Norway and, having invaded the latter it would be in the Soviet interest to secure all of Norway, including the North Cap area, to deny NATO bases in Norway from which to attack Warsaw Pact troops in the south. The question now, however, is no longer limited to the region, but has already been extended into the North Sea, which means Europe, and indeed the systemic level because of attack on a neutral and on two NATO countries. Although the Soviet Union and the Warsaw Pact have the capability to carry out such an action, the enormous manpower and cost required for this would be completely disproportionate to the advantages gained: preventing NATO intrusion into the Baltic and keeping it open to Soviet shipping and air activities, at the price of involving Europe and the United States-NATO in war. The answer to the question whether a campaign would be fought with conventional or tactical nuclear weapons depends on both NATO and Soviet willingness to use nuclear weaponry, on NATO and/or Soviet fears of escalation, on the success of the respective blocs in the battle over Danish/Swedish/Norwegian territory, and on the speed with which the campaign is carried out. Denmark, Sweden and Norway have no say in the matter since none possesses nuclear weapons.

Although the scenario is fanciful in the 1970s, it was realistic in the immediate post-war years. Moreover, it was underscored by the race between the Soviet Union and the Western Allies to liberate Denmark from Nazi occupation, and by the brief Soviet occupation of Bornholm. Danish and Norwegian membership

of NATO, however, made the scenario highly unlikely. The reason
for this is twofold. First, Danish territory is of little
importance for NATO at the regional level unless, of course, NATO
wishes to control the Baltic Sea or has objectives of conquest in
the littoral states. Neither objective, however, is realistic,
since none of the major NATO countries has interests in the
Baltic, with the possible exception of West Germany which could
conceivably wish to expand its control over East Germany and to
the former German territories in Poland. The North Cap area is
also of relatively little importance for Norway at the regional
level, unless NATO intends to invade Finland and attack the
Soviet Union. That neither of these objectives has even been
mooted by NATO is shown by the miniscule Norwegian military presence in the Finnmark and the absence of any foreign NATO troops
in Norway.

2.2 The European Level

It is at the European level of hostilities that the analyses of
and preparations for a defence of Danish, Norwegian and Swedish
territories have been concentrated during the quarter-century
since the formation of the bipolar system. It is at this level
that control of Danish and Norwegian territories would play a
strategic role, for the three means listed above: 1) naval and
air transit; 2) denial of this to the enemy; and 3) a beachhead
and/or forward defence perimeter. The scenario would unfold as
follows. There would be either a concentrated attack by the
Warsaw Pact on the central front, and/or a simultaneously amphibious attack on the North Cap, moving south to cut off trans-
Atlantic supply lines through the Norwegian Sea and the North
Sea, and to establish a beachhead at the northern continental
flank. In both cases Danish and Norwegian territory would prove
crucial. On the one hand, occupation of these areas would deny
NATO access to the Warsaw Pact's northern flank, and on the
other, the occupation of Denmark would ensure supply lines in the
Baltic Sea to support the central front. Another advantage to
Warsaw Pact occupation of Danish and Norwegian territory would be

the establishment of a beachhead from which to attack the United Kingdom and NATO's western continental flank.

Then again, as in the regional case, it would be necessary for the Warsaw Pact to occupy southern Sweden in addition to southern Norway in order to ensure domination of not only Danish territory but the Kattegat and Skagerrak. Such action, however, because of Denmark's and Norway's adherence to NATO, would immediately involve the whole of NATO and would escalate the conflict to the systemic level.

For NATO, Denmark's and Norway's geographic locations are equally important. From the defensive point of view, these provide NATO with a continuous line of defence against Warsaw Pact penetration from the Baltic into the North Sea and from the Barents Sea into the Norwegian Sea. Sweden in this regard is less important because of the narrowness of the Skagerrak and the possibility of a naval line of defence there. Nevertheless, in Danish, Norwegian and other analyses of a possible Soviet attack on Denmark and southern Norway, Sweden is included as a target for the Warsaw Pact.[3] In the totalling up of capabilities, Western analysts include Swedish forces in the Western column, though only insofar as defence of Swedish territories is concerned. Moreover, although there are no ties whatever between Sweden and NATO, informal consultations among Swedish, Danish and Norwegian military establishments take place as a matter of course within the framework of Nordic cooperation.

Danish territory also provides NATO with a forward base from which to launch attacks on the Warsaw Pact's flank support shipping in the Baltic, and possibly even attacks behind the Elbe line on the Warsaw Pact's central flank. Norwegian territory in the North Cap area provides at least a potential hornets' nest from which to harass the Soviet Union's naval, shipping and air installations in the Kola Peninsula, and thereby provides a much

---

[3]See ibid., vol. II, Appendix 6 for analysis of Denmark's military and political role by General Wolf Graf von Baudussin, General André Beaufre, Colonel Bjørn Egge, Professor L.W. Martin and Docent Ingemar Ståhl.

needed delaying tactic to prevent the Soviet Union from closing
the northern arm of the pincer. As a forward attack base against
the Kola Peninsula, northern Norway is not particularly well-
suited because of its difficult mountainous terrain and lack of
all-weather roads and major airfields. In any case, the Kola is
so heavily defended that a NATO land and/or amphibious attack for
purposes of occupation would be too costly to be worth the
effort.

2.3 The Systemic Level

The importance of the Baltic Straits area in a conflict between
the two poles of the system has been declining steadily since the
introduction of nuclear weapons, and in particular since the
mutual deployment of ICBMs by the two superpowers. Whereas at
one time Danish and north German airspace provided access for
American SAC bombers to Soviet territory, and conversely played a
similar role for the Soviet long-range nuclear bomber forces, the
introduction of ICBMs has caused this airspace to decline progressively to marginal importance. Similarily, the importance of
the Baltic Straits as egress routes for the Soviet Baltic fleet
has declined, particularly since the 1960s. The reason for this
is the increased emphasis placed by the Soviet Union on naval
installations in the Kola Peninsula for its operational Atlantic
high seas fleets, including the surface fleet equipped with
cruise missiles, the submarine attack fleet, and half of its
total SLBM-equipped Polaris type submarine forces, a total of
approximately 500 high seas ships. The Baltic fleet, though it
has a larger number of capital ships, including a number of
cruisers, and numbers 135,000 men as contrasted to 100,000 in the
Northern fleet, has become regarded by the Western allies during
the past decade as a local Baltic defence fleet and a training
fleet. It is no longer believed that the Baltic fleet is desig-
nated by the Soviet Union to play any role in the North Sea after
the outbreak of hostilities. Before the outbreak of hostilities,
of course, ships can be sent out from the Baltic through the

Baltic Straits and deployed in the North Sea and the Atlantic.[4] These considerations seem to accord with the Sokolovskii position on the conduct of a future war in which it is projected that the initial exchange of ICBMs would be followed by a prolonged territorial campaign with Soviet forces fighting on foreign soil.[5] In such a situation the defensive and logistical role of the Baltic fleet is imperative, and it is also in such a situation that the 'European' level of hostilities discussed above would take place.

In contrast to the Baltic Straits area, the North Cap has become more important in considerations of systemic conflict, particularly since the sixties. This is the result, not only of the increased Soviet installations in the Kola, but also of the increased Soviet land and air build-up to two motorised divisions, two airborne divisions in the Baltic and Leningrad military districts, and one infantry brigade, with 3,000 men with landing craft and amphibious tanks, in the northern district. In addition the Soviet Union has 15 to 18 army divisions in the Leningrad and Baltic districts and 10,000 Ministry of the Interior troops in the Finnish-Norwegian border areas. The Air Force has 200 to 300 offensive aircraft based on forty airfields in the Kola Peninsula and two IRBM bases south of Murmansk. The Leningrad and Baltic districts have an additional 500 aircraft. Clearly, the Soviet Union regards the North Cap as of strategic importance for transit and beachhead purposes in North Atlantic naval warfare, and to spearhead an attack on the British Isles and continental western Europe. For the Western alliance the North Cap area is considered useful for defensive purposes, i.e. to deny the Soviet Union the offensive advantages of transit route and beachhead. Finnmark in Norway and Swedish Lapland are considered of little importance in a Western offensive strategy

---

[4]There is a canal link between the Baltic and the White Seas through Lakes Ladoga and Oneshkoe through which smaller ships are exchanged between the two fleets.

[5]See V.D. Sokolovskii, *Soviet Military Strategy* (Rand Corporation-Prentice Hall, 1963), pp. 304-15.

against the Soviet Union.

3. The Policies of Security

Whereas the security policies of great powers are usually *alterative* in character, having as the principal objective the changing of the political and military environment in their favour, the security policies of small powers are usually adaptive in character, attempting to adapt or change their security requirements to those of the environment -- other states and the international system. The Nordic countries depart to some degree from this generally observed rule. Though small and relatively powerless, the Nordic countries follow various mixtures of adaptive/alterative security policies. In this respect Finnish policy is more consistently active than are the policies of the other Nordic countries. The most significant difference between the security policies of Finland and the other Nordic countries is that the latter have a high military defence content whereas the former is almost exclusively political, diplomatic and psychological.

3.1 Finland

For comparative purposes the security policies of the four countries may be conceptualised in the form of three concentric circles where the innermost circle represents the primary security policies, the middle circle secondary strategies, and the outermost circle the supportive political-security systemic outlook. In the case of Finland the innermost circle represents the Paasikivi-Kekkonen line, the middle circle Finnish Nordic area policies and the outermost circle Finnish commitment to the restructuring of the bipolar security system. In all three conceptual areas Finnish policy tends to be adaptive, in the sense that Finland perceives Soviet security policy in highly pro-Soviet and conservative terms; yet Finnish policy is also attempting to change, or influence change, in the status quo, particularly in the latter two policy areas. While it may be

difficult to distinguish between adaptive and alterative policy
orientations in the Finnish case, it is even more difficult than
usual to distinguish between what is primarily security-oriented
and what is primarily politically or economically oriented, since
Finnish security, foreign and economic policies are carefully
orchestrated to take advantage of the minutest possibilities of
advancing or emphasizing the political independence of Finland.
Although the effectiveness of such political moves may be moot
from the external point of view, internally they satisfy the
psychological need for the Finns to strengthen their sense of
independence and to disassociate themselves, in however small a
way, from the overwhelming presence of their giant neighbour
which conditions all Finnish security considerations.

Classical security strategy was almost wholly military in
content and was designed so to deploy the military and political
forces of a state in peacetime that the latter would be in an
advantageous position *vis-à-vis* a potential enemy before the
outbreak of hostilities. In the current bipolar nuclear system,
the emphasis has shifted towards a strategy of preventing the
outbreak of war between the two nuclear powers and their allies,
while the classic concept of military strategy is used as insurance in case the newer strategy fails. While the other three
Nordic countries consider strategy in these dual terms, Finland
does not. Finnish security considerations are limited to the
newer keeping-the-peace strategy because it neither has the
military capability nor wants it, since that would lead to a
Soviet demand that it become a member of the Warsaw Pact.

What makes it possible for Finland to disregard classic
strategy almost entirely, and at the same time to gain credibility for keeping-of-the-peace strategy, is Finland's interpretation of the Soviet security position. This view holds that
Soviet foreign policy, far from being expansionist is conservative, that the Soviet Union is not interested in world conquest
or even European domination, but that it is instead committed to
total defence of its own territory. The commitment to building
enormous military capability and the need to push the defensive

perimeters as far from Russian territories as possible -- even to Cuba -- is seen as a psychological need stemming from at least as far back in history as Napoleon's march on Moscow. This sense of insecurity was reinforced by the German devastation of Russia in both World Wars as well as by the hostile anti-communist stance of Western nations both before and after the Second World War. In fact it can be argued -- as the Soviets do -- that it is the West that is aggressive and that, far from having a policy of containment toward the Soviet Union, it has instead a policy of invasion and destruction, which is based on both irrational anti-communism and big power *Realpolitik*. The Finnish interpretation, of course, does not include the last anti-Western point. As a matter of fact the Finns also accepted the declared Western position in the bipolar security system: they do not believe that the West will initiate an attack on the Soviet Union. They believe that war would break out only in the event of misperception at a time of high tension.

Hence the objective of Finnish security policy: to reduce tensions and to remove Finland as much as possible from areas of possible tension. To this end the Paasikivi-Kekkonen line is central, for by consistently reassuring the Russians of their appreciation of Soviet security perceptions and by refusing to become even a minor irritant to the Soviet Union, the Finns hope to remove successfully most of Finnish territory and all of Finnish-Soviet relations from the field of bipolar attention.

The second policy area, the Nordic, is a natural extension of the Finnish policy of keeping-the-peace by reducing tensions and removing Finland as far as possible from tension areas. It is also fully in line with the psychological interpretation of the Paasikivi-Kekkonen line and serves as reassurance to the Soviet Union of Finland's continuing appreciation of Soviet security needs. The heart of Finnish Nordic policy is neutrality. Kekkonen introduced this policy in his "pyjamas speech" on 23 January 1952, while he was prime minister.[6] Thirteen years

---

[6]On account of illness the speech was never delivered but

later the President expanded on this policy when he proposed "... treaty arrangements with Norway that would protect the Finnish-Norwegian frontier region from possible military action in the event of a conflict between the great powers." He continued:

> The agreement which I have outlined would be in the interest of both Norway and Finland as it would lessen military tension in the northern area in times of international crisis, and help both countries to preserve their territorial inviolability in the event of a conflict between the Great Powers. Such an arrangement would be a link in the friendly cooperation between the Nordic countries.... Finland's land frontiers would then be as safe as they can be made through treaties. With the USSR, there would be the Pact of Friendship, Cooperation and Mutual Assistance; with Norway, the treaty to maintain peace on both sides of the Finnish-Norwegian frontier. As for Sweden, her traditional recognized non-alignment would suffice to ensure peace on our western boundary.[7]

While all three aspects of Kekkonen's Nordic security policy are plausible and logical extensions of the basic Finnish desire to remove Finland from possible tensions between the two superpowers, there is some question of the sincerity with which these proposals were made. Johan Jørgen Holst puts it as follows:

> In Finnish foreign policy I perceive a certain tension between two conflicting images: 1) The image of the Nordic balance providing a bargaining lever towards the Soviet Union, and 2) the image of a neutralized Nordic system which would eliminate any Soviet pretexts for exerting pressure against Finland. The dichotomy in the Finnish perspective perhaps reflects a communications dilemma. The surrounding states entertain conflicting expectations concerning Finland's role in the Nordic region. Such a state of affairs may not be altogether undesirable from a Finnish point of view. Helsinki, however, is confronted with a problem of assigning credibility to dissimilar positions to the two audiences (the Scandinavian countries on the one hand and the Soviet Union on the other). The problems arise when both parties "listen in" on the communications in both directions.[8]

---

was published in the newspaper _Maakansa_.

[7]U.K. Kekkonen, _Neutrality in the Finnish Position_ (London, 1970), pp. 188-89: Speech given at a meeting of the Foreign Policy Youth Society in Helsinki, 29 November 1965.

[8]J.J. Holst, "Norwegian Security Policy", _Cooperation and Conflict_, 1966: 2, p. 73.

Holst's point is underscored by two facts. First, from the
beginning the Soviet Union has been quite consistent in its
disapproval of any Nordic neutral alliance, such as was under
serious discussion during 1948-9, because it would be neutral in
name only but in fact an extension of the Western security
system. Secondly, both the nuclear-free zone[9] and the Norwegian-
Finnish North Cap treaty proposals were made in public speeches
in Helsinki, without prior notification have been given to the
respective governments. This is hardly diplomatic practice any-
where, and particularily not in the Nordic countries, where
foreign ministers consult each other regularly as a matter of
course both in person and by telephone.

Although it is possible to interpret the three policy
positions differently, the most plausible explanation seems to
bear out Holst's point. The Finnish Nordic neutrality position
appears to have been designed to remind the Soviet Union of the
role of bipolarity in the Nordic balance. The nuclear-free zone
proposal seems to be a combination of the Finnish desire to
reassure the Soviet Union of Finland's continuing appreciation of
Soviet security needs, and a genuine desire to further de-escal-
ate tensions in the Nordic area. Kekkonen's Norwegian-Finnish
North Cap proposal seems designed to reassure the Soviet Union
but at the same time to focus attention on the interrelations in
the Nordic balance.

The third conceptual area of Finnish security policy, that
of Finnish international efforts, is much more recent in origin
and began only in the 1960s, as was the case with the similar
policies of the other Nordic countries. The main purpose here is
to decrease the likelihood of a bipolar conflict confrontation by
reducing both psychological tensions and military levels.
Finland bases its participation -- and its leadership -- in this
area of activity on the principle of global security. Risto
Hyvärinen, Director of Political Affairs in the Finnish Ministry

---

[9]Kekkonen, op. cit., pp. 143-5: "The Creation of a
Nuclear-free zone in Scandinavia." Speech delivered to the
Paasikivi Society in Helsinki, 28 May 1963.

for Foreign Affairs, put it as follows:

> ... It has become increasingly evident that the security
> of an individual country no longer rests merely on its
> relations with its neighbours, but is largely dependent on
> whether all political conflicts, even those in which the
> country is not directly involved, can be settled by peace-
> ful means or whether it is necessary to resort to arms.[10]

The security aspect of Finnish activities in this area is closely followed by the desire to promote the credibility of Finland as a politically independent and sovereign nation. As Hyvärinen puts it,

> Finland's efforts to promote peace have obtained recogni-
> tion in the political activity of the United Nations; in
> the same way, Finland has found for herself a task in
> relieving tension in Europe that far transcends her imme-
> diate borders.[11]

Finland has limited its active role in international secur-ity efforts to that of middleman between East and West, capital-izing on its position of neutrality and its special relationship with the Soviet Union. Its success in this role is based on a highly astute capability in the art of the possible. By waiting until both poles are psychologically ready for talks before making its proposals, Finland has managed to give the impression of political leadership. Thus, in the case of the Strategic Arms Limitation Talks between the Soviet Union and the United States, Finland offered to host the conference at the psychologically right moment. The result was that it became co-host along with Austria for the SALT talks, thereby helping -- however precar-iously -- to decrease tensions between the two superpowers while at the same time reaping political benefits for itself. The role of Finland in the European Security Conference illustrates even more clearly its cautious astuteness. The idea of such a con-ference was originally raised by the Soviet Union in 1954, but at the time it was supported only by the Soviet bloc. Other na-tions, including Finland, considered the idea unrealistic in the

---

[10]Ministry of Foreign Affairs, *Finnish Features*, No. 6, 1972 (an English-language press release series).

[11]Ibid.

circumstances. The proposition was renewed on several occasions by the Soviet Union and its bloc partners, but without success. In 1966 the Finnish Government expressed its view on the matter for the first time in a communiqué after Premier Kosygin's visit to Finland: "The parties also exchanged opinions on a conference on European security considering the convening of such a carefully prepared conference to be beneficial in the light of the present situation; all states concerned should participate in such a conference."[12] At the same time, in July 1966 the Warsaw Pact renewed its proposal, but NATO did not reply until June 1968 when it agreed that the possibilities of improving the East-West relationship should be explored. The events in Czechoslovakia during the summer prevented further explorations and consequently it was not until March 1969 that the Warsaw Pact was able to carry the matter further. This time it proposed far-reaching preparations for the convening of a conference on European security. When NATO replied within six months that it was willing to start negotiations about regional disarmement in Europe, the stage was set for Finnish intervention.

Finland began its initiative by repeating the standpoint of 1966 in a communiqué of the Nordic foreign ministers' meeting held in Copenhagen on 23 and 24 April 1969. The communiqué emphasized that the "preconditions for conferences on security problems are that they should be well prepared, that they should be timed so as to offer prospects of positive results, and that all states whose participation is necessary for achieving a solution to European security problems should be given opportunities to take part in the discussions."[13] Immediately following, on 5 May 1969 Finland offered its good offices to the preparation of a conference on European security and cooperation and stated its willingness to act as host country.

Although the value of the Helsinki Agreement is moot insofar as the creation of stability in Europe is concerned -- mainly

---

[12] Ibid.

[13] *Ulkopoliittisia Lausuntoja ja Asiakirjója 1969*, pp. 85-6.

because the Western participants had objectives diametrically opposed to Soviet ones -- the fact that thirty-five states took time to work out a compromise indicates that the conference was in the mainstream of the pursuit of the psychology of détente. To the Finns this is all that matters; for as long as there is movement towards lessening of tensions, the objectives of the outermost circle of Finnish foreign policy -- to restructure the bipolar security system -- are being secured, and Finland can comfortably claim a role in this alterative process without having had to sacrifice the trust of the Soviet Union. On the contrary, Finland has again, by sleight of hand, increased the trust of the Soviet Union while at the same time its visibility in the eyes of the Western world has increased. Indeed the psychological impact of acting as host to a conference of all European states (and the United States), signing a convention as the equal of the Soviet Union, the United States and the rest of Europe, and signing it in its own capital city, gives an enormous boost to Finland's sense of independence, which makes it much harder for the Soviet Union to put pressure on Finland in the future.

3.2 Denmark and Norway

In the case of Denmark and Norway the primary and secondary security policies differ in content from the Finnish, whereas the supportive political-security systemic outlook is very like the Finnish. Using the concentric circle approach, it may be shown that the innermost circle of Danish and Norwegian security policies consists of the principle of collective security anchored in NATO; the middle circle represents defence strategies; and the outermost circle consists of what may be called "global security".

The basic principle of collective security was laid down by Foreign Minister Halvard Lange in his speech to the Norwegian Labour Party's annual meeting on 19 February 1949:

> The government has come to the conclusion that the Soviet
> Union will not take any steps against us or any other
> state, which they think will be likely to lead to a new

general war. Precisely because we evaluate the Soviet
government's position in this way, we believe that a solidarity anchored in a treaty with the great democracies of
the West will give us the greatest degree of security that
it is possible to reach in this imperfect world.[14]

The Norwegian Government has not changed its position since,
either in its interpretation of the Soviet Union's aggressive
potential, or about the basis of Norwegian security. And, since
Denmark's adherence to NATO has virtually the same basis as
Norway's, the statement by Lange may be taken as representing
both.

Although both Denmark and Norway have for over a quarter of
a century regarded the NATO alliance as the primary military
safeguard, both have from the beginning operated strategies of
security which are politically, diplomatically and psychologically oriented in the same way as Finnish security policy. The
fundamental reason for this is simply that both quickly came to
the conclusion that there was little likelihood of a local
attack on them by the Soviet Union since their territories
per se were of little interest to it, and that in the event of a
general war both would be involved because of the strategic
importance of their territories to the Soviet Union for both
transit and beachhead purposes for North Atlantic naval warfare,
and to spearhead an attack on Britain and continental western
Europe. For the Western alliance the territories of Norway and
Denmark were judged to be useful for defensive purposes: to deny
the Soviet Union the offensive advantages of transit route and
beachhead. The territories of the two countries were considered
to be of little importance in a Western offensive strategy
against the Soviet Union. These considerations led to Danish-
Norwegian defensive strategies of dependence on the United
States-NATO -- first, to prevent the break-out of a general war
and, secondly, for military support in case of war.

Danish and Norwegian defence strategies contain three

---

[14]Halvard Lange, *Norsk Utenrikspolitikk siden 1945* (Oslo,
1952), p. 122.

rationales: political independence, maximum security with
minimum provocation, and détente politics. Thus, for example,
Norway early in the life of NATO on 1 February 1949 undertook in
a note to the Soviet Union not to permit the basing of foreign
troops in peace time on Norwegian soil, while reserving the right
to do so if danger of war increased.[15] Denmark made a similar
decision on 5 October 1953. The base policies were extended in
1957 when a decision was made to arm NATO with tactical nuclear
weapons. Both countries stated that neither country would
accept the stationing or stockpiling of tactical atomic devices
on their territories. To the psychological fear of provocation
deep-seated in the Danish and Norwegian psyches the expectation
of European détente which arose in the 1960s was added. In an
article published in *Dagens Nyheder* on 23 January 1961 Poul
Hansen said, 1997029

> As far as it concerns a primary task: to avoid war, and
> to hold the way open to détente and disarmament, it is
> essential to ensure that it should be too great a risk to
> attempt an attack on our country; but it is just as impor-
> tant that no step is undertaken which can distract efforts
> at détente. As the situation exists today, it could be
> doubtful whether Denmark would obtain greater security
> against attack especially if Europe attacked us if we did
> establish a Danish nuclear capability.[16]

The above Danish reaction was the more significant since in
November 1960 a series of discussions was instituted in NATO
concerning the development of arrangements which would give the
non-nuclear European powers some influence on NATO's nuclear
policy. The discussions included both the MNF (Multilateral
Nuclear Force) and the ANF (Atlantic Nuclear Force). Throughout
the discussions, the Danish and Norwegian governments made it
very clear that they would not participate, nor permit the
stationing or the passage of any sea-borne nuclear weapons in

---

[15]See exchange of notes between Norway and the Soviet Union
reprinted in Johan Jørgen Holst, *Norsk Sikkerhetspolitikk i
Strategisk Perspektiv* (Oslo, 1967), Vol. II, pp. 65-7.

[16]*Dansk Sikkerhedspolitik 1948-1966* (Copenhagen, 1970), Vol.
I, p. 119.

their waters. At the same time, however, both also made it clear
that they would not obstruct or veto NATO establishing multilateral nuclear forces.

In contrast to the refusal to have anything to do with
nuclear weapons, when Robert McNamara, the American Secretary of
Defence, on 31 May 1965 proposed the establishment of a committee
of defence ministers to examine how and in what way non-nuclear
members of the alliance could obtain a voice in nuclear affairs,
Denmark and Norway changed their tune: "This proposal was hailed
with satisfaction in Denmark."[17] And when in 1966 the Nuclear
Defence Affairs Committee (NDAC) and the Nuclear Planning Group
(NPG) were established, Denmark and Norway agreed to participate.
The reason for this apparent reversal was, of course, that
Denmark and Norway needed to hedge their bets. The result is an
ambivalence of policy: while Denmark and Norway insist on
keeping their territories and the whole Nordic area free of
nuclear weapons in peacetime, and thus presumably reduce tensions
by not engaging in possible provocation, they at the same time
participate fully in nuclear planning activities, and thereby
contribute to the solidarity of the alliance. Moreover, having a
voice in NATO's nuclear activities Denmark and Norway increase
their political influence.

The outermost ring of Danish and Norwegian security policy
-- the policy of global security -- differs marginally from
similar Finnish and Swedish policies. Like the Finns, the Danes
and Norwegians have, since the inception of the United Nations,
consistently supported increasing multilateralization of international decision-making and the "democratization" of international politics. In particular, all the Nordics have been
active in promoting the welfare and the interests of the Third
World nations, to the extent that they have actively encouraged
the Group of 77, and have reduced tariff rates for developing
countries' manufactures to virtually nil. Moreover, and more
directly within the sphere of military-security matters, all have

---

[17]Ibid., p. 125.

assiduously supported the various attempts at détente, from the
Antarctic Treaty in 1959 to the 1972 Biological-Weapons Convention.[18] In addition they have vigorously supported the various
bilateral American-Soviet agreements from the 1963 Hotline
Agreement, to the 1974 SALT II ABM Treaty, 1974 SALT II Thresh-
hold Nuclear Test-Ban Treaty and in 1974 SALT II Interim Offensive Arms Agreement.[19] Furthermore, all were industrious participants in the Conference on Security and Cooperation in Europe.
However, there is little question that though a great deal of
effort is expended by the Danes and Norwegians on global security
through détente politics and the building of multilateral webs of
relationships on a world-wide basis, it nevertheless remains true
that in this collective effort the Danes and Norwegians are but
bit players. The main lines of the play will still be developed
by the United States and the Soviet Union. All that the Nordics
can do is to play adaptive and supportive roles, not instrumental
and alterative roles, despite the alterative ethos of their policies. And, since the main players, despite détente, continue to
balance military strategies, the Nordics must pay primary attention to the effect of these factors on their own interests and
policy objectives. Hence the Nordic dilemma: how to integrate
the conflicting strategic interests of the Soviet Union and the
United States in the Nordic area, and these strategic interests
with the idealistic objectives of the web of democratic multilateral relations which would reduce world tensions and create a
world security system with stable safeguards for the independence
of the Nordic states.

---

[18]The other treaties were: the 1963 Partial-Nuclear Test-
Ban Treaty, the 1967 Outer-Space Treaty, the 1968 Non-Prolifera-
tion Treaty, and the 1971 Sea-Bed Treaty.

[19]Other bilateral agreements were: the 1971 Hotline Re-
organization Agreement, the 1971 Nuclear-Accidents Agreement,
the 1972 High Seas Agreement, the 1972 SALT I ABM Treaty, the
1972 SALT I Interim Offensive Arms Agreement, the 1973 Protocol
to the High Seas Agreement, and the 1973 Nuclear-War Prevention
Agreement.

38.

3.3 Sweden

Swedish security policy may be summed up by the term "armed neutrality". The objectives of this policy are the continuing
preservation of Sweden as a sovereign and independent "Swedish"
entity by the means of non-alignment and the maintenance of
capability of arms to enforce both non-alignment and the primary
objective of sovereign independence. Taken separately none of
the three components of policy are particularily startling or
even noteworthy. Just about every contemporary state includes in
its foreign policy objectives continued sovereignty, many states
pursue policies of non-alignment, and sufficiency of military
capability is a common though seldom reached policy objective.
What makes Sweden noteworthy is that the objectives and means
have been pursued single mindedly -- and successfully -- during
the period since the Second World War. And what makes the
Swedish case unique in the contemporary world is that one of the
means -- non-alignment/neutrality -- has become the measure of
Swedish security and foreign policy. Professor Nils Andrén puts
it this way: "It is no overstatement to regard non-alignment as
an extraordinarily fixed foreign policy doctrine (so fixed that
even balanced bystanders sometimes regarded it as a 'sacred
cow')."[20]

Using the concentric circle approach in the analysis of
Swedish security policy it is evident that the innermost circle
(the primary policy) consists of the policy of non-alignment/
neutrality, the middle circle of the supportive defence strategy,
and the outermost circle of policies of global security. Clearly
the Swedish security policy set differs considerably from both
the Finnish and the Danish-Norwegian ones, but it also exhibits a
considerable amount of commonality with both sets, in addition to
the common Nordic policies of "global security". For one, like
the Finnish Swedish security policy is posited on psychology (the

---

[20] Nils Andrén, *Den Totala Säkerhetspolitiken* (Stockholm,
1972), p. 55. It should be noted that "neutrality" and "non-
alignment" are used synonomously by Swedes in reference to
Swedish neutrality.

psychology of non-alignment/neutrality) which because of its
long-held pride of place has become a socio-cultural value held
with all the tenacity of ideology. Hence it colours all aspects
of Swedish foreign policy to a greater extent than does the
Paasikivi-Kekkonen line in Finnish foreign policy since the
latter is after all devoid of ideological value and is clearly
understood by the elites (except for the pro-Soviet Communist
Party) as an exercise in pragmatism designed to safeguard Finnish
sovereignty. But Swedish security policy also has a great deal
in common with the Danish and Norwegian security policies in that
it, like the latter, emphasizes military defence. However,
unlike the latter, because of the historical doctrinal centrality
of neutrality Swedish defence strategy cannot be permitted to
depend on considerations of external assistance in the fulfill-
ment of its objectives.

The security that neutrality can bring a state depends on
the credibility of the government's statements and actions and in
the growth of the external meaning of these; on a realistic
analysis of the international system and the strategic position
of the neutral within that system; and on the credibility of the
neutral's capability. Though all parts of this statement are
interdependent it is, nevertheless, necessary to separate them
for purposes of analysis.

Two government statements eloquently describe the importance
attached by Sweden to the credibility of neutrality. The first
appeared on 9 February 1949:

> ... neutrality politically and in international law does
> not demand that a nation renounce the right for its citi-
> zens to participate in debates about international
> questions or democracy or freedom of speech. In general
> neutrality is a concept which relates to the conditions of
> war time. When one speaks of neutrality in peacetime the
> meaning can only be that a state, in order to attempt to
> keep itself outside conflict during war time, does not
> during peacetime bind its freedom of action through
> alliance arrangements, which make neutrality during war
> time impossible....
> ....
> Our policies must, according to our understanding, be
> directed to keeping our territory pacified in the sense

that it can not be placed at the disposition of any external power for purposes of military preparation. We must
not take on such responsibility or enter such agreements
with the one power group that the other power group pre-
ceives our territory being used by its opponent as a
forward support area. This type of non-alignment policy
makes great demands on defence. Truly we have not chosen
it in order to escape our burden cheaply.[21]

What Nils Andrén calls the most authorative statement of the
goals of the Swedish policy of neutrality appeared in the Foreign
Affairs Committee Report of 26 April 1956:[22]

There is no doubt, either in this country or abroad, that
the principle of the Swedish Government of holding fast to
its chosen policy of not acceding to any one of the Great
Power blocs reduces the chances of our country being drawn
into any possible conflict between the Great Powers. This
policy is well known everywhere. It has met with increasing understanding and respect.[23]

To build this kind of credibility demands a great deal of
agreement -- in fact, orthodoxy -- insofar as neutrality/non-
alignment is concerned. The orthodoxy of unity and uniformity in
the pursuit of this was apparently so successful by 1962 that
Foreign Minister Östen Undén was forced to protest the self-
congratulatory sense of superiority that Swedes exhibited about
neutrality. In a speech on 4 July 1962, titled "Realism and
Idealism in Foreign Policy" Undén pointed out that to relate
morality and neutrality is "boastful self-complacency". Nevertheless, he said, "The motivation for the foreign policy chosen
is to be found, so to say 'beyond good and evil'." But he
insists, "... nor do we consider that a neutral attitude ... [is]
non-moral. We are realists in regard to our policy. The motive
behind our attitude is a political one."[24]

---

[21]Nils Andrén and Åke Landqvist, *Svensk utrikespolitik efter
1945* (Stockholm, 1965), pp. 110-1; document reprinted in full,
pp. 101-02.

[22]Andrén, op. cit., p. 56.

[23]*Documents on Swedish Foreign Policy, 1956*, p. 114.

[24]Ibid., 1962, p. 34; note that Undén was the father of the
postwar policy of neutrality.

As the above demonstrates neutrality rapidly became an end in itself and the criterion against which both internal and external political actions were to be measured. It is thus no exaggeration to label the Swedish policy of neutrality/non-alignment as a doctrine. Indeed, by the mid-sixties orthodoxy in neutrality/non-alignment was so thoroughgoing that it did not admit even the possibility of the kind of expansion of the neutralist concept to the neutral alliance envisaged in the ill-fated Scandinavian defence union negotiations of 1948-49.

The continuity of orthodoxy of the policy of neutrality/non-alignment was reiterated by Olof Palme at the Social Democratic Party congress in October 1969 when he was chosen to succeed Tage Erlander as party leader (which meant that he automatically became prime minister):

> The Swedish policy of neutrality, as it had been formed by Östen Undén and Torsten Nilsson, remains fixed. It has survived the proof of history. It is grounded in Sweden's real situation in the strategic and power political fields of tension. We believe that it has assisted in providing the peace and the stability which in large measure have characterized conditions in the Nordic area since the war. In the formation of our policies we take into account especially the other Nordic countries. We respect the lines of foreign policy that they have themselves chosen.[25]

The second and third conditions necessary for the operationalization of a policy neutrality (a realistic analysis of the international system and the strategic position of the neutral within the system, and the credibility of the neutral's defence capability) demand careful and constant attention to defence strategies. There is no question that Swedish neutrality is not of the legal type, like Swiss neutrality, in which there are guarantees by the great powers that they will respect Swiss neutrality, provided the Swiss respect the obligations of neutrality, should war break out. Nevertheless, Swedish neutrality depends as much as on the undeclared willingness of the great

---

[25]Cited in *Problemer Omkring Dansk Sikkerhedspolitik* (Copenhagen, 1970), Vol. II, p. 74.

powers to respect that neutrality as Swiss neutrality depends on the declared willingness of the great powers to respect it. The difference is that in the Swiss case international law acts as an additional set of moral suasions, whereas in the Swedish case the Swedes must make their unilaterally declared intention of remaining neutral in the case of outbreak of war believable prior to the outbreak of war. Hence, there is a greater demand on Sweden to show _positively_ the credibility of their declaration whereas the Swiss need but _passively_ observe the provisions of the Congress of Vienna which recognized its permanent neutrality.

Sweden has had to depend on a combination of lack of strategic interest by the great powers in its territory, credibility that it will not enter war on one side or the other, and the maintenance of a sufficient capability to dissuade potential aggressors from believing that they could conquer Sweden and thus make inexpensive use of its territory in pursuit of their aggressive intentions. Of the three conditions only the first is largely beyond the control of Sweden, while the latter two depend virtually on unilateral Swedish efforts. But even the first demands a certain amount of Swedish input, namely a correct and realistic analysis of the contemporary international system and Sweden's strategic position within it. Throughout the period since the formation of the East-West bipolar system, Swedish analysis has regarded the ideological level of the conflict as relatively stable, but continuing in conflict, despite the fluctuations of the international "tension ratio". The military aspect is a contributory aspect of this ideological conflict: military capability is both the defender of a particular ideological position and the means to further its ends at the expense of the other ideological position. It follows then that a balance of military capability provides for non-outbreak of hostilities between the ideological blocs. Military balance, however, is complicated by the problem of stability. Instead of stability technological development and scientific breakthroughs in physics brought about an increase in the "arms race" during the 1950s and 1960s.

The problem is further complicated by the fact that the international security system is _in fact_ a two-nation one involving a balancing of Soviet and American capabilities. The alliance systems that have been built up by the two superpowers have been pushing the defence perimeters of the two as far from their own borders as possible. The introduction, successively, of nuclear weaponry and of intercontinental missiles has changed military strategy and consequently the importance of the extended defence perimeters of alliance. The political and psychological commitments made in the early days of the alliance systems, however, remain largely unchanged. The result is that superpower military strategy has continuously taken into account not only technologically _preferred_ military strategy but has had to marry it with the politically _demanded_ alliance needs. The result has been, not a narrowing of the military potential of confrontation, but a widening of it from the original direct confrontation of the European theatre to, in addition, a potential direct confrontation between the American and Soviet homelands. The threat of destruction inherent in a centre-to-centre nuclear confrontation, however, produced during the 1960s a subconscious stability in the nuclear missile balance and a deliberate political strategy to decrease the possibility of conflicts.

That Swedish analysis of its strategic situation within the existing international security system is realistic is shown by the following excerpt from the report of the 1970 Committee on Defence relating to the 1968 defence decision:

> Swedish Defence policy ought to ... proceed from the position that the political and military situation in Europe during the foreseeable future shall be conditioned by the existence of two power blocs with at least partly opposed political goals. It may be expected that even in the future a power balance between the great powers shall exist with a significant degree of parallelism between the military resources of the great powers. This balance has led to the great power forces being primarily directed towards each other, where only limited forces could be used against us.... If one of the parties attempted to use Swedish territory for her own needs this would bring with it losses for the opposing party ... Sweden's geographic position and the structure of her defence, its composition

and its grouping, etc., could give one party greater
possibility of advantage than the other.[26]

It is, however, not believed that Sweden would be attacked
in isolation from a great power general attack in which Swedish
territory would be but a means, and not a goal in itself. But
this also means that no matter how much Sweden builds up its
defence capabilities in order to dissuade an attacker, it can
never reach total security. Consequently,

> Swedish defence policy must therefore be based on the
> position that attack against the country is a part of a
> great power strategy where the value of the advantages
> that a great power can reach through the occupation of the
> whole or parts of the country are determined first and
> foremost by the advantages that this great power wishes to
> deny to its main opponent. Great power interest is greatest
> in the areas which are near its own territory and in other
> areas which are of great strategic importance. No part of
> the world, however, is so unimportant that great powers do
> not watch developments and follow up their opponents' even-
> tual possible gains. If a conflict should break out in our
> neighbourhood, the areas of strategic importance for the
> great powers would be the Baltic Straits and northern
> Scandinavia. The importance of Gotland ought also be noted
> in this context.[27]

It ought to be added here that the reference to Gotland is
an indication that control of Sweden would give the Western
alliance the power to deny the Soviet Union control over the
whole of the Baltic Sea. In contrast, a strict observation of
neutrality by Sweden will provide virtually the same advantage to
the Soviet Union. Thus it can be seen that were the Soviet Union
to fear that Western powers would wish to occupy Sweden in order
to deny the Soviets domination of the Baltic, a pre-emptive
conquest of Sweden by the Soviet Union would deny the Western
powers that objective. With respect to the Baltic Straits
similar arguments apply. It is only in order to deny the opponent land-based air control over the North Sea waters leading to
the Baltic Straits that Swedish territory would be significant.
But as pointed out in the excerpt, there would have to be an

---

[26]*Säkerhets- och Försvarspolitiken* (SOU 1972: 4), p. 20.

[27]Ibid., p. 21.

objective greater than merely that of control over the area in order for an attack to be mounted against Swedish territory. The objectives would obviously have to be extra-Nordic.

In the northern part of the Scandinavian peninsula, Swedish Lapland is relatively less important strategically. Its only value is in denying an opponent a vantage point from which to attack the Finnmark (Norway), Finnish Lapland, or the Kola Peninsula. As far as the question of permitting transit of troops between Norway and Finland to belligerents is concerned, there is no reason to believe that Sweden would act any differently in any future conflict than it did during the Second World War.[28]

Clearly in order to prevent the possibility of any kind of pre-emptive attack on its territory, Sweden must conduct a credible neutrality policy, and maintain a credible military capability to support that policy. Apparently Sweden has been successful in this, at least insofar as the Soviet Union is concerned, if one believes the Soviet statements expressing satisfaction with the Swedish security policy and with Swedish defence capability as a stabilizing factor in northern Europe.[29]

The direct and close relationships between the two main components of Swedish security policy, the policy of neutrality and the defence policy, are emphasized by Prime Minister Palme:

> Externally we must create a credibility that we have the capability in case of war to prevent initiatives which would encroach on Swedish territory. To do otherwise would create doubt or expectation among the great powers. In order to fulfil these obligations we must have a strong defence relative to our condition. Defence is an instrument of our foreign policy. It strengthens the credibility thereof. But on the other hand it is only through a fixed foreign policy that our defence remains credible.[30]

---

[28]Interviews with Swedish officials tend to confirm this.

[29]See Börje Lindkvist, 6 Debatt-inlägg om säkerhet och försvar (Stockholm, 1971); also V. Prokofjev, Nordeuropa och Freden (a mimeo translation from the Russian into Danish), pp. 55-61. Original published in Moscow, 1966.

[30]Andrén, op. cit., p. 88.

Swedish defence policy has been consistent in maintaining the two goals: first, that defence must be "so prepared for war that it effectively maintains the peace"; and secondly, that "Sweden's defence must be so built up that an attack would not prove gainful to any party."[31] To make the latter more specific, Swedish forces shall have "such strength, composition, and preparedness that an attack against Sweden demands such great resources and would require such a long time that any gains that an attack must bring would not be deemed worth the input."[32]

Throughout the period since the end of the Second World War there has been general agreement between the government and the opposition parties (excluding the Communist Party) about the necessity of maintaining strong defence forces to fulfill the twin main goals of Swedish defence policy. However, the agreement on goals has not prevented periodic disagreements about the strength and size of the forces, resulting from differing interpretations of the level of the international threat. Such disagreements, nonetheless, have not prevented agreement on periodic reformulations of defence objectives or the force levels necessary to fulfill them, if for no other reason than because Swedish politicians have always understood the necessity of considering defence costs within the framework of the priorities of the total national budget.

In general the re-evaluations of specific defence objectives have led to a narrowing and more detailed statement over the two-and-a-half decades, 1948 to 1972. The basic reasons for the change were the rapid increase in technological developments in weaponry, the consequent equally rapid escalation in costs, and the pressures that these placed on the annual budgeting system. The initial result of this during the late 1950s was the integration of planning/programming/budgeting of defence matters with the national budget/national resources allocation processes, and

---

[31]SOU 1972: 4, p. 20.

[32]Andrén and Landqvist, op. cit., p. 78; see 1963 goals of total defence and 1964 goals for Swedish forces.

the institution of a concept of total defence for civilian, economic and military aspects of defence to be included in integrated defence planning/programming/budgeting. The total integration process, however, did not take place until 1972 when, in addition, long-term programming covering the period 1972-7 was introduced. The 1972 system was a direct result of ten years of increasing concern with costs, experience in planning for two-year military budgets, and the increasing realization that the concept of total defence implicit in the original goals required more extensive planning and increasing resource input, the further one moved away from the psychological experience of the Second World War. There was also a realization that the continuing world development in military and industrial technology demanded not only greater efforts on Sweden's part to keep its military effort credible in the changing military technology and the resultant changing strategy, but also that it made Swedish military/industrial technology more and more dependent on the Western industrial nations for components at competitive costs. Clearly greater specifying of defence objectives consonant with changing interpretations of military strategy and with internal/external economic structures were becoming necessary, and led directly to emphasis on long-term planning and budgeting.

In the event, the 1972 re-organization of goals within an explicit concept of "total defence" planning was a rationalization which brought the goals more in line with the resources that Sweden had available, and produced a more "realistic" defence posture. A large part of the realism was achieved by a reduction in the role previously assigned to the defence forces -- to prevent major invasions simultaneously in the three elements of air, sea and land, as well as any other possible attempts at invasion -- to stiff resistance and no more. As the report puts it:

> Defence against invasion shall be the armed forces' most important responsibility. The armed forces shall resist as long as possible the attempt by an attacker to gain a foothold on Swedish territory in order to use our country for its own purposes. Stiff opposition shall be offered

in all parts of the country even in the form of guerrilla war if necessary.[33]

Such a reduction in the level of ambition may be interpreted as a more realistic one for a country with Sweden's resources, which consequently provides greater credibility for Sweden's attempt to convince possible attackers of its real intentions to make an attack as expensive as possible. Of course, this reformulation of goals has led to significant reductions in the economic resources allocated to defence, with the immediate consequence that the military and the Conservative Party are highly critical of the weakening of the Swedish defence stand. The criticism is valid if one considers Sweden's current defence goals, and the resources allocated to them, in relation to the earlier ones. The criticism, however, is not valid when one compares Sweden's current military effort with the efforts of other European countries, including members of NATO. Such a comparison would show that Sweden spends a greater amount of its Gross National Product annually on military defence than any western European country with the exception of France.[34]

---

[33]Cited in Andrén, op. cit., pp. 90-1.

[34]See IISS, *The Military Balance*, annual.

CHAPTER 3. THE STRUCTURE OF TRADE

That the fundamental economic relationships among sovereign
nations are conducted by means of trade in commodities is a fact
which remains true even though, in the increasingly complex world
of rising rates of inter-action, services and services to services -- including transportation, tourism, insurance and international financial activities -- are rapidly approaching the
relative importance of trade in commodities to a nation's economy. But even in such economies as the American, where the total
value of "invisibles" approaches that of goods, the relative
health of the "invisibles" market is based on the strength of the
"goods and commodities" market. Moreover, though total trade
forms but 5% or 6% of the American GDP, the trade dependence of
two key sectors of the economy -- agriculture and machines and
machine tools -- is significantly higher.

In economies that are much smaller than the American, such
as the Nordic, the importance of trade to the health of the
economy is much greater, and the relative dependence of key
sectors on trade is very much greater. It is for this reason
that our analysis of the economic value of the relationship with
other market economies, specifically those of western Europe as
they have formed themselves into a common market with financial

arrangements, legal rules, political authorities, and customs barriers against third countries, will focus on trade as an initial indicator of "integration" or relative dependence of the Nordic economies on the EEC ones.

A search for economic rationales for the Nordic countries' attitudes towards Europe as an economic or political entity produces both inconclusive and confusing answers. It is possible to argue on economic data alone that particular Nordic countries would be both better off in joining the Economic Community and equally well-off if not joining the Community. The reason the seemingly contradictory arguments are possible is that the economies of the four Nordic countries have been actually integrating with those of the European Economic Community for the two decades, 1950-70, without benefit of formal state treaties. What has been happening is a natural tendency of like-developed economies in geographical proximity to grow along the same lines and to practice economies of scale by integrating their productive capabilities at the firm and industry levels. Despite this, no spill-over took place between 1950 and 1970 into the political level. However, it was a political stimulus and not an economic one that first forced the four Nordic countries to pay attention to the growing entity of the Common Market. It was the same political reality that brought about the second Nordic approach to the Common Market in 1967. And once again, the 1970 approach was a continuation of the same political reality. This chapter attempts to analyse the essential economic background of trade against which the political decisions -- beginning with the formation of EFTA as a result of the EEC, continuing through the three rounds of application and the abortive Nordic attempt to create a Nordic Economic Community, to the partial solutions of 1970-2 -- took place. The succeeding chapters of the study will analyse the political rationalizations, decisions, and moves of the "Europeanizing" or "integrating" processes in the four Nordic countries.

1. Exports and Imports of the Nordic Region

An analysis of the trade statistics of the four Nordic countries
shows a number of common characteristics as well as considerable
differences including wide variations within the common characteristics. First, it is to be noted that the export-generated
share in the Gross Domestic Products of the four countries falls
in the range of 20% to 25%.[1] During the twenty years, 1950-70
all four countries experienced fluctuations in the ratio of
exports to GDP with Denmark moving from 21.2% in 1950 to 25.5% in
1960, and down to 22.0% in 1970. The Finnish experience was
somewhat different, with the ratio standing at 13.8% in 1950,
moving up to 22.5% in 1960, and again up slightly to 23.6% in
1970. Norway's graph shows a similar U-tendency, with the ratio
standing at 15.9% in 1950, moving up to 21.4% in 1960 and upward
again to 23.6% in 1970. Sweden presents a more static picture
with a ratio of 20.5% in 1950, 20.2% in 1960 and 23.1% in 1970.

A comparison of direction of exports of the Nordic group by
region from 1950 to 1970 shows marked changes in structure. It
is interesting to note that the EFTA countries form the largest
customer group in 1950, ten years before EFTA was organized, but
that by 1970 the increase in the share of exports going to EFTA
countries was only 6 percentage points above that of 1950.[2] This
does not take into account the traumatic reversal of the trend
evident in 1960 when the EFTA share of exports declined to 36%
but increased to 43% five years later. The next five years,
however, produced only a slight change to 46%. The reasons for
the EFTA twenty-year trend are not hard to discover. Almost the
whole of the EFTA countries' share of Nordic exports is made up
of a combination of intra-Nordic and United Kingdom trade. The
static level of intra-Nordic export trade was abruptly changed
between 1960 and 1965 with the formal organization of EFTA, but
the market was apparently quickly saturated and the intra-Nordic

---

[1]See Table 1 in Appendix I.

[2]See Table 2 in Appendix I.

exports market share between 1965 and 1970 was nearly static. A different situation took place in the United Kingdom's share of Nordic exports, with the static level of 1950-5 abruptly dropping between 1955 and 1960, and continuing to decline during the next ten years. EFTA clearly brought about a liberalization of trade and increased the intra-Nordic component but did not affect the United Kingdom's share at all. The result was that, while the intra-Nordic share of exports increased to second place after the EEC (third if all EFTA is included), the United Kingdom share dropped to third place.

The EEC countries' share of total Nordic exports has fluctuated very little, increasing from 27% in 1950 to 28% five years later, to 29% in 1960 and in 1965, and dropping to 26% in 1970. That this has been the case, despite the enormous increase in consumption in the EEC countries in all commodity sectors, is an indication that the customs union and other impediments to free trade that the EEC pact has created have affected the Nordic countries' export trade.

When we look at the change in total export figures between 1950 and 1970 we notice an almost sixfold increase. A comparison of the percentage changes in each ten-year and five-year period with the corresponding total export percentage changes indicates that the structural change in Nordic exports took place as a result of long-term ten-to-twenty-year trends in the rate of increase within a market area rather than as a result of sudden very large changes. This also shows that the decline in EEC exports began already during 1960-5 although these exports represented the same 29% of total exports at the end of that five-year period as at the beginning. Similarly, EFTA increases, which are made up of two opposing trends, the intra-Nordic and the United Kingdom trade, may be seen to have begun earlier than either the absolute figures or the structure of percentage distributions indicate. The United States and Canada category and that of East Europe are interesting in that they both represent similar and steady shares of the Nordic export market between 1950 and 1970. The North American five-year increases have been above or at total export increases in percentage change for three of the five-year periods; the Communist market has exceeded the total increase only in one of the five-year periods. This despite the fact that the East European market is physically much closer to the Nordic countries than is the North American one.

Clearly Nordic export markets during the twenty years remain concentrated in the EEC, in themselves and in the United Kingdom. The 65% share that these had of Nordic exports in 1950 fluctuated but little: to 66% in 1955, 65% in 1960, 68% in 1965, returning to 65% in 1970.[3] When the rest of EFTA is added, the share of the group in Nordic exports shows a slightly higher level: 67%, 69%, 69%, 71%, and 72% in each of the five-year periods respectively.[4] If we now add the EEC and EFTA minus Nordic countries' share of Nordic exports, we get the following configuration for the five-year periods mentioned: 52%, 55%, 52%, 49% and 49%, respectively.[5] In other words, half of all Nordic exports go to the Common Market and non-Nordic EFTA countries. An even greater dependence of the Nordic countries' exports on the EEC and non-Nordic EFTA markets is shown when we calculate the share of the EEC plus non-Nordic EFTA markets of world markets minus intra-Nordic trade.[6] The results are as follows for the five-year periods: 61%, 64%, 63%, 63% and 63%, respectively. It is to be noted that despite the changes in the structure of direction of exports the ten West European countries' share of Nordic exports outside the Nordic area has remained more or less constant during the twenty-year period.

Extrapolating from the analysis above, it would seem that markets change slowly, that changes in the structure of export

---

[3] EEC + Nordic + UK.

[4] EEC + EFTA.

[5] EEC + (EFTA - Nordic).

[6] $\dfrac{\text{EEC + (EFTA - Nordic)}}{\text{(World - Nordic)}} \times 100 = \%.$

markets are the result of varying rates of increase rather than decrease in exports which manifest themselves in trends over ten- or fifteen-year periods, and that barriers to trade such as customs duties may or may not significantly affect the structure of export markets. In the case of the EEC the effect of customs barriers (which were the only trade barriers in effect during the period of our analysis) appear to have had some effect on Nordic exports in reducing the rate of growth. In the case of the United Kingdom, even the removal of customs and other trade barriers through the formation of EFTA did not halt the decline in exports. But in the case of intra-Nordic trade, the liberali- zation of trade which resulted from the formation of EFTA led to a dramatic increase in exports. This, however, was short-lived. The Nordic market apparently reached saturation shortly after 1965 as a result of the small size of the Nordic populations, which totalled 20.9 million in 1965 and increased by 3.25% to only 21.6 million in 1970. Furthermore, the fact that the Nordic market was already a highly sophisticated industrialized one akin to the western European market in general would indicate that the 1960-5 EFTA liberalization merely produced a shift in the level of competition which is not likely to be repeated.

A brief look at imports is necessary to determine the foreign dependence of the intra-Nordic market and to compare it with the Nordic export market.

An initial comparative glance at export and import figures produces an immediate realization that the Nordic balance of trade has been negative and stable for each of the five-year periods with exports forming four-fifths of imports. No such steady state is exhibited by the regional divisions. The regions may, however, be divided into those that exhibit a negative balance below the total negative balance and those with a higher balance. Only two regions, the EEC and North America, exhibit a consistently negative balance. The EEC's consistency of balance of trade has one exception: in 1950 it stood at 87%, but after that was unable to climb out of the sixties with 68%, 63%, 68% and 69% respectively at each five-year interval. The North

American balance of trade is even worse, beginning with 52% in 1950, moving to 55%, 54%, 65% and 66% of exports to imports over the five-year periods to 1970. It may be remarked that these two regions represent the most sophisticated industrial markets of the world. The consistently negative balance of trade with these two would indicate that the Nordic countries, far from being able to compete in their markets, apparently cannot even compete with them in their own markets, as is shown by the consistently negative balance at a much greater level than with any other region or with the Nordic countries' total balance of trade average. The high excess of imports over exports with the EEC and North America and the consistency of this also indicate a certain degree of actual integration of the three regional economies, based on the economies of scale inherent in large-scale production in the EEC and the United States which is not possible in the Nordic countries. It also indicates a certain division of labour between the Nordic and the two other regions where certain industrial manufactures and semi-manufactures are produced more efficiently in one or other of them. A glance at commodity breakdowns of exports and imports supports both contentions as regards basic manufactures, machinery and miscellaneous manufactured goods (SITC nos. 6 to 8).[7]

Considering the ratio of imports to exports of the seven regions in Nordic trade, it is notable that the EEC plus intra-Nordic plus United Kingdom share in 1950 and 1970 is approximately the same for imports as for exports, standing at approximately two-thirds of total trade. If we take the EEC plus EFTA minus Nordic imports as a percentage of world minus Nordic imports, we get the following figures for the five-year periods: 58%, 63%, 65%, 62% and 62%.[8] As in the case of export trade, so

---

[7]See U.N., *Yearbook of International Trade Statistics* (annual), tables for the four countries on imports and exports by Standard International Trade Classiciation.

[8]$\frac{EEC + (EFTA - Nordic)}{(World - Nordic)} \times 100 = \%$.

in the case of the import trade as well, the Nordic internal
market depends for two-thirds of its imports on the ten West
European countries. Again, it is noteworthy that despite structural changes in the share of imports according to regions these
changes have been largely internal between the EEC and EFTA,
including the Nordic countries themselves, and relatively insignificant as far as the North American and East European markets
are concerned.

2. Denmark

An analysis of the direction of trade for Denmark shows a greater
structural change during the twenty years of our study than for
any other Nordic country. This is true for both exports and
imports. A glance at export-import data quickly shows the reason
for this: at the beginning of the period Denmark was simply
over-dependent on a single market.[9] In 1950 42% of Danish
exports went to Britain and 32% of its imports came from there.
No other Nordic country had such a degree of trade dependence on
any other single market. Clearly diversification of markets was
necessary, and did take place during the next twenty years. It
was not, however, an easy task to carry out, primarily because of
the composition of Danish exports, which in 1950 constituted 74%
agricultural products. The fact that by 1970 agricultural
products formed only 34% of total exports indicates that trade
deflection was accompanied by extensive reorganization and
diversification in commodity production in Denmark. During the
period 1950-70 agricultural production increased by 246% while
the total export trade increased by 537% (as valued in current
prices including the inflation factor).

Despite the strenuous efforts and upheavals of the internal
economy, the diversification of direction of exports was confined
largely to the EEC and EFTA countries, which together accounted
for 84% of Danish trade in 1950 and 71% in 1970. Of the thirteen

---

[9]See Table 3 in Appendix I.

percentage points removed from the EEC-EFTA group over the twenty
years, seven went to the United States and Canada, with the
largest increase taking place between 1950 and 1960, and the rest
of the world, where the twenty-year change constituted a slow but
steady expansion from an 11% share in 1950 to a 17% share in the
Danish export market by 1970.

Breaking the EEC plus EFTA share into two, we note that
EFTA's extraordinarily high share of 58% in 1950 declined to 50%
in 1955 and 44% in 1960 but picked up to 47% in 1965 and to 50%
in 1970. The reason for this was a steady decline in the share
of the major market, the United Kingdom, which declined from 42%
to 33%, to 27%, to 22% and 19%, in each of the five-year periods
from 1950 to 1970 respectively. The decline in the United
Kingdom share is the result, not of absolute decreases in exports, but in a consistently low rate of growth. The other
component of EFTA trade, Danish-Nordic trade, increased only a
percentage point in each of the five-year periods from 13% in
1950 to 15% in 1960, but then rose dramatically in the next ten
years to form 26% of total exports by 1970. The reason for this
is found in the formation of EFTA in 1960, which liberalized
intra-Nordic trade but did not reverse or even halt the declining
trend of Danish-British trade.

Between 1950 and 1955, the EEC share of Danish exports
increased from 26% to 29% as a result of a 170% increase in the
value of trade in the five years, well above the total Danish
world increase. After 1955, there was a decline both in the
share of Danish exports and in the rate of increase of the value
of exports going to the EEC countries. The decline, slow at
first but rapid between 1965 and 1970, may be attributed to the
establishment of the EEC in 1958 and the institution of the
Common Agricultural Policy in the mid-1960s. The latter effectively imposed a barrier preventing Danish agriculture from
competing in the EEC market. This development was of serious
consequence to Denmark, since it produced a situation by 1970
where 40% of Danish trade was dependent on two declining markets,
the EEC and the United Kingdom, with the remaining 26 percentage

points of West European trade (which took 71% of total exports)
dependent on the other Nordic countries, which represented a very
small and virtually saturated market.

A comparison of export and import data shows a greater
imbalance in the excess of imports over exports than the Nordic
average. The balance of trade fluctuated over the twenty years
as follows: in 1950 exports formed 77% of imports, in 1955 88%,
in 1968 81%, in 1965 80%, and in 1970 74%. The upsurge of
exports as compared to imports between 1950 and 1955 was wiped
out by 1960, with a further decline in 1970 to below the 1950
level. An important factor in the negative trend of the balance
of trade has been the EEC trend, which declined steadily from a
high of 76% of exports to imports in 1950 to 67% and 58% by 1960,
rose to 62% in the ensuing five-year interval, and dropped to an
all-time low of 46% in 1970. Interestingly enough, the EEC
sector is the only one that exhibits a steady trend, either
negative or positive. All others fluctuate after showing considerable increases between 1950 and 1955. The only market
sector that shows a consistently positive balance of trade is the
United Kingdom which moved from 103% in 1950 to 118%, 114%, 135%
and 102% respectively in each of the five-year intervals. The
Nordic sector, after showing an increase from 68% to 86% between
1950 and 1955, decreased to 82% in the following five-year
period, then increased to 84%, and to 86% in 1970.

It is most interesting, when comparing share of import and
export market by trade partner, to note that the trade dependence
of Denmark on imports from the ten non-Nordic European countries
that made up the EEC and EFTA before 1973 provided the following
shares of total imports in each of the five-year intervals: 61%,
66%, 62%, 52% and 51%. In contrast the same ten countries
provided the following share of Danish exports in the same five-
year intervals: 71%, 65%, 58%, 54% and 45%. Hence, though both
import and export percentages show a steady decline over the
twenty-year period, the decline in exports is greater than that
in imports. Despite the decline it is obvious that both the
import and export sectors of the Danish economy have remained

consistently dependent on the ten European countries during the twenty years. This dependence is brought out more fully when we eliminate intra-Nordic trade from the export and import totals. In that case the ten European countries forming the EEC and the non-Nordic EFTA account for the following import and export trends.[10] In imports in each of the five-year intervals from 1950 to 1970, they provided 72%, 76%, 76%, 65% and 67% of imports. In the same years they took 82%, 74%, 67%, 67% and 60% of non-Nordic exports, and produced a balance of trade as follows for each of the five-year periods: 91%, 87%, 75%, 83% and 63%, respectively. Hence, whichever way one regards the Danish import and export markets, there is a very heavy dependence, ranging from half to two-thirds (depending on the base of calculation) on the ten non-Nordic West European countries. This kind of dependence, though it has declined from the peak of the 1950s, nevertheless, indicates what may be called a large degree of *de facto* integration of the Danish import-export markets with those of western Europe.

It is this dependence which made Denmark particularily aware of the necessity of assuring access to West European markets for its exports. The awareness was heightened by the fact that such a large portion of Danish exports was composed of agricultural products -- 55% in 1960, 46% in 1965 and 45% in 1970. The natural -- indeed the only -- outlet for these had been, and continued to be, the western European markets. Hence, access to these was vital to the continued prosperity of the Danish economy. It could be assured only by some form of membership of the European Economic Communities. It is for this primary reason that Denmark was quick to apply for membership of the EEC in 1961-2, along with the United Kingdom, and it is for the same reason that Denmark kept up its pressure for membership through the two additional rounds of applications, and that it finally -- alone of all the Nordic countries -- became a full member of the

---

[10] $\frac{EEC + (EFTA - Nordic)}{(World - Nordic)} \times 100 = \%.$

EEC on 1 January 1973.

3. Norway

Although Norway is the only other Nordic country that has pursued
full membership of the EEC, the structure and direction of Norwegian trade differs considerably from the Danish. For example,
in contrast to the Danish, the trend of Norwegian exports to the
EEC is largely positive: the 27% share of exports to the EEC in
1950 dropped slightly to 24% in 1955, then increased by one
percentage point in the ensuing five-year period, dropped by one
percentage point in 1965, and then increased dramatically by five
percentage points to 30% in 1970.[11] This makes Norway the only
Nordic country with a larger share of exports to the EEC at the
end of the twenty-year period than at the beginning. Similarily,
the share of Norway's exports to the United Kingdom exhibits a
trend completely different from the Danish, with the share of
exports standing at 18% in 1950, rising to 22% and 23% respectively in the ensuing five-year periods, but returning to 18%
in 1965, where it remained in 1970. Norway is thus the only
Nordic country whose exports to the United Kingdom remained at
the same structural level at the end of the twenty-year period as
at the beginning. The only two export areas where deflection of
trade took place are the Nordic and the Rest of the World sectors. The former began at a 16% share of exports in 1950,
increased to 17% in 1955, then took off to 20% in 1960 and 25% in
1965, before settling down to a very slight one percentage point
increase in 1970. The latter -- the Rest of the World sector --
in contrast exhibits a steady decline from 21% in 1950 to 20%
five years later, to 17% in 1960, at which it remained in 1965,
and dropped then to 15% in 1970. In both the Nordic and the Rest
of the World sectors the Norwegian experience is different from
the Danish and is closest to the Swedish. It is noteworthy that
the increase in exports to the Nordic countries began in 1955,

---

[11]See Table 4 in Appendix I.

five years before the formation of EFTA, and ended in 1965. In
the case of Denmark the increase began in 1960 and proceeded
apace until 1970.

The above changes in structure add up to increasing concentration of exports going to the thirteen EEC and EFTA countries
beginning with 64% of total trade in 1950, increasing to 65% and
71% in the following five-year periods, then dropping slightly to
70% in 1965, and increasing to 76% in 1970. If we remove the
Nordic countries from this composition, the share of the remaining ten West European countries in total Norwegian exports for
each of the five years is: 48%, 48%, 51%, 45% and 50%. In other
words, a concentration of exports took place with half of total
exports going to the ten non-Nordic West European countries, and
a quarter going to the three Nordic countries, at the end of the
twenty-year period. In both cases, trends completely opposite to
the Danish trends in the same two sectors took place. The
importance of the EEC plus the non-Nordic EFTA countries to
Norwegian exports may be more dramatically shown by removing
Nordic exports from total exports and calculating the exports to
the ten as a percentage thereof.[12] The resulting percentages are
as follows: 57% in 1950, 58% in 1955, 64% in 1960, 60% in 1965,
and 68% in 1970. Hence, an increase over the twenty-year period
from just under three-fifths of non-Nordic exports to just over
two-thirds takes place, or roughly a 10% increase in dependence
on the ten non-Nordic European countries. Denmark, in contrast,
exhibits a decrease from four-fifths of total non-Nordic exports
going to the ten European countries in 1950 to three-fifths in
1970, a decrease in dependence of roughly 20% over the twenty-
year period.

Comparing import and export data, we discover that Norway
has the worst balance of trade record of all the Nordic countries. During the five-year intervals in our study exports form
the following percentages of imports: 57%, 58%, 60%, 65% and

---

[12] $\dfrac{EEC + (EFTA - Nordic)}{(World - Nordic)} \times 100 = \%.$

66%. The twenty-year trend shows a slight increase from just
under three-fifths to two-thirds of exports to imports. The
Nordic regional arithmetic mean in contrast fluctuates between
86% and 96% of exports to imports. The Nordic country with the
closest balance of trade record is Denmark, where the respective
percentages for each of the five-year intervals are as follows:
77%, 88%, 81%, 80% and 74%. Clearly the consistently dismal
showing of the Norwegian balance of trade requires an explanation. This is found in an analysis of the balance of payments
tables which indicate that in 1960 Norway earned U.S. $412
million for shipping which increased to $651 million in 1965 and
$981 million in 1970.[13] These earnings met almost the whole of
the balance of trade deficit, the remainder being made up of
other invisible earnings, transfer payments and foreign capital
investments in Norway.

An analysis of the structure of the balance of trade by
trade partner over the twenty-year period under review shows a
small increase in exports over imports in the Nordic sector,
which remains consistently below the total balance of trade
percentages. From 1950 to 1970 the figures for the five-year
intervals are: 49%, 46%, 58%, 59% and 59%. For the United
Kingdom the balance of trade figures are generally in favour of
Norwegian exports but fluctuate heavily during the last ten years
of the period: in 1950 Norwegian exports to the United Kingdom
formed 47% of imports, 62% five years later, increased then to
90% in 1960, and to 134% in 1965, but declined to 96% in 1970.
The third major trade partner, the EEC, shows even more confusing
figures: beginning with 85% of exports to imports in 1950, the
balance dropped to 50% in 1955, and to 47% in 1960, then increased to 56% in 1965 and to 79% in 1970. The fourth industrialized trade partner, the North American area, shows the
heaviest import dependence of all: beginning with 41% of exports
to imports in 1950, the balance moved five years later to 44% and

---

[13]See *Yearbook of Nordic Statistics*, 1966, Table 96; *Yearbook of Nordic Statistics*, 1972; Table 138.

then dropped to 33%, increased again to 57% and dropped to 34% in 1970. The only trade areas, apart from the United Kingdom, that show consistency in trends as well as a consistent level of exports to imports that is substantially higher than the Norwegian world balance of trade level are the Rest of the World and the East European sectors. Both increased substantially between 1950 and 1955 and then began a slow decline to 1970; the latter, however, remained higher than the 1950 balance of trade level.

In considering import dependence, the data shows that the combined EEC-EFTA share of imports increased from 61% to 71% between 1950 and 1960, where it remained in 1970. Though the initial increase is primarily due to the increase in exports from the EEC, the long-run increase was due to a shift in favour of imports from the other three Nordic countries, particularily between 1960 and 1965. The ten non-Nordic country dependence (EEC plus non-Nordic EFTA) shows an inverted U-curve: beginning with 42% in 1950 the share of the ten in Norwegian imports moves to 50% in 1955, stays there for 1960 and drops to 44% in 1965, and to 41% in 1970 -- actually below the 1950 level. However, this apparent deflection of imports is misleading, as indicated by the share of imports from the ten non-Nordic EFTA and EEC countries as a share of non-Nordic total imports. In 1952 52% of total non-Nordic imports came from the ten West European countries. The share increased to 63% in 1955, 64% in 1960, dropped to 60% in 1965 and to 57% in 1970. Hence, over the twenty-year period a slight increase in import dependence from just over half to just under three-fifths of total non-Nordic imports took place. Nevertheless, it is important to note that there was a slight decrease in import dependence in 1960 and 1970, the result of diversion of trade, however slight.

4. Sweden

Sweden, the largest of the Nordic countries both in territory and in population, had in 1970 a Gross National Product that was twice the size of the Danish and three times that of the Norwegian and Finnish. It formed almost half the combined Gross

National Products of the Nordic countries. It is thus no surprise to discover that half of all Nordic exports, including
intra-Nordic exports, originated in Sweden, or that one-third of
all Nordic imports, including intra-Nordic trade, was destined
for Sweden. More specifically, Swedish exports and imports were
three times the size of Finnish exports and imports; were three
times the size of Norwegian exports, but only twice the size of
Norwegian imports; and were roughly twice the size of Danish
exports and imports.

As a result one would expect greater stability in the structure of trade in Sweden than in the other Nordic countries. This
is the case with the Swedish export trade; relatively little
dislocation took place over the twenty-year period under review.
In imports, though some restructuring took place, there was much
less dislocation than in the import configurations of the other
three Nordic countries. Moreover, because of the size of the
Swedish economy and of Swedish exports relative to the sizes of
the other Nordic economies and their exports, it may be expected
that Sweden exerts a dominating influence on the import markets
of the other Nordic countries while remaining relatively un-
affected by the export trade of the others.

Aggregating the share of Swedish exports going to the EEC
and the EFTA countries, we get the following figures: 63% in
1950, rising to 72% in 1955, remaining steady at 71% in 1960,
rising again to 74% in 1965 and dropping slightly to 72% in
1970.[14] The share of Swedish exports destined for western Europe
increased by nine percentage points between 1950 and 1955 and
remained relatively steady for the next 15 years. If we remove
the exports going to the other Nordic countries from the previous
totals, we get the following share of Swedish exports destined
for the ten West European non-Nordic EFTA and EEC countries: 46%
in 1950, rising to 54% in 1955, and declining thereafter to 51%
in 1960, to 48% in 1965, and to 45% in 1970. In other words,

_____

[14]See Table 5 in Appendix I.

after an initial rise of eight percentage points during the first
five-year period, there is a slow but steady decline over the
following fifteen-year period to a point just below the initial
share.

The two diverging patterns, the aggregate EEC plus EFTA and
the non-Nordic EFTA plus EEC, are composed of three interacting
component trends, the EEC, the Nordic and the United Kingdom.
The EEC share of the Swedish export market trend over the twenty-
year period under review represents a shallow inverted U-curve
with the percentage figures moving as follows at five-year
intervals from 1950 to 1970:   29%, 32%, 32%, 31% and 28%.   The
United Kingdom share of Swedish exports shows a sharp initial
rise from 15% to 20% in the first five years, and then a steady
steep decline to 16% in 1960 and 13% in 1965, with a further
marginal decline to 12% in 1970.   Since the EEC and the United
Kingdom make up the lion's share of the total non-Nordic West
European exports, it can readily be seen why the non-Nordic West
European aggregate trend has been negative since 1955.   It is
harder to determine why the share of exports to the United
Kingdom declined as steeply between 1955 and 1965 as it did.   A
partial answer is provided by the data on relative increase by
trade partner.   The percentage change of exports going to the
United Kingdom falls short of the total increases in each of the
five-year intervals between 1955 and 1965 by considerable amounts,
and constitutes the lowest increase in the two periods in any
area, except the East European between 1960 and 1965.   Hence, one
may conclude that though no absolute decline in exports to the
United Kingdom took place, the rate of increase was so low that
higher rates of increase in exports to other markets led to a
decline in the relative importance of the United Kingdom as an
export market.   The reasons behind the low rate of increase in
the value of exports may be found partially in the relative
weakness of the British economy, including the British balance of
payments position, in contrast to the rapidly expanding Nordic
economies.   The trend of the share of Swedish exports going to
the three other Nordic countries is a strongly positive one.

Though the increase in the Nordic share was low at first, moving from 17% to 18% to 20% in the ten years from 1950 to 1960, it rose rapidly to 26% in the ensuing five years and leveled off at 27% in 1970. Clearly there was an underlying attraction in the Nordic market for Swedish exports, reinforced by the liberalization of trade produced by EFTA between 1960 and 1965. The increase in share of exports by trading partner supports this view: in each of the five-year periods, exports to the other Nordic countries exceeded Sweden's total exports to other markets, and exceeded the increase in exports to all other markets in the 1960-5 period by a considerable percentage. The fact, however, that the rapidity of expansion of exports declined in 1965-70 to just above the total Swedish world export increase indicates that the Nordic market may be becoming saturated as an export market. This is supported by the comparable data in the Norwegian and Finnish export tables, though not by the Danish export data.

The result of these interactions is an increasing dependence over the twenty-year period on West European export markets, as shown by the aggregate EEC plus EFTA trend data: a situation which appears to show a continuing more balanced structure of export markets than is the case with any of the other three Nordic countries. This, however, is a superficial and misleading conclusion. What has happened with the Swedish export trade is that it has been concentrating on western Europe. This is shown by the three export market areas not so far referred to: the steady North American share of the export market; the fluctuating but relatively steady share of the East European export market during the fifteen-year period 1955-70; and the declining share of the Rest of the World from a 24% share of the market in 1950 to only 16% in 1970. In addition, if we consider the EEC plus non-Nordic EFTA exports as a share of Swedish non-Nordic world exports, we get the following percentage figures for each of the five-year intervals: 55%, 66%, 63%, 65% and 62%. It is interesting to note that the Swedish export dependence on the ten non-Nordic West European countries, when intra-Nordic trade is

excluded from calculations, increased by seven percentage points
to 62% during the twenty years under review, whereas Norwegian
export dependence similarily calculated increased by 11 percentage points to 78%, and Finnish by seven percentage points to 56%.
Only Danish export dependence on the ten declined by 22 percentage points to 60% over the twenty-year period.

But the import dependence on western Europe has increased
even more than the export dependence. Again this is demonstrated
by considering Swedish non-Nordic imports from the EEC and the
rest of EFTA as a share of non-Nordic world imports. The calculation gives the following percentages for imports originating in
the ten non-Nordic West European countries for each of the five-
year intervals during the twenty-year period under review: 55%,
63%, 62%, 65% and 65%, giving a total increase of ten percentage
points. This compares as follows with the other three Nordic
countries' comparable calculations: Norwegian imports rose by
five percentage points to 57%, Finnish by six percentage points
to 57%, and Danish imports declined by five percentage points to
67%.

Comparing the ten countries' exports and imports respectively, as a share of total exports and imports, we discovered that
Sweden has a greater import than export dependence on the ten
along with Denmark, that the share of the exports is roughly
balanced by the share of imports in Finland, and that in Norway
the export dependence is greater than the import dependence.

The increasing Swedish import dependence on the ten West
European countries has been brought about primarily by the steady
decline in the share that the Rest of the World has in the
Swedish market, from a high of 26% in 1950, to a low of 14% in
1970. It is to be noted that imports from the United Kingdom,
after an initial decline from 20% to 14% between 1950 and 1955,
have tended to remain around that level for the rest of the
period under review. If we include intra-Nordic trade in our
calculations we get an even greater Swedish dependence on western
Europe, rising from 59% in 1950 to 65%, 66%, 71%, and 72% by
1970 -- an increase of 13 percentage points. The shares of the

North American market and the East European one have remained
relatively steady.

In comparing the balances of trade, we discover that in
terms of total trade Sweden has a better, though negative,
balance of exports to imports than Denmark or Norway, and since
1960 a better balance than even Finland. Between 1950 and 1970,
Sweden's exports formed 93%, 86%, 89%, 90% and 96% of imports
at each of the five-year intervals. Hence, after an initial
reversal between 1950 and 1955, the balance of trade steadily
improved with exports moving closer to imports in terms of total
value. The main market for Swedish trade, the EEC and EFTA --
the latter with its main sub-markets of the Nordic countries and
the United Kingdom -- exhibits similarily healthy trends towards
a balance of exports and imports. The EEC balance of trade
trend, after an initial drop from 94% to 67% during the first
five-year interval, has steadily improved, to 70% in 1960, 75% in
the next five-year period, and to 78% in 1970.[15] It is to be
noted that though the trend is positive there is still a considerable import excess over exports, indicating a need for greater
market penetration by Sweden in the EEC. The fact that the
improvement trend has been relatively steady between 1955 and
1970, however, indicates that the Common Market barriers to trade
against third countries have not significantly impeded Sweden's
competitive performance in its markets.

The EFTA balance of trade, consistently positive, is not
interesting in itself but one of its component markets, the
Nordic, is. The Nordic market exhibits a positive trade trend
which declines markedly and steadily between 1950 and 1970 from
208% to 207%, 186%, 167% and finally 139%. The trend towards
balance of trade within the Nordic market indicates that it is
rapidly moving to saturation and that the liberalization of trade

---

[15]The high balance of trade percentage of 94% in 1950 may be
explained by the fact the Swedish economy remained intact during
the Second World War whereas the economies of the six members of
the EEC were shattered to different degrees and had not been re-
built by 1950.

that EFTA brought about after 1960 is not solely responsible for
the increase in Nordic trade since that began in the preceding
five-year interval. This view is further substantiated by
increases in Norwegian and Finnish exports to the Nordic --
primarily the Swedish -- market. Danish Nordic exports -- again
primarily to Sweden -- also run above increases in Danish total
exports between 1955 and 1960, though they did not take off until
after 1960. The reason for this is found in the composition of
Danish exports and the composition of Swedish imports. In the
former there is a very heavy emphasis on agricultural products,
which formed 74% of total exports in 1950 and 55% in 1960,
whereas Sweden has been largely self-sufficient in agricultural
products, its imports of these forming only 14% in 1950 and 10%
in 1960.

The other balance of trade trends are inconclusive, with the
exception of the North American one, where exports ran at 70% of
imports in 1950, dropped to 46% in 1955 and have since risen to
49%, to 63%, and 75% in 1970, indicating an increased sophistication in industrial production which is able to penetrate the
North American market on better terms than before.

5. Finland

Of all the Nordic countries Finland is the only one which, consistently throughout the twenty-year period under review, had
the widest and most balanced distribution of export markets.
Excluding EFTA as a unit, we get the following distribution of
exports among the six market areas in 1960: a cluster composed
of the EEC, the United Kingdom and Eastern Europe with respectively 23%, 20% and 20% of exports, and a cluster made up of the
Rest of the World, the Nordic countries and North America with
respectively 16%, 11% and 9% of total exports.[16] By 1970 the
clustering effect has disappeared and there is a hierarchy of the
EEC taking 23% of exports, the Nordic countries 23%, the United

---

[16]See Table 6 in Appendix I.

Kingdom 17%, Eastern Europe 16%, the Rest of the World 12% and North America 6%.[17]

The main reason for the wider distribution of markets in the case of Finland than in the other Nordic countries is the importance of the East European -- specifically the Soviet -- market, which is relatively insignificant for the other Nordic countries. Secondly, the relative evenness of distribution among five market sectors may be attributed to the growth of the Nordic market, particularily in the five-year period between 1965 and 1970.

Aggregating the share of Finnish exports going to the EEC and EFTA countries, we get the following figures: 55% in 1950, a slight drop to 53% in 1955, a relatively steep rise to 62% in 1960, where it still remained in 1965, and a further rise to 66% in 1970. The increase of nine percentage points from 1955 to 1960 is composed of a 4-percentage-point increase in the EEC market, a 3-percentage-point increase in the Nordic share, and a 1-point increase in the United Kingdom's share. These increases in the share of exports came about as a result of increases in exports significantly above the increase in total exports in the five-year period beginning in 1955. In the next five-year period, the EEC's share remained constant while a 4-percentage-point drop in the United Kingdom's share was exactly compensated by an equivalent increase in the Nordic share in Finnish exports. The increase in the period 1965 to 1970 in exports to the EEC and EFTA from 62% to 66% is made up of a 5-percentage-point decline in the EEC share, a 3-percentage-point decline in the United Kingdom share and a dramatic 10-percentage-point increase in the share of exports to the other Nordic countries, thus producing the four-percentage-point change in total export to the EEC and EFTA.

During the twenty-year period under review exports to the EEC show a declining trend in the size of change in successive periods. In the case of exports in the United Kingdom there is a

---

[17]The remainders of 1% in the 1950 configuration and 3% in the 1970 configuration consist of the other EFTA countries not included.

similar trend which, however, appears to reverse itself in the last of the five-year periods, when the increase is larger than in either of the two preceding periods. In the case of the Nordic export market, the trend is a reverse one showing a large change in the second five-year period, amounting to almost a doubling of trade, a slight increase in the third five-year period, and a virtual tripling of exports in the fourth five-year period (between 1965 and 1970).

There are a number of underlying reasons for the restructuring of the configuration of Finnish export markets. The most important of these are the reparations demands imposed by the Soviet Union as a condition of the conclusion of peace at the end of the "Continuation War" agreed to on 17 December 1944. Accordingly, Finland was required to pay war reparations of goods in kind amounting to the value of 300 million U.S. gold dollars within six -- later extended to eight -- years. The breakdown of products was as follows: machines, installations and complete sets of capital machines, $100.9 million; new ships, $60.2 million; paper products, $59 million; wood products, $41 million; cable products, $25 million; and existing ships, $13.9 million. Hence metal products, exclusive of ships, accounted for 62% of war reparations. To meet this demand Finnish industry had immediately to double its capacity in ship-building and engineering industries. That Finland was able to begin restructuring at an accelerated rate -- even though it had been crippled by the loss of 12% of its territory and by five exhausting years of war -- is indicated by the size of deliveries of reparations goods to the Soviet Union, which accounted for 15% of Finland's national income during the first year and 11% during the second year. By the end of 1947 about 60% of the total reparations obligations had been met.

The importance of the reparations to the future development of the configuration of Finland's export industries and markets is twofold: first, in the short run there was an enormous diversion of exports and imports to the Soviet market; secondly, there was the rapid expansion and development of a strong metals industry. It was reparations that provided the basis of the restructuring of Finland's export industry. And reparations forced the development of a sizeable metals industry which has had psychological fallouts in other sophisticated industrial sectors, not least in terms of providing a spillover in proving that it is possible to build up an industrial sector rapidly.

When the reparations were completed in 1952, Finland was faced with a dual dilemma: on the one hand, almost a quarter of its total exports were going to the Soviet Union and its metals and machine-building industries were very heavily dependent on the Soviet market; on the other hand, continued growth of the standard of living demanded a steady growth in exports -- for which the Soviet market was unsuited for two reasons, one political and the other economic. The political reason produced a complex dilemma, for though in the interests of continued independence the Finns had to show unwavering friendship towards the Soviet Union and to Soviet political and economic interests, Finland could not afford to become too one-sidely dependent in exports on the Soviet market because of the political leverage which this would have given the latter in Finnish political affairs. The reality of the danger of economic dependence was demonstrated by an incident in 1958 when the Soviet Union applied economic sanctions to force Finland to form a government that it approved of. As K.J. Holsti puts it,

> In November 1958, the Soviet Government abruptly halted all trade with Finland, including goods which had already been ordered. This action had the most serious effect, since many Finnish metal and machinery products sold in the Soviet Union could not be sold in Western markets because their prices were not competitive. In other words, since no alternative markets existed, the Soviet cancellation of trade threw many Finnish workers out of jobs, adding to an already severe winter unemployment problem.
> Recognizing that such economic pressures could seriously damage the Finnish economy and worsen an already large unemployment problem, several members of the cabinet resigned and a new government more to the liking of the Kremlin eventually formed. The Soviet economic

pressure in this case worked very efficiently.[18]

However, from the strictly economic point of view the
economic advantages of relatively large Soviet trade outweighed
the political and economic disadvantages indicated by Holsti. In
this connection three facts must be noted. First, the metals and
machine tools industry that Finland built up as a result of
reparations is still largely based on the Soviet market, which
has provided it with a certain amount of stability and shelter
from the vagaries of Western industrial competition while at the
same time providing a margin of safety for the development of
sophistication, and thereby competition, in the Western markets.
Secondly, trade with the Soviet Union has provided greater
stability than trade with the market economies because of the
methods of agreement by which this trade is carried on. It
consists of contracts that extend over several years and comprise
fixed quotas for both import and export goods. The first of
these contracts, signed in the spring of 1950, extended for a
period of five years with detailed annual agreements made within
the framework of the five-year contract, including the setting of
prices according to prevailing market prices and with payments
arranged through central clearing. This type of contract arrangement continues to the present day. Thirdly, the import
aspect of Soviet trade cannot be underestimated, for it provides,
on a long-term basis, most of Finland's demand for cereals,
petroleum products, coal, coke and synthetic fertilizers. Apart
from the fact that Finland has been assured of adequate deliveries at fixed prices in these commodities, which have fluctuated widely in availability and price on Western markets during
the twenty years under review, Finland has also been able to
stabilize its foreign currency problem in that payment for Soviet
raw materials and producers' goods need not be made in hard

---

[18]K.J. Holsti, *International Politics* (Englewood Cliffs,
1967), p. 288. See also Holsti, "Strategy and Techniques of
Influence in Soviet-Finnish Relations", *The Western Political
Quarterly*, Vol. 17, pp. 63-84.

currency but is settled within the separate Soviet-Finnish central clearing arrangements of bilateral trade.

That Finland has been successful in increasing its natural markets in western Europe during these twenty years, may be seen when we aggregate the EEC and the EFTA shares of Finnish exports, giving an increase from a 55% share to a 66% share between 1950 and 1970. However, the aggregate EEC plus EFTA twenty-year increase is somewhat misleading, since a great deal of it is the result of the very rapid and spectacular rise in Finnish exports to the other Nordic countries between 1955 and 1970 -- in particular between 1965 and 1970. The increase in the Nordic markets is due to three factors: first, at the end of 1957 the devaluation of the Finnish mark increased the rates of foreign exchange for currencies by 39% and was combined with the so-called "Helsinki Club" arrangement. The latter consisted of an agreement between Finland and the OEEC states which removed the strict restrictions on Finland's foreign exchange and made the Finnish mark convertible reciprocally with the OEEC currencies. In addition, there was a free listing of imports up to 70% of Finland's trade with the OEEC members which led to Finnish exports being treated on the same basis as intra-OEEC exports.[19] In fact, Finland had become a *de facto* member of the OEEC. Initially, this appears to have assisted the growth of exports to the EEC more than to the other Nordic countries as witnessed by the increases between 1955 and 1960. The second factor of importance is the formation at the beginning of 1960 of EFTA, which Finland was able to join on 30 July 1961; this assisted in the growth of Finnish exports to the Nordic countries in the ensuing period. Interestingly enough, Finland's membership of EFTA did not assist its exports to the United Kingdom whose share dropped between 1960 and 1965 by four percentage points, and a further three points in the following five-year period. Con-

---

[19]Only France stayed outside the agreement; trade with France was conducted on a bilateral basis until 1960 when it joined in the multilateral OEEC-Finnish arrangement.

versely, the formation of the EEC in 1958 appears not to have
hindered the growth of Finnish exports to the EEC countries as
witnessed by the five-percentage-point increase in the EEC market
share in Finnish exports between 1955 and 1960. The third
factor influencing the increase in Finnish exports to the other
Nordic countries is undoubtedly a combination of proximity,
aggressive salesmanship, good design and the awareness of Finland, particularily in Sweden, produced by the heavy influx of
Finnish labour into the Swedish market during the 1960s.

What is worrying from a long-term growth point of view is
that such a large percentage of growth has been based on exports
to Sweden and to the other Nordic countries -- which, because of
the limited market, are becoming saturated, while during the last
five-year period declines have taken place in the share of the
other three main markets, the EEC dropping from a 28% to a 23%
share, the United Kingdom from a 20% to a 17% share and the East
European from a 20% to a 16% share of exports. The problem is
particularily worrying in that the EEC and the United Kingdom
trends of percentage change in the five-year periods have been
declining since the 1950-5 period. If we remove the Nordic
market from EFTA and add the EEC countries, we get the following
share of exports going to the ten West European countries: 44%
in 1950, 47% in 1955, 53% in 1960, 49% in 1965, and 43% in 1970.
Removing Nordic exports from Finnish world totals we get the
following shares for the ten West European countries in non-
Nordic world exports: 49% in 1950, 50% in 1955, 58% in 1960, 56%
in 1965, and 56% in 1970. In other words, an increase took place
between 1950 and 1960 -- where, for practical purposes, the West
European share has remained.

The main problem for Finland appears to be the securing of
markets in the United Kingdom and the EEC for the products of the
wood-processing industry. But according to export data, these
markets simply have not grown at steady rates -- nor have they
grown lately (1970-5) at or near the growth rate for Finnish
total exports.

Comparing exports with imports, we discover that in the
five-year intervals during the twenty-year period of the study
Finland had total trade balances as follows: 101%, 102%, 93%,
86% and 87% of exports to imports. For the EEC market the
balance of trade was as follows: 91%, 105%, 77%, 78% and 75%.
The United Kingdom balance of trade figures are: 123%, 139%,
167%, 129% and 116%. For the Nordic countries the figures are:
77%, 58%, 60%, 62% and 93%. The 1950-5 period is not particularily interesting since during that time Finnish foreign economic policy demanded a strict controls over imports. Nevertheless, it should be noted that even in those early years Finland
exported more than it imported from the United Kingdom, and that
imports from the Nordic countries were far below Finnish exports
to them. It is more interesting to note that Finnish exports to
the United Kingdom have continued to exceed imports, though at a
declining rate, which may indicate a certain weakness in the
competitiveness of the United Kingdom providing goods for the
Finnish market. At the same time, after the restrictions were
removed and the Finnish mark was devalued in 1957, a change took
place in Finland's trade relations with the EEC with imports exceeding exports by a sizeable margin, which has remained largely
unchanged since, indicating that the Finnish penetration of the
EEC market has been insufficient because of Finland's inability
to overcome the tariff barriers. The Finnish-Nordic balance of
trade figures remained more or less steady for the years 1955,
1960 and 1965, indicating that the interpenetration of the Nordic
markets and the Finnish market was proceeding in phase. The
rapid increase in the balance between 1965 and 1970 indicates a
movement to a rapid saturation of the Finnish market for Nordic
goods and, perhaps also, the reciprocal saturation of the Nordic
markets for Finnish goods.

Since such a heavy percentage of Finnish exports derives
from the forest industries, Finland's continued well-being will
depend heavily in the short term on its ability to continue
increasing the share of its goods entering the ten West European
non-Nordic markets. The problem, however, is that both Norway

and Sweden are competitors in the same West European markets for the same products. Equality of access is consequently mandatory for continued Finnish exports and Finnish domestic growth.

CHAPTER 4. EUROPE VERSUS NORDEN

1. The Necessity of Europe

Although the European option has been pursued with varying
degrees of enthusiasm in a number of European countries since
Count Coudenhove-Kalergi founded the Pan-Europa Movement in 1924,
it gained almost no attention in the Nordic countries until the
late 1950s when the Europe of the Six became an operative entity,
and until necessity of choice forced Denmark to consider the
option.[1] A scepticism with regard to anything involving *Grosspolitik* until forced by necessity is evident throughout the fifty
years since the Pan-Europa Movement was founded. A Danish
Europeanist, C.F. Herfordt, published plans for a European

---

[1]As Erling Bjøl points out, "One might ... compare the in-
sular and continental positions of Sweden and Denmark and conclude that as far as Denmark is concerned possibilities for
"freedom of choice" have been consistently de-emphasized since
1864 and that Danish foreign policy has been dictated by external
conditions, by 'la force des choses', which leave only a small
margin for manoeuvre. This point is strengthened by the fact
that 'European necessity' was one of the main arguments of the
'realists' before 1864, ridiculed by the nationalists who
steered the country into the abyss.... After this great calamity no one was inclined to deride the argument of 'necessity'
any longer." "Foreign Policy Making in Denmark", *Cooperation
and Conflict*, Vol. II, 1966, p. 2.

community involving a customs union and common policies in foreign, defence and economic affairs, in two volumes in 1924 and 1926.[2] Herfordt attempted to gain the support of the Danish political parties and the other Nordic governments for a joint Scandinavian initiative to further his cause, but was rebuffed with complete indifference on the part of all except a few politicians who endorsed his plans as individuals.[3] According to the memoirs of Danish Foreign Minister Peter Munch, a similar scepticism was shown towards French Foreign Minister Briand's plan in 1929 to create a European union within the framework of the League of Nations: "It was rather cool ... but it was realized that we could just turn it down."[4] The memorandum giving the official Danish response to the proposal made this scepticism clear. While giving only vague support to the concept of European unity, it spelled out clearly the Danish conditions for considering participation in the proposed union: (1) the United Kingdom would have to join the union; (2) the union should be open to all European states; (3) new organs besides those existing within the framework of the League of Nations should not be created; and (4) the problems raised by tariff barriers in Europe should be given the highest priority.[5]

---

[2]C.F. Herfordt, Et Nyt Europa, Vol. I and II (Copenhagen, 1924), 1926.

[3]See Peter Hansen, Denmark and European Integration, Co-operation and Conflict, Vol. V (1969), p. 15.

[4]P. Munch, Erindringer, 1923-33 (Copenhagen, 1964), p. 204, cited in Peter Hansen, "The Formulation of Danish European Policy", English typescript completed in December 1972, later published in German, "Die Formulierung der dänischen Europapol-itik", Österreichische Zeitschrift für Aussenpolitik, Vol. 13, No. 1 (1973). The English manuscript is referred to exclusively in this study.

[5]See Munch, p. 205, and Folketingstidende, 1930-1, Tilaeg A., Column 6147 passim., from Hansen, referred to in op cit., 1972, p. 7. Hansen adds: "If to these four points we add the need for the dismantling of agricultural trade barriers and the desirability of Nordic unity, and subtract a little from the resistance against international institutional machinery, we

In the immediate post-war years Nordic scepticism towards any form of *Grosspolitik* was at a very high level, having been given new impetus by the experiences of the Second World War. The antipathy was not limited to the continental European states but extended to the developing Soviet-American antagonism as well. There was general agreement that the Nordic countries should try to remain neutral in the East-West confrontation, perhaps trying to play the role of intermediary, but definitely not consider joining any bloc against the Soviet Union. The Marshall Plan and its successor, the OEEC, were not regarded by the Nordics as anti-Soviet Western instruments, although the fact that these efforts at cooperation became restricted to the western part of Europe was deplored.[6] In early 1945 an attempt at "bridge-building" mediation was made: an unsuccessful application was made to Moscow for supplies of armaments, and in the summer of 1946 trade agreements were made with the Soviet Union.[7]

The general foreign policy orientation of the Scandinavians in the immediate post-war years was one which might best be described as "neutralism within the United Nations", combined with a Nordic regionalism. As Danish Prime Minister Hans Hedtoft said on Danish Radio: "We shall not, in general, place our country in any bloc. We're members of the United Nations, and we will do our duty there as a Nordic country."[8] However, this orientation was fundamentally changed in little over a year when in 1949 Denmark and Norway, after the breakdown of the Nordic Defence Union negotiations, decided to join the Atlantic Alliance.

This radical departure from Denmark's traditional policy of

---

obtain a complete catalogue of the main elements in Danish post-war European policy." Hansen, op. cit., 1969, p. 16.

[6]See *Dansk Sikkerhedspolitik 1948-1966* (Copenhagen, 1968), p. 21.

[7]Ibid., Vol. I, Chapter I, p. 22.

[8]Ibid., p. 22.

neutrality brought about a period of highly vocal reactions from a strong anti-NATO grouping consisting of the left wing in the Social Democratic Party and the Radical Party. In the opposition's view, joining NATO was a negation of both the Nordic and the universalist-United Nations policy orientations, which would lead to a surrender of national independence. The NATO issue enlivened Danish political discourse well into the second half of the 1950s, and did not abate until the Radical Party reversed its position in 1957. The intensity and the long duration of the NATO controversy had a dual impact on Danish foreign policy. On the one hand it led to a moderation in Denmark's participation in NATO, eventually leading to what might be called a formal "semi-neutrality".[9] On the other hand, the controversy so dominated the foreign policy debate that the various European unification efforts of the early 1950s were almost totally ignored. In Norway, by contrast, accession to the NATO treaty was calmly accepted by everyone -- except a small left-wing minority -- as inevitable, and as time went on became regarded as one of the necessary bulwarks to Norway's sovereignty. The Norwegian counterpart of Danish semi-neutrality -- the Norwegian base and nuclear policy -- was the result, not of political, partisan or public issue agitation, but of rational calculation of the strategy of deterrence.[10]

The European efforts of the period 1947-8 to 1956-7 were impressive, and in the main followed two general courses, the one leading to the formation of the European Communities, and the other towards greater European cooperation along the lines of the OEEC. Early on, an attempt was made to combine the two approaches into one with the objective of a grand European union. The "Congress of Europe" was held at The Hague from 8 to 10 May 1948 with 663 delegates from sixteen European countries and fifty

---

[9]W.J. Alcock, "The Evolution of Scandinavian Foreign and Defence Policies, 1919-1969" (M. Phil. thesis, Kings College, University of London, 1973), pp. 91-103.

[10]See Hansen, op. cit., 1969, pp. 16-17.

observers from ten others.[11] The direct result of The Hague
meeting was the establishment of the Council of Europe on 5 May
1949, which for the next two years proceeded to debate approaches
to the formation of a grand integrated Europe. The Scandinavian
governments' reactions throughout were ones of lack of interest
and opposition to the establishment of supranational institutions. In general, the response was similar to the position that
the Danish Government had taken in the 1920s in replying to the
Briand memorandum.

Throughout the "grand debate" in the Council of Europe the
Danes, the Swedes and the Norwegians adopted an identical position and shared the British "functionalist" as opposed to the
"federalist" or "supranational" approach. The basic Scandinavian
argument was that the "small things" should be done first, along
the lines of Scandinavian experience of the multilateral coordination approach to integration. There was also an economic reason
for the Scandinavian rejection of the federalist approach.
Because of the high standard of living in the Scandinavian
countries, it was feared that European economic union schemes
would result in unemployment in Scandinavia when the continental
labour forces flooded north in search of jobs. In addition the
Norwegians, who were the most outspoken opponents of federalism,
emphasized that "membership in the Atlantic community through
NATO was much more important for Norway than any European organization for, contrary to many Continental European arguments, the
ocean unites rather than divides."[12]

But there was also a political argument which the Scandinavians found was an important reason for rejecting European
federalism. Along with the British they found that those who
wished to federate Europe were reflecting traditions of political

---

[11]A.H. Robertson, *European Institutions* (London, 1966),
lists these in a footnote on p. 10.

[12]Gunnar P. Nielsson, "Denmark and European Integration: A
Small Country at the Crossroads" (Ph.D. dissertation, University
of California at Los Angeles), 1966, University Microfilms, Inc.,
Ann Arbor: Michigan (Xerox reprint), pp. 288-9.

instability rather than expressions of "political maturity".[13]
The Anglo-Nordic group, on the other hand, saw itself as representing states

> some of whose existence (Norway and Denmark) had been
> disrupted by the war, but unlike the Continental states
> whose very foundation had been shaken and whose future
> was more uncertain. This difference of experience had
> prompted the Continental Europeans toward greater will-
> ingness to seek solutions in regional terms....[14]

The basic difference between the Anglo-Scandinavian and
continental approaches is summed up in the two words frequently
used at this time, "functionalism" and "federalism". While the
latter approach implied the establishment of constitutional
arrangements whereby either a United States of Europe along the
lines of the American model or supranational organs with authority superior to national parliaments and governments would be
established, the former approach is summed up in Lord Boothby's
terminology as "the approach which occupies itself with extending
and multiplying the working arrangement between the States of
Europe". In Arnold Zurcher's words it becomes even more mundane
and pragmatic: an approach to "merely ... specific international
problems on the usual intergovernmental basis of negotiation and
treaty".[15]

To the extent that the Scandinavians were interested in
European integration, it was limited to the functionalist approach. Danish Foreign Minister Gustav Rasmussen put it this
way: "We prefer to proceed less rapidly [than the six 'federalist' countries], to work for the solution of concrete problems
... and in this way gradually build up European cooperation at

---

[13]Ibid., p. 288.

[14]Idem.

[15]Arnold J. Zurcher, *The Struggle to Unite Europe*, 1948-
1958 (New York: University Press, 1958), p. 51; and Boothby,
see Consultative Assembly, Council of Europe, *Reports*, First
Session, August 10-September 8, 1949 (Strasbourg, 1949), p. 98.

the government level."[16] Consequently, at the official level the Scandinavians largely disregarded the "federalist" debates in the Council of Europe and elsewhere. Little time was spent in parliamentary debate on these matters, and the level of awareness among Scandinavian parliamentarians of European integration questions was very low. To a survey asking the question "Are you in favour of a European federation within the frame of the United Nations?", which Count Coudenhove-Kalergi conducted among European parliamentarians during the winter of 1946-7, only 14.7% of the members of the Danish lower house even bothered to reply. This was the third lowest level of replies in Europe, Norway's and Sweden's being even lower. In contrast the replies in the lower houses of five of the six EEC countries -- Germany being excluded -- varied from 54% in Belgium, France and Holland, to 64% in Italy and Luxembourg. The favourable response among those replying in the latter countries was very high, mostly over 90%.[17]

The main reason for the general lack of interest in "federalism" among Scandinavian politicans is aptly explained by one of the few Danish parliamentarians interested in it, Frode Jakobsen, the chairman of the Danish European Movement until 1964 and Social Democratic Party parliamentary spokesman on European affairs, when he said in the Folketing, "For a Dane there is no doubt that a larger area with a smaller degree of unity is preferable to a smaller area with a larger degree of unity."[18] Hence, the Scandinavians concentrated their efforts on possibilities of broadly applied functional solutions, such as the OEEC and the various cooperative agencies set up under its aegis.

But the pursuit of broad European solutions was only partly based on political reasons: economic reasons were just as

---

[16]Hansen, op. cit., 1969, p. 17.

[17]Nielsson, op. cit., pp. 278-9.

[18]*Folketingstidende*, 1952-53: Column 764, cited in Hansen, op. cit., 1969, p. 17.

important. An important aspect of Scandinavian "European" policy
was the need for trade liberalization. And, since politically as
well as economically the Scandinavian countries had similar ties
with the United Kingdom, it is not hard to see the reason for a
similarity in the Scandinavian and British approaches to both
"political" and "economic" Europe at that time. An early concrete example of this was the formation of Uniscan in 1949, a
loose and informal mechanism for multilateral coordination of
economic policies that fulfilled entirely the Anglo-Scandinavian
objectives of the functionalist approach as expressed by Lord
Boothby and Foreign Minister Rasmussen.

In structure Uniscan was very simple: it consisted of
continuous regular consultations and negotiations among senior
civil servants in the four countries' ministries of finance and
foreign affairs, interspersed with periodic ministerial meetings.
Functionally, its operation was more complex. Beginning with
such immediate practical problems as convertibility of currency,
capital transfers and double taxation, it soon became a forum for
ironing out more complex and cross-cutting economic problems in
the four countries. For example, the Norwegians called a meeting
of Uniscan in March 1952 to discuss the implications of a newly
instituted British price policy on imported wood pulp; similarly,
an expert committee met in April 1953 to discuss ways of coordinating Scandinavian trade and payments with a proposal by the
Commonwealth Conference to expand the use of sterling as a world
currency.[19]

But the value of Uniscan was not limited to the review and
negotiation of multilateral -- in practice United Kingdom/Scan-
dinavian bilateral -- economic relations. It also became the
main forum for the Anglo-Scandinavian group to review and consult
each other about the progress of general European economic
integration, and to formulate reactions to the continental
"federalist" drive for supranational European institutions. More

---

[19]Nielsson, op. cit., pp. 211-2.

than twenty ministerial conferences took place within the Uniscan framework during the 1950s in which OEEC policies, the Schuman plan, the "Green Plan" proposal, the Maudling proposal for a Wide Free Trade Area in Europe, and the formation of the EEC were discussed.[20] Indeed it is suggested that it was because of the habits of continuous consultation and solution of common problems that EFTA was established so rapidly, after only a few consultations in 1959.[21]

It should be noted that almost all economic, as well as security and even political démarches relating to Europe and/or *Grosspolitik* made by the four Nordic countries and the United Kingdom since the Second World War have been reactive rather than initiatory in character. This was the case with the establishment of Uniscan, which was formed as one expression in response to American pressure for evidence of regional cooperation in post-war European economic reconstruction as a prerequisite for the disbursement of Marshall Plan funds. Its counterpart was the much more ambitious Finebel Customs Union project which began as a French, Italian and Luxembourger response in the first instance -- the Frialux Customs Union -- and was later expanded to include the Benelux Customs Union already established in 1948. Neither Frialux nor Finebel, however, got off the ground.

2. The Historical Dimensions of Scandinavianism

Denmark, Norway and Sweden had begun discussions and negotiations for the formation of a Nordic Common Market -- Danoswe -- along the lines of the Belenux Customs Union. This is not to say that

---

[20]The term Wide Free Trade Area or WFTA was coined after the European Free Trade Association, EFTA, was formed to distinguish the two. Originally the EFTA proposal was referred to as either the Free Trade Area or the European Free Trade Area.

[21]Nielsson, op. cit., pp. 312-3; this view is postulated as a basic thesis in G. St. J. Barclay, "Background to EFTA; in Episode in Anglo-Scandinavian Relations", *Australian Journal of Politics and History*, Vol. XI, No. 2 (August, 1965), pp. 185-97.

the three Nordic countries, as well as Finland and Iceland, did not have a long history of cultural, political, security and economic cooperation. They did, but it was sporadic and uneven, and largely dependent on external factors. Thus, for example, although Scandinavian jurists, after an initial meeting in 1872, had been slowly developing far-reaching uniformity in the administration of justice in Scandinavia, it was not until 1946 that a permanent Scandinavian Committee for Legislative Cooperation was established. The objective of the Committee is to keep legislation in the Nordic countries under constant review to ensure conformity with the principles of Nordic cooperation; to submit proposals for cooperation in new fields; to initiate joint preparation of commentaries on Nordic laws in order to produce uniform legislation; and to coordinate Nordic views on the agendas of international conferences.

In the security and economic fields, however, cooperation has less continuity. In 1872, at the instigation of Danish, Norwegian and Swedish economists and leading businessmen, the governments of the three countries decided to establish a currency union with a common medium of exchange based on gold. The agreement was ratified by Denmark and Sweden in the following year and by Norway in 1875. But, as so often in Nordic economic activities, both the impetus for its formation and its disappearance came about as a result of external factors. The impetus came from the formation of the Latin Monetary Union centred on France in 1865, and from the new German *Reich* which adopted a uniform currency and the gold standard in 1871. The suspension of the monetary union was similarly the result of external factors, namely the outbreak of war in 1914, which led to the suspension of the gold standard and to such extensive dissimilarities in economic conditions in the three Nordic countries that even with the restoration of the gold standard at pre-war parity, it was impossible to re-establish the union.

Though economic cooperation among the Nordic countries was largely limited to the monetary union and, indirectly, to rendering legislation uniform, the more ambitious idea of a customs union has been present since shortly after the establishment of the German *zollverein* in 1834. In 1843 and 1845 Viggo Rothe, a young Danish civil servant, published a two-volume study titled *Denmark's Industrial Conditions, with Particular Reference to the Question of Forming Customs and Commercial Unions*,[22] in which he proposed the removal of intra-Scandinavian tariffs and the introduction of a common tariff wall. In the 1880s, when the continental powers had reverted to protectionism, the debate on a Scandinavian customs union resumed, with the Danish financier C.F. Tietgen vigorously advocating the establishment of customs union to create a common market which would enable the Nordic countries to hold their own against the continental industrial powers. Though the matter was discussed at a number of private and intergovernmental Nordic meetings no action was taken, mainly because of the growing disagreement between Norway and Sweden over their political union and the differences arising out of their tariff cooperation which had been established by the 1825 Intra-Union Act. Under this arrangement a number of Swedish and Norwegian commodities could be imported into the other country at half the normal tariff rates if they entered by ship, and entirely free of duty when imported overland. As time went on more and more commodities were incorporated into the system. In 1874 the intra-union system was extended and, with the abolition of all import duties between Norway and Sweden, became a common market for the two countries. There was, however, no common external tariff. As long as both Sweden and Norway pursued a liberal trade policy, the difference in the external tariff caused little difficulty. But as soon as protectionism became the order of the day in the 1880s, Swedish manufacturers began to exert pressure on the government to renounce the Intra-Union Act because they felt that Norwegian industry was taking advantage of the lower Norwegian tariff for raw materials to compete unfairly with Swedish industry. The Norwegian manufacturers, who had

---

[22]Referred to in Frantz Wendt, *The Nordic Council and Co-operation in Scandinavia* (Copenhagen, 1959), p. 88.

feared earlier that the abolition of intra-union tariffs would give Swedish industry unfair advantage, now became the champions of the Act because they realized that it had given them free access to the Swedish market and thus provided a strong base for Norwegian industrialization. In the event, the Swedish manufacturers won the pressure game and the Act was terminated in 1897. The immediate result was a considerable drop in trade between the two countries; indirectly, the abolition of the "common market" contributed to the 1905 dissolution of the Swedish-Norwegian political union.

Though the termination of the Swedo-Norwegian intra-union system was a serious blow to the hopes of continued and increasing Nordic economic cooperation, and though the problems of the First World War led to the breakdown of the monetary union, the idea persisted in political and economic circles. In 1919 the governments of Denmark, Norway and Sweden instructed the treaty commissions, set up to study post-war problems of commercial policy, to appoint committees for joint investigation of ways and means to promote economic cooperation in Scandinavia. Unfortunately, the work of the committees came to naught mainly because there were neither external nor internal unifying forces, and in 1922 the committees were dissolved.

In the 1920s, despite considerable attempts to negotiate the reinstatement of the Scandinavian monetary convention and continuing cooperation among the Scandinavian central banks -- cooperation which has since been extended to rotational Nordic representation on the governing boards of a number of international monetary organizations such as the Bank for International Settlements, the International Monetary Fund, the International Bank for Reconstruction and Development, etc. -- all the activity yielded only one result, the "escape clause". By this the Nordic countries agreed to attempt to incorporate into trade agreements with outsiders an escape clause which would reserve their right to grant each other mutual concessions that would not automatically benefit other trade partners. Potentially the escape clause was of some importance in that it would have

permitted the Scandinavians to circumvent the Most Favoured
Nation trade rules of the inter-war years and thereby to introduce some form of customs union. In the event, the escape clause
came to mean very little since the main trading partners of the
Scandinavians -- Germany, France, Italy, the United Kingdom and
the United States -- did not accept it.

In contrast to the 1920s, the 1930s saw the greatest increase up to that time in economic cooperation among the three
countries. This was mainly due to the international depression,
which led the Scandinavian foreign ministers to resume their
meetings in 1932 after a break of twelve years. The main theme
of their deliberations was joint action in currency and trade
matters, but the immediate result of the first meeting was the
establishment of an official in each of the foreign ministries to
handle mutual relations. In 1934 the foreign ministers met again
and decided to set up committees in each country to cooperate
with each other and with representatives of industry and trade in
the promotion of intra-Scandinavian trade and the improvement of
Scandinavia's position in external markets. It is worth noting
that the Delegations for the Promotion of Economic Cooperation
between the Nordic Countries (or Neighbour Country Boards) were
established as a result not of governmental initiative but rather
pressure by the Norden Association formed in Denmark, Norway and
Sweden in 1919, in Iceland in 1922 and in Finland two years
later.[23] With the war clouds on the horizon in 1937 the Neighbour Country Boards began preparing for war, and set up expert
committees to organize an exchange of commodities and a joint
Nordic rationing system so as to obviate the problem of supplies
which had been acute during the naval blocade of Scandinavia in
the First World War. Immediately after the outbreak of war in
1939 the Nordic prime ministers and foreign ministers held a

[23]The Norden Association was formed to promote cultural
contact among the Nordic peoples. It has 500 local branches
throughout the five Nordic countries including Iceland, and is
headed by a national organization in each of the states.

meeting in Copenhagen at which an announcement was made that the four countries would attempt to alleviate war problems by maintaining the closest possible cooperation in all possible areas.

Unfortunately again, as in the past, external realities prevented the carrying out of Nordic ideas and ideals.

3. Functional Nordic Cooperation: the Nordic Common Market Proposal

After the war economic cooperation began with the successful launching of SAS (Scandinavian Airlines System) on 1 August 1946, a joint enterprise of two Swedish, one Norwegian and one Danish airline company underwritten by the three national governments. This was followed a year later by a Norwegian proposal, at a conference of the Nordic foreign ministers on 9 July 1947 in Copenhagen, to establish a special committee to investigate the expansion of economic cooperation among the Nordic countries. The Norwegian initiative was given impetus by the Marshall Plan negotiations taking place at the same time in Paris, where the Americans first pressed for the establishment of a general European Customs Union; when this was rebuffed, they replaced it with a proposal for the establishment of regional economic unions along the lines of the Benelux. It was apparently with this in mind that the Nordic foreign ministers, at a later meeting in August 1947, decided to pursue the Norwegian initiative. A committee, known as the Joint Nordic Committee for Economic Cooperation, was established at a meeting of the foreign, and trade and commerce ministers of Denmark, Iceland, Norway and Sweden held in Oslo on 23-24 February 1948. The committee chairman was C.V. Bramsnaes, head of the Danish National Bank, and there were three members each from Denmark, Norway and Sweden, with an observer from Iceland. The Bramsnaes Committee was given four general areas to study: the establishment of a common external tariff; the reduction of tariffs and removal of non-tariff barriers among the Nordic countries; the implications of division of labour and of industrial production; and the possibilities of expanding the process, already in existence, of

coordinating external trade policies and relations. Despite the
urgency of the security question which arose during the late
winter and spring of 1948, and the associated negotiations on
the Nordic Defence Union proposal, the Bramsnaes Committee proceeded apace and submitted a provisional report in January 1950.
The report was discordant in character. In general it concluded
that the abolition of Nordic tariff walls and the establishment
of a customs union would be beneficial to the economies involved,
and that the establishment of a Scandinavia-wide market with
concomitant large-scale production, specialization and rationalization would bring great advantages. Further, the committee
concluded that a Nordic Customs Union would fit into the general
plans for a reconstructed Europe, so that there would be no
external reasons for not going ahead with the plan.

But unfortunately the idea was doomed to failure -- although
another four years were to pass before discussions were suspended
-- because of parochialism. It was the Norwegian sense of self-
interest, which differed markedly from the Swedish and Danish,
that proved the main stumbling-block to closer economic integration. The Norwegian uneasiness was expressed in a minority
report, in which the Norwegian members of the committee pointed
out that present conditions did not permit Norway to join a
customs union at that time; war damage had been much heavier in
Norway than in Denmark, with the result that, while Norway had
been concentrating its efforts on reconstruction of export
industries and the rebuilding of its merchant fleet, Denmark and
Sweden had been able to concentrate on economic growth and
development. Consequently, Norway's domestic industry was in a
very weak condition, and could not hope to compete against the
Danish and Swedish industries, even on its home ground, without
the protection of tariff barriers. The Norwegian position notwithstanding, the Danes, Icelanders and Swedes on the committee
adhered to the idea of a customs union, believing that it would
work to everyone's advantage in the long run by developing an
industrial region which could compete with other regional en-
tities being created in the reorganizing world. More immediately,

they agreed, there would be transitional problems, not only for
Norway but for the others too; however, these could be overcome
by joint effort. Nevertheless, the committee came to the final
conclusion that

> those difficulties [raised by the Norwegians] are so sig-
> nificant that they cannot at present be solved by the
> participating countries. Therefore, there is no basis
> for the establishment of a customs union encompassing
> Denmark, Iceland, Norway and Sweden.[24]

The reaction of Danish Scandinavianist and business circles
was to pressurize the government for the formation of a Danish-
Swedish Customs Union which Norway could join later. Bramsnaes,
the chairman of the Joint Nordic Committee on Economic Cooperation, was particularly active in the pressure operation. However, nothing came of it because the Swedes were not interested
and because there was general concern among the Nordic governments about the effects of yet another split among the Nordic
countries in addition to the split in security systems a year
earlier when Denmark and Norway opted for membership of NATO.
The problem was resolved in typical Nordic fashion: if you
cannot reach consensus at a higher level, you attempt to reach it
at a lower level. This, of course, required the establishment of
a committee to analyse the implications. Thus the foreign and
commerce ministers, meeting in Copenhagen on 28 November 1950 on
Norway's initiative [sic], decided to ask the Bramsnaes Committee
to examine the various branches of industry in the Nordic countries in order to establish the feasibility of abolishing existing tariffs on specific categories of goods to be determined by
joint consultation, and whether such a "limited" customs union
could be expanded gradually to cover more and more branches of
industry as economic conditions became equalized in the Nordic
countries. For the next four years the Joint Nordic Committee
for Economic Cooperation thoroughly studied the manufacturing

---

[24]*Nordisk Økonomisk Samarbejde*, Report of the Joint Nordic
Committee for Economic Cooperation (Copenhagen, 1950), p. 43, as
cited in translation by Nielsson, op. cit., pp. 250-1.

industries of the three Nordic countries. These studies were
supported by additional research and investigations carried out
by the Federation of Nordic Farmers Organizations (on the role of
agriculture) and by the Scandinavian Labour Union's study of
labour's position in a Nordic Common Market.

Before the committee was ready to present its report, a new
development took place in Nordic integration. The Nordic Council
was formed in 1952, originally as a body for the purpose of
"consultation among the [parliaments of Denmark, Finland -- which
formally joined in 1956 -- Iceland, Norway and Sweden] as well as
the governments of these countries in matters involving joint
action by any one or all of these countries."[25] Ever since its
establishment, the Nordic Council has been the central forum for
Nordic cooperation and integration efforts, and has operated not
only as a parliamentary sounding-board but also as a forum for
the five member-governments to discuss, deliberate and coordinate
their Nordic-related policies. Indeed, the latter operation
became of such moment that in 1971 the Council Treaty was amended
to provide for a formal Council of Ministers to coordinate
cooperation among the governments, and between the governments
and the Council, which also entailed the setting up of a formal
continuing secretariat of officials in 1973, with headquarters in
Oslo.

Hence, it is not strange that the JNCEC report, completed in
the spring of 1954, became the key issue at the August session of
the Nordic Council. The report covered twenty-one branches of
industry, but came to the same schizophrenic conclusion as the
committee's interim report four years earlier. And for the same
reasons. The Danish and Swedish members of the committee concluded that all twenty-one branches of industry could profit
through a gradual branch-by-branch institution of common markets,
beginning with the most promising -- furniture, heavy chemicals,
paint and varnish, porcelain, leather and shoes, textiles,

---

[25]The Statute of the Nordic Council, Art. 1.

agricultural and machine tool industries, and broadcast receiving equipment. The Norwegian members of the committee, on the other hand, concluded that Norwegian industry needed protection in most of these areas. In contrast, Norwegian industrialists had indicated willingness to institute common markets in fish canning, aluminium semi-manufactures and iron alloy manufactures. In June the Norwegian Government published a commentary on the Bramsnaes Committee report in which it suggested alternative areas of cooperation other than the institution of a common market.

The two reports became the basis for consideration of the common market issue at the August session of the Nordic Council. After lengthy debate -- and despite a public struggle between the Norwegian Labour Party (the government party) and opposition parties' delegates over whether even to proceed with the question -- the Nordic Council in plenary session passed Recommendation 22/1954 which asked the governments of the three countries to take over the task of clarifying the possibilities of establishing partial customs unions on the basis of the data submitted by the Bramsnaes Committee, and to initiate negotiations to this end. At an intergovernmental conference held at Harpsund, Sweden, a Committee of Ministers of Economic Cooperation, consisting of one cabinet member from each country, and a Nordic Economic Cooperation Committee (NECC), consisting of three members and a secretary -- all civil servants -- from each of the three countries, were appointed.[26] The NECC was instructed to go over the ground of the JNCEC sectoral study, to analyze the external effects of a Nordic Common Market, to examine the competitive ability of industries in the three countries, and to prepare a uniform customs nomenclature on the basis of the Brussels nomenclature.

The NECC published a technical and statistical study of 50

----

[26]In August 1956, the Government of Finland appointed its finance minister to the ministerial committee and three members to the NECC.

pages in June 1955, and followed this in October 1957 with a
final report in five volumes: the first outlined a plan for a
Nordic market to include 80% of current intra-Nordic trade; the
second analyzed specific branches of industry; the third covered
special problems of cooperation; the fourth proposed a common
schedule of tariffs and concessional measures; and the fifth
presented a common nomenclature for trade statistics.[27] Two
supplementary reports followed: one in 1958, of 500 pages, and
the other in 1959, of nearly 200 pages.

Though extensive debates based on the NECC reports took
place during the 1956 and 1958 sessions of the Nordic Council and
though a number of ministerial committee and intergovernmental
meetings also considered the question of the Nordic Common
Market, the work of the experts and the effort of the politicians
over the years did not materially change the positions of the
respective countries as presented in the 1950 Interim Report of
the Bramsnaes Committee. If anything, the battle lines were
hardened, as shown by the views of the two members of the Nordic
Council's Standing Committee on Economic Matters in 1956: they
felt that, despite all the work done so far, the only thing that
had been demonstrated was that a common Nordic market would on
the whole be disadvantageous for Norway.[28] Also, the Norwegian
Prime Minister, Einar Gerhardsen, stated at the 1958 session of
the Nordic Council that his Government had not yet taken a stand
on a Nordic Customs Union. This, despite ten years of thorough
analysis and wide-ranging and heated debate!

The Nordic Common Market interlude is aptly summed up by
Recommendation 26/1958 of the Nordic Council:

> ... that the Governments of Denmark, Finland, Norway and
> Sweden commence negotiations, based on [prior] reports
> and in contact with the Council on the forms of Nordic
> economic co-operation, with a view to presenting the

---

[27]Stanley V. Anderson, *The Nordic Council* (New York, 1967),
p. 131.

[28]Ibid., p. 130.

matter to the Parliaments when the preconditions for a
decision are present.[29]

4. Nordic Decision-Making: Consensualism of the Lowest Common Denominator

The Nordic Common Market episode illustrates the peculiar character of the Nordic region and its regionalism more comprehen-
sively than does the earlier unsuccessful attempt at the formation of the Nordic Defence Union. A brief look at the factors
which militated against the successful establishment of a Nordic
Customs Union or Common Market, but which kept the discussions
and negotiations open for a decade, goes a long way towards explaining the subsequent different approaches of the Nordic
countries towards the European Common Market.

As so often in the Nordic Countries' external political,
security and economic matters, two facts stand out: the importance of external factors and the peculiarly Nordic manner of
handling the internal responses to these. A Nordic "filter"
appears to exist through which external stimuli pass before they
are converted to responses by the individual country's decision-
making system. While it is not uncommon for small countries to
be adaptive rather than initiatory in their external responses,
the existence of a filter such as the Nordic one is unique to the
Nordic countries. The filter consists of each country's decision-
making system making a careful appraisal of the likely effects of
its alternative responses on each of the other Nordic countries.
This does not mean that each country's response necessarily
incorporates the results of the filter, but it does mean that
each response is made in the full awareness of the possible
effects on the other Nordic countries. The operation of the
filter has produced, with the passage of time, a tendency to
coordinate policies as far as is practicable, given the differing
political, security and economic conditions of the countries
involved. Since the Second World War, in fact, there has been a

---

[29]Ibid., p. 134.

steady increase in the formalization of the operation of the filter, first by means of *ad hoc* ministerial and ambassadorial meetings to coordinate responses at international conferences and forums, such as the Marshall Plan negotiations in Paris in 1948 and the United Nations annual general assemblies; and, with the inception of the Nordic Council, at more structured regular meetings of ministers of foreign affairs and commerce, culminating in the formation of the Council of Ministers in 1971 as part of the Nordic Council.

The "obligation to consult" which this entails was already so strong by the mid-1960s that, when Danish Foreign Minister Per Haekkerup disregarded it in 1965 by taking a stand on South African apartheid at the United Nations without prior consultation with the other Nordic representatives, there was a strong reaction. The matter became an issue which was discussed in the national parliaments and taken up at the subsequent Nordic Council session in 1966. In the Danish Parliament the Foreign Minister defended his negligence on grounds of urgency, but was nevertheless heavily criticized by the leading opposition parties. This happened despite the fact that the actual policy position taken by the Foriegn Minister on the apartheid question was generally approved by Danish parliamentarians.

In the Nordic Council Poul Møller, spokesman for the Danish Conservative Party, said that he did not

> ... venture to say whether one should go as far as to request every Nordic government to consult other Nordic governments on actions related to foreign policy, but as a Danish parliamentarian I would like to stress here today that it was unfortunate and regrettable that we last autumn experienced an instance in the South Africa policy, in which the Nordic governments voted in different ways. Our votes do not mean very much when we take our stand separately, but a united Nordic voice in the UN carries quite different weight....[30]

John Lyng, Norwegian Foreign Minister, minimized the significance of the Danish action by emphasizing that it was atypi-

---

[30]Nils Andrén, "Nordic Integration", *Cooperation and Conflict*, 1967, pp. 11-12.

cal and that there was generally a good "relationship of consultation". He regarded the whole matter as an exceptional episode
"which we now bury and disregard". Tage Erlander, the Swedish
Prime Minister, agreed that "the Norwegian Foreign Minister has
fully clarified how the Swedish and Norwegian governments look
upon these matters".[31]

In addition to discussion of the Danish neglect of the obligation to consult in the apartheid case, there was also an
attempt to formalize the requirement to consult. Three private
members, representing Sweden and Norway, requested that the
Nordic Council Treaty be amended by substituting "must" for
"should" in Article 30 of the Treaty. (The article reads: "The
contracting parties should, whenever possible and appropriate,
consult one another regarding questions of mutual interest that
are dealt with by international organizations and at international conferences.") Though there was widespread support for
the idea the amendment of the treaty was not supported simply
because "it was not thought to secure the desirable effect,
especially as it was proposed that the general, limiting condition 'whenever possible and appropriate' should be retained in
the Article".[32] The point was well taken, and is *inter alia* an
illustration of the operation of the Nordic "filter", since joint
consultation obviously cannot take place on matters which concern
the special relations that particular Nordic countries have with
outside powers. Nevertheless, the general filtering action of
one Nordic country taking into consideration the other Nordic
countries' interests and positions, even in these special external relations cases, is amply illustrated by the "Nordic balance"
policy activities where joint consultation is specifically
prohibited in the case of the adherence of Denmark and Norway to
NATO, is virtually excluded in the case of the Finnish-Soviet
relationship, and is theoretically precluded by the Swedish

---

[31] Ibid., p. 12.

[32] Ibid., p. 11.

stance of neutrality.

If the "filter" operates even in the area of security, it is not surprising that it operates even more fully in matters of overt common interest, such as economics. For example, the possibility of an agricultural common market was not even raised by the Danes for serious consideration throughout the Nordic Common Market discussions because the damage of a free flow of Danish agricultural products to Sweden and Norway would be unacceptable to the agricultural sectors of the latter. Agriculture is politically sensitive in both Norway and Sweden, and was even more so in the immediate post-war years. It was the general opinion in both countries that farming had to be kept viable in order to ensure at least a minimum supply of food in the event of a blockade resulting from war. Secondly, it was felt that the depopulation of the countryside, which would come about as a result of a decline in farming, would have undesirable social consequences and reduce national security. This is not to say that the matter was not discussed at all; it was, but only by competent experts -- in this case the farmers. The Board of the Federation of Nordic Farmers Organizations agreed in a report issued in April 1951 that even if a free and common market were established for industrial products, agricultural trade would still have to be subject to restrictions.[33]

Similarly, when pressure was exerted -- in 1950 by the Danish industrialists and in 1954 by the Danish non-socialist opposition elite -- to establish immediately a Danish-Swedish Customs Union which the Norwegians could join later, the three governments acting in concert rejected any hasty action and decided to carry out yet another investigation by experts. Why? Because the Swedish and Danish governments did not wish to isolate Norway or to add to the political difficulties of the Norwegian government, which already had to contend with an

_____

[33] Nordens Bondeorganisasjoners Centralraad, *Jordbruket og en Nordisk Tollunion* (mimeo), Norwegian edition, April 1951.

internal split over the question of the Nordic Common Market.

As can be seen, the Nordic filter operates at both the particular (in security matters) and the collective (at the Nordic Common Market) levels. And at both levels -- but particularly at the collective level -- the filter tends to lead to temporizing and dilatory tactics while consensus is sought. Indeed, the hallmark of Nordic collective politics is the Consensus, which is courted assiduously in order to avoid not only open conflict but even the possibility of it. The overriding purpose of this appears to be the preservation of the "Nordic concept". When situations arise in which consensus is impossible for external reasons, then each Nordic country goes its separate way while carefully using the Nordic filter in order to obviate the possibility of open conflict. And when consensus is not possible for internal reasons, then collectively either no decision is made or the matter is kept alive and under discussion without positions being taken which could lead to conflict, until either conditions change to make consensus possible, or events overtake and make consensus irrelevant.

Consensus is of overriding importance in Nordic collective policy-making. Indeed, it may be suggested with some justification that the attempt at forming the Nordic Common Market failed precisely because of the overriding emphasis on consensus. This is certainly suggested by Danish Foreign Minister Per Haekkerup,

> Our approach was to ask experts to determine and describe the difficulties that had to be overcome before such a customs union could be formed. No stone was left unturned, no question unanswered. The outcome of concentrated work in the Nordic Council was 18,000 pages of arguments for and against a customs union. But while we were discussing and elaborating these problems from every conceivable angle, developments in Europe passed us by.[34]

Of course, such other factors as differing economic conditions, differing security-political conditions, and national

---

[34]Anderson, op. cit., p. 137, cited Haekkerup, "Nordic Cooperation and the World Around Us"; address to the annual meeting of the Danish Norden Association on June 13, 1964.

parochialism, played an important role in the failure to reach
agreement on the Nordic Common Market. Nevertheless, this does
not detract from the remarks of Foreign Minister Haekkerup or
from those of Knut Getz Wold, the chairman of the Norwegian
section of the Nordic Economic Cooperation Committee:

> The Nordic countries ought to ... prevent their foreign
> economic policy from becoming a one-sided accommodation to
> situations which are created for them by other countries.
> They ought to be willing to make political decisions in
> this area without always demanding comprehensive and
> detailed study beforehand. The Six made the political
> decisions first, and then asked the experts for help in
> carrying them out.[35]

The point is well taken, for is one to imagine that the Six
did not have their differing economic conditions, their differing
security-political conditions, and national parochialisms? And,
is one to believe that when the Benelux was formed in 1947-8, that
these factors were absent?

That the search for consensus has become something of a
"sacred cow" in Nordic collective political decision making is
again demonstrated in the Nordek negotiations which took place a
decade after the collapse of the Nordic Common Market episode.

5. The NORDEK Chimera

In April 1968, the Danish Government at a Nordic Prime Ministers
meeting, held jointly with the Presidium and the Economic Committee of the Nordic Council, resuscitated the question of the
establishment of a Nordic economic community. According to Per
Haekkerup, this initiative was "a natural reaction" to the
failure of the second attempt by the United Kingdom, Denmark and
Ireland to initiate negotiations with the Six to enlarge the
membership of the EEC. In Haekkerup's words,

> In the Danish view the Nordic countries could in this way
> try to make a constructive contribution during the stale-
> mate in European market integration efforts, which had
> occurred against Denmark's will and desire. At a time
> when an impasse appeared to have been reached elsewhere in

---

[35]*Nordisk Kontakt*, 1963: 10, p. 581.

Europe it seemed worthwhile for the Nordic countries to extend the process of integration in their part of Europe, while ensuring that it would run parallel to developments within the EEC. In this way the Nordic countries might actually prepare themselves for the day when the door to a broad European integration will be opened.[36]

The April meeting decided to follow up the Danish initiative, and at the next meeting of the prime ministers and the Presidium of the Nordic Council at Oslo in October, it was decided that an interim report on the matter, to be prepared by the Nordic Committee of High Officials on Nordic Economic Co-operation (Nordek), should be submitted before 1 January 1969, and should be presented to the Presidium of the Council and the Council's Economic Committee not later than 15 January 1969. Subsequently a meeting of the prime ministers, the Presidium and the Economic Committee of the Council was to take place about 1 February. In fact, the meeting took place on 1 and 2 February and the report was considered in detail by the Nordic prime ministers, the Presidium of the Nordic Council, and the Economic Committee of the Council. At a follow-up meeting of Nordic prime ministers in Helsinki on 18-19 February 1969, the Nordic Committee of High Officials was instructed to complete its work and to submit by 15 July 1969 proposals for solutions in all areas of cooperation. On the proposal of the Economic Committee the seventeenth session of the Council meeting at Stockholm in March adopted the following Recommendation on the Nordek question:

The Nordic Council recommends the Governments of Denmark, Finland, Norway and Sweden:

(1) to complete the work of enquiry and negotiation in such a way that proposals for solutions in all co-operation areas treated in the official report and a draft for a treaty on comprehensive and diversified economic co-operation may be ready not later than July 15, 1969, ...
....

(3) to fix a date in the autumn of 1969 for the next meeting between the Presidium, the Economic Committee and

---

[36] P. Haekkerup, "The Role of the Nordic Countries in European Economic Cooperation", *Annuaire Europénne*, Vol. 16, 1970, p. 81.

the Prime Ministers of the Nordic countries for a discussion of the draft treaty and the other materials as well
as the planning of the future work, ...

....

(5) to plan the negotiations between the Governments in
such a way that proposals for such comprehensive extension of economic co-operation may be submitted to the
Nordic Parliaments as soon as possible, ...[37]

The Presidium of the Nordic Council and the Prime Ministers
met on 4 November at Stockholm, accepted the 15 July report of
the Nordic Committee of High Officials, and planned the eighteenth session of the Nordic Council to be held in Reykjavik in
February 1970.

The eighteenth session of the Nordic Council expressed
satisfaction that negotiations of the Nordic Customs Union and
comprehensive economic cooperation had led to an agreement
approved by the prime ministers. The Council recommended to the
four governments -- Iceland was excluded from Nordek -- that they
should submit proposals to their parliaments for the implementation of the treaty on the establishment of Nordek in sufficient
time for proceedings in the parliaments to be concluded during
the spring sessions of 1970, after which ratification documents
should be deposited immediately. The prime ministers agreed to
submit proposals to their respective parliaments at the beginning
of April 1970. It seemed then that the quest for a Nordic Common
Market, which had failed twelve years earlier despite a decade of
investigations and discussions, was finally within the grasp of
the Nordic countries -- and in less than two years of discussions
and after only two short reports.

Alas, it was not to be. On 24 March 1970 the Finnish Government decided that it was unable to sign the Nordek treaty on the
basis of reservations expressed by it on 12 January 1970, in
which it pointed out that Finland, because of its policy of
neutrality, did not consider Nordek an appropriate organ to
further European integration. As Foreign Minister Ahti Karjal-

_____

[37] *Annuaire Européenne* Vol. 17, 1969, p. 621.

ainen put it in an interview in January,

> We wish to have a clear demarcation between Nordek and
> the EEC -- for our country Nordek means a commercial
> grouping based on the Nordic concept, which we hold very
> dear. During the negotiations it has become clear that
> there are difficulties if one emphasizes the creation of
> Nordek as a manoeuvre in order to strengthen our position
> towards the EEC, so that one could increase one's power
> in the discussions about joining the Community. We do
> not criticize any of our Nordic neighbours for their in-
> terest in the EEC -- for we, in our particular way, are
> also interested. But when other Nordic countries desire
> membership and regard Nordek as a strength in this speci-
> fic connection, then we must point out that our interests
> do not coincide with theirs.[38]

Contrast this with the following, written by former Danish
Foreign Minister Per Haekkerup:

> ... It is the stated policy of Denmark that Nordic econ-
> omic integration is in no way an alternative to our
> European objective. It is a *conditio sine qua non* for
> Denmark that a Nordic treaty be worked out in such a way
> that it positively improves the possibilities of the
> Nordic countries to participate in an enlarged European
> community.[39]

Given the fact that the above was published in the *European
Yearbook* in 1969 and that Haekkerup's views corresponded closely
with those of the Baunsgaard Government (1970) in Denmark, it is
impossible to believe that the Finnish Government was not fully
aware of the intentions of the Danes insofar as the purpose of
Nordek was concerned. Indeed, Haekkerup continues in his *European Yearbook* article to make it explicit,

> First, the substance of Nordic integration must be con-
> ceived in such a way that it approaches Nordic policies
> to those of Common Market. Secondly, strong institutions
> inspired by the Common Market institution should be
> established within the Nordic framework. Thirdly, a
> Nordic treaty must include an article for the revision of
> the treaty and, if necessary, the withdrawal from the
> treaty of one or more member countries. This article
> would come into play in the case of one or more member

---

[38]Interview granted by the Foreign Minister to *Veckans
Affärer*, January 1970, No. 5, reprinted in *Ulkoministeriön Asiakirjoja ja Lausuntoja*, 1970, p. 282.

[39]Haekkerup, *European Yearbook*, Vol. 16, 1969, p. 88.

countries opening negotiations for membership of, or
association with, the European Communities.[40]

It is clear from the above that in Denmark the Nordek experiment was regarded as a prelude to not only a Danish, but a
Nordic, accommodation with Europe. As such it involved two
gambles: first, that each of the other Nordic countries could
overcome the national considerations of parochialism -- different
economic, political and security conditions -- which frustrated
the earlier attempt to form a Nordic Common Market; and secondly,
that the negotiations could be concluded and the Nordek common
market instituted, before the EEC opened the door for membership
application. In retrospect it appears that the former was not
much of a gamble at all, as shown by the rapidity with which the
negotiations proceeded and were concluded; clearly, the free
trade period of EFTA had removed many of the economic fears of
the previous decade. The possibility of setting the political
and security considerations aside, however, was another matter,
and dependend entirely on the second gamble. That this was
understood by the Danes is indicated again by former Prime
Minister Haekkerup in the article cited:

> One of the basic ideas of the present Nordic exercise is
> through a constructive approach to solve the particular
> problems of Sweden and Finland in relation to the Euro-
> pean Communities. If it takes a long time before a
> European break-through becomes possible, the Nordic
> countries will at least have done something worthwhile in
> the meantime. If a European break-through comes sooner,
> as may be hoped after the departure of General de Gaulle,
> the Nordic efforts will at least have produced sensible
> drafts for the solution of the particular problems of
> Sweden and Finland.[41]

In the event, General de Gaulle left office in April 1969
and thereby opened the way for an expansion of the EEC. The
death knell for Nordek was sounded at a meeting at The Hague in
December 1969 when the heads of government of the Six agreed to
begin negotiations with the membership applicants and discussions

---

[40]Idem.

[41]Ibid., p. 88.

with the non-membership-seeking EFTA countries. It was in December, at a Nordek debate in the Finnish Parliament, that it became clear that both the Government and opposition were leery of the economic, political and security implications of Nordek and the opening for membership application by the Six.[42]

If Finland was gambling on the EEC's tardiness to open the door for expansion, and if Denmark was "bridge building", what then were Norway and Sweden hoping to accomplish with Nordek? The position of the former was made clear at a debate on market policy which took place in the Storting on 3 February. The broad cross-party position on the entire market question was well expressed by Commerce Minister Kåre Willoch: "The realistic solution to the market situation -- if Great Britain joins it -- is that the Nordic countries stand as one before the EEC -- with a distinctive position."[43] The chairman of the Foreign Affairs Committee, Bent Røiseland, suggested that all the Nordic countries should reach an arrangement with the EEC. If, he added, the negotiations with the EEC failed, then the Nordek arrangements could be put in operation as planned. If, on the other hand, the negotiations with the EEC led to a result, then the Nordek arrangements could be revised and fitted into the framework of the EEC's regulations.[44] In other words, for Norway the purpose of the Nordek negotiations was virtually the same as for Denmark: to make preparations for accommodation -- preferably Nordic-wide -- with the EEC. The value of Nordek *per se* was strictly secondary, and was to be considered only if accommodation with the EEC either failed or did not come about in the near future.

In the case of Sweden, the whole Nordek question raised little enthusiasm. Indeed when the market debate, postponed because of the Government's taxation proposals from March 18 to

---

[42]See *Nordisk Kontakt*, 1970: 1, p. 21.

[43]*Nordisk Kontakt*, 1970: 3, p. 163.

[44]Ibid., p. 164.

April 29, finally took place, the Government simply noted that it
understood the Finnish Government's difficulties -- particularly
since the results of the Finnish general election of March had
led to a serious loss for the coalition parties and created a
government formation crisis -- and that a new government had to
be formed in Finland before the Nordek question could be raised
again. And that was all the Swedish Government had to say about
Nordek. Among the opposition parties a half-hearted suggestion
was made by the former leader of the Liberal Party, Sven Wedén,
that since it would undoubtedly take several years before the EEC
questions could be solved, therefore Denmark, Norway and Sweden
ought to immediately accept the Nordek agreements, with a proviso
for Finland to join later. The Vice-President of the Nordic
Council, Leif Cassel, spokesman for the Conservatives, added his
voice to that of Mr. Wedén. The leader of the Centre Party,
Gunnar Hedlund, on the other hand, disagreed about the possibilities of forming a Skandek which did not include Finland.
According to him, "freer trade with the EEC ought to be sought,
but Swedish neutrality must be respected...."[45]

There is an element of unreality and ennui about the attitudes expressed in the above statements on the Nordek question,
particularly in the case of Norway and Sweden. The reason may
very simply be that for those two countries trade with the United
Kingdom and the EEC far outweighed in importance any advantages
that the formation of Nordek could possibly bring. Additionally,
in the case of Sweden, the formation of a Skandek without Finland
would be politically and, from the security-political point of
view, as impossible as Finland's joining a Nordek that was a part
of the EEC.

For Finland the purpose of the negotiations was not so much
to broaden its economic arrangements with the other Nordic
countries, but to expand its political contacts with yet another
formal Western organization. It was important, however, that
this Western organization be independent of the EEC -- parti-

---

[45]*Nordisk Kontakt*, 1970: 7, p. 420.

cularly an EEC which had just approved the Werner and the Davignon reports. Quite apart from the neutrality-infringing aspects of the latter reports, Finland also had to be careful not to antagonize the Soviet Union with further approaches towards the EEC, particularly in the company of NATO members such as Denmark and Norway.

For Denmark the Nordek attempt had a substantial purpose: to build as strong a Nordic bridge as possible before the inevitable economic attraction of the EEC weaned it too far politically from the Nordic fold. And it made clear that it did not matter much whether the formation of Nordek was successful or not, as long as the exercise was carried out. If, however, Nordek by some miracle were to succeeed, then Denmark would obviously be able to take greater advantage of it than any of the other Nordic countries, particularly if the opening of the doors of the EEC were delayed; this was because of Denmark's heavy dependence on agricultural produce.

But why did Nordek fail? The reasons are very similar to those advanced in the case of the failure of the Nordic Common Market in 1958. The only difference is that at this time the reasons were more clearly political. The Nordic "filter" had become perfected over the twelve years separating 1970 from 1958. This time consensus was reached on the substance of Nordek in short order but, since there was no consensus -- from the beginning -- on the political objectives of Nordek, even the mere expectation of external events was enough to suspend the further search for consensus.[46]

Following the Finnish declaration of March 1970 no attempt was made by the other Nordic countries to persuade Finland to

---

[46]As Bertel Dahlgaard, a leading Radical Liberal and later Danish Minister for Nordic Economic Cooperation, noted in 1953, "in Denmark we are quite agreed that in this area one cannot go farther than each country wants to go and can gladly go, and not farther than popular opinion in each single country [permits]." Cited in Anderson, op. cit., p. 147 from 1953 *Record of First Annual Session of Nordic Council*, Column 214. Dahlgaard reiterated this view in the 1955 *Record*, p. 57.

change its mind, nor to go ahead with a Skandek without Finland. This again supports the view that when a situation arises where consensus is not possible for external reasons, then each Nordic country goes its separate way while carefully using the Nordic "filter" to obviate the possibility of open conflict which might destroy the "Nordic concept".

CHAPTER 5. THE PREFERRED ALTERNATIVE: FREE TRADE

1. Pragmatic Idealism

In the economic field nothing has been sought as conscientiously
by the Nordics as the ideal of free trade. This is true despite
the twelve years of Nordic Common Market and Nordek negotiations
and the decade of EEC applications. It is not difficult to
understand why free trade should be so attractive to the Nordics,
for all are small economies that depend heavily on external
trade. Hence, free -- or at least freer -- access to other
countries' markets is vital to the continued health of their
economies.

Essentially, two ways exist whereby wider access to markets
can be provided: general trade liberalization and the creation
of a common market. In addition, a number of intermediate
arrangements are also available -- e.g. free trade areas, commodity agreements, bilateral trade arrangements and customs
unions. Each has its attractions, but also its drawbacks. To
take only the two extremes, general free trade and the common
market, the former is attractive because (theoretically, at
least) all barriers to trade are removed, but free trade also
removes all barriers to competition, which means that larger

economies, either because of efficiency resulting from economies
of scale, or because of intrinsic lower costs, or because of
other -- including political -- reasons, are able to take advantage of non-competitive economies. Common markets, on the other
hand, provide protection against competition from outside while
at the same time producing conditions for equitable rationalization of productive resources within an enlarged market area.
This requires the establishment of a central institution, or
institutions, to coordinate and control the industrial rationalization and the external economic relations of the members of
the common market. And this involves the delegation of authority
from the national government to the common institutions. Whether
the latter have constitutionally independent "supranational"
authority or whether they operate on confederal or federal
principles is immaterial: the point is that the common decision
is binding on all members. It is the principle of common decision which for small countries constitutes the greatest drawback
to membership. It is particularly disadvantageous when the
common market consists of some large countries and several
smaller ones, for the larger ones will inevitably dominate
because of their superior power, capability and interests even if
the simple federal principle of representation according to size
is not the prime basis for decision-making.

For the Nordic countries -- consciously nationalist, historically neutralist and therefore anti-bloc in orientation -- it is
the threat to sovereignty and independence of action implied in
the common principle of a common market consisting of unequal
partners that has been the greatest deterrent to membership. The
same fear operated in the case of the Norwegian refusal to enter
into the Nordic Common Market in 1958, even though all the
partners were of more or less similar size -- with the exception
of Sweden, whose domination the Norwegians therefore very much
feared.

Hence, it is not hard to see why free trade -- or at least
freer trade -- has had the greater attraction for the Nordics.
As Frode Jakobsen, one of the few Europeanists among Denmark's

parliamentarians, has said, "For a Dane there is no doubt that a larger area with a smaller degree of unity is preferable to a smaller area with a larger degree of unity."[1] Unfortunately, there can also be little doubt that the Nordics -- and especially the Danes -- have been unable to remain true to the ideal of free trade because of the thrust and momentum of the idea of an exclusive common market among the main trade partners of the Nordic countries -- Germany, France and finally even the United Kingdom. When a quarter to a third of a country's trade is affected by a common market, that country must consider accommodation with it, but when the proportion is more than half, accommodation is inevitable. This, very simply, explains the search for alternatives by the Nordic countries from 1948 to 1970, and the negotiations and arrangements entered into subsequently when Great Britain entered the EEC.

Over the years the Nordic countries' pursuit of the ideal of free trade fits into three categories: the European, the Universal and the Developing Countries. The first category consists of the Organization for European Economic Co-operation (OEEC) and its successor, the Organization for Economic Co-operation and Development (OECD), the Wide Free Trade Area (WFTA)[2] negotiations in 1956-8 and the European Free Trade Association (EFTA). The Universal category consists mainly of the General Agreement on Tariffs and Trade (GATT), the International Monetary Fund (IMF) and the United Nations Conferences on Trade and Development (UNCTAD). The latter may also be considered an example of the Nordic countries' activities in the Developing Countries category which is much less well defined than the other two, since the industrialized world's interest in the developing countries has till recently been largely exploitative. UNCTAD is almost the only attempt made by the former to assist the trade-related

---

[1] *Folketingstidende* [Records of the Folketing] 1952-3, Column 764, cited in Hansen, op. cit., 1969, p. 17.

[2] The term Wide Free Trade Area (WFTA) is adopted to distinguish from EFTA.

problems of the developing countries by at least talking about
the possibilities of liberalizing tariff and non-tariff barriers
to the manufactures of the latter. The Nordic countries, on the
other hand, have been much more systematically sympathetic to the
trade problems of the developing world, and have lost few opportunities in the United Nations and within other international and
European trade related organizations to present suggestions aimed
at assisting the developing world with their trade and growth
problems. In pursuit of this objective the four Nordic countries
have from the mid-1950s -- but particularly from the early 1960s
-- developed a three-pronged attack: first, they have instituted
preferential tariffs for most of the products of the developing
countries; secondly, they have developed aid programmes on a
cooperative basis with the goal of increasing aid to at least 1
per cent of the respective Gross National Products, of reducing
"tied" aid, and of increasing the multilaterally distributed
component thereof; and thirdly, beginning with the Kennedy round
in the GATT negotiations of 1964-7 where the Nordic countries
first cooperated in their economic external negotiations to the
extent of having only a single representative, they have extended
this to the IMF and IBRD where they are also represented by a
single director. In addition, the Nordics have agreed to rotate
membership in the various United Nations organs, and have coordinated their policies at the negotiations at all four UNCTAD
conferences. The Nordics' common "liberalizing" thrust towards
the developing countries is contained within the policy positions
taken by the four at the UNCTAD conferences of 1964, 1968 , 1972
and 1976.

The juxtaposition of the Nordic countries' cooperative
activities above is not intended to suggest that there is any
moral, or immoral, thrust to the Nordic countries' commercial,
financial and aid-related "liberalization" activities. Rather,
the juxtaposing and interweaving is a reflection of reality, and
shows the wide-ranging efforts of the Nordic countries to
maximize their external political standing. It demonstrates that
the Nordics, by cooperating closely on matters on which they

agree anyway, can increase their voice and hence their visibility
as a group of countries seemingly independent of any political
blocs. Moreover, from the strictly economic point of view,
increasing contacts with the developing world through trade and
aid will assist in reducing their market dependence on either
Western or Eastern Europe. But more important, vocal activity in
any support of developing countries will assist in increasing the
likelihood of reaching the objectives of liberalization of trade
through GATT's Kennedy and Tokyo rounds and the restructing of
the IMF's system of international credit. To the extent that the
latter activities are successful, the importance of the EEC and,
for that matter, any common market or customs union declines, and
the Nordic countries will have increased their chances of pre-
serving independence.

The high-point of trade liberalization activities for the
Nordic countries was reached during the Wide Free Trade Area
negotiations between 1956 and 1958. This is not to say that the
Nordic countries have since abandoned the idea of free or freer
trade, as their activities at the GATT, IMF and UNCTAD conferences in the 1960s and 1970s have clearly demonstrated. Nevertheless, it is true that after the failure of the WFTA negotiations, the hope of achieving European free trade receded and the
reality of the EEC began to occupy the Nordic countries' attention.

Hindsight also suggests that the WFTA experience had a
number of long-term effects. First, it disabused everyone
concerned in the negotiations of the notion that any kind of
universal norms or normative ideals motivated European economic
politics. Pragmatic self-interest was the order of the day.
Clearly, neither the idealistic politically unified Europe of
Count Coudenhove-Kalergi and his Pan-Europa Movement, on the one
hand, nor the American-inspired cooperative Europe which the
Marshall Plan and the OEEC had been working for, on the other, was
developing. Instead, a self-centred and inward-looking competitive structuring had become the operative central factor in
European politics. Ironically, it was the WFTA negotiations

which led the EEC Commission to begin to formulate a Community doctrine in order to obviate further pressures for a WFTA-type Europe-wide looser multilateral arrangement.[3]

For the Nordic countries the WFTA negotiations had the salutary effect of exposing the pragmatic basis of their adherence to the principle of trade liberalization. This is most clearly shown by the Danish arguments for the WFTA as well as by Denmark's willingness to make special arrangements with the EEC when it became clear that the WFTA was being aborted.[4] And, the failure of the WFTA and the consequent establishment of the EEC as a self-centred community led directly not only to the more realistic freer (as opposed to free) trade GATT-wide Kennedy and Tokyo rounds and the UNCTAD conferences, but also to a much more realistic Nordic appraisal of the politics of economics: on the one hand, accommodation had to be reached with the Europe of the Six, but on the other hand support for world-wide trade liberalization and a judicious cultivation of the countries of the developing world would reduce the impact of the EEC on the Nordic countries -- at least politically.

2. The WFTA Negotiations: Conflict of Pragmatics

The OEEC Council decision in February 1957 to try to establish a Europe-wide free trade area was a direct reaction to the decision at Messina early in June 1955 by the ministers of the European Coal and Steel Community to proceed to the next stage on the road to European unity with joint action on the development of atomic energy and the establishment of a general common market among the Six. During the rest of the year a committee under the chairmanship of the Belgian Foreign Minister, Paul-Henri Spaak, proceeded to examine the means for achieving these ends. The committee's deliberations resulted in the "Spaak Report" in April 1956,

---

[3]See Leon N. Lindberg, *The Political Dynamics of European Economic Integration* (Stanford, 1963), Chapter 8.

[4]See Section 2.2.1, *The Danish Record*, below.

which contained a detailed plan for the joint development of
atomic energy (Euratom) and a general plan for the progressive
establishment of a common market. In May the report was accepted
by a meeting of the foreign ministers of the Six as the basis for
negotiation for Euratom and Common Market treaties, and M. Spaak
was appointed to direct the negotiations.

It was in the light of these developments that the OEEC
Council at its July 1956 meeting decided first to establish
Working Party No. 17 to study possible forms and methods of
association between the proposed customs union of the Six and the
remaining OEEC countries, and more specifically, the possibility
of establishing a free trade area of western Europe in which the
customs union would be an element; and secondly, to delegate to
the Steering Board of Trade the examination of a plan for the
reduction of tariffs on a Europe-wide basis. The former study
was proposed by the United Kingdom and the latter by a group of
low-tariff countries including Denmark and Sweden. It was agreed
that the Council would decide early the following year which of
the lines proposed by the two committees to pursue. In January
1957 Working Party No. 17 reported that the establishment of a
free trade area was "technically possible". This was followed in
February by a White Paper published by the British Government
presenting its views on the form of the proposed free trade
area.[5] Thereupon the OEEC Council in mid-March decided to
establish three more working parties to study the question in
further detail. Working Party No. 21 was established to

> enter into negotiations in order to determine ways and
> means on the basis of which there could be brought into
> being a European free trade area, which would, on a
> multilateral basis, associate the European Common Market
> with other Member countries of the Organization, and to
> prepare the necessary instruments.[6]

---

[5] A *European Free Trade Area*, Cmnd. 72 (London, HMSO,
February 1957).

[6] *Negotiations for a European Free Trade Area, Documents
Relating to the Negotiations from July 1956 to December 1958*,
Cmnd. 641 (London, HMSO, January 1959), pp. 8-9.

Working Parties Nos. 22 and 23 were to examine arrangements that might be made to accommodate the problems of agricultural trade and the special problems of the underdeveloped members of the OEEC, respectively. It was agreed that the committees report to the Council in time for it to be able to make a decision as its June-July summer session. The summer session of the Council, however, was postponed at the request of the French Government to avoid prejudicing the Treaties of Rome ratification debate scheduled for July in the French National Assembly.[7]

The postponed Council meeting took place in October 1957, and declared

> its determination to secure the establishment of a European Free Trade Area which would comprise all Member countries of the Organization; which would associate, on a multilateral basis, the European Economic Community with the other Member countries which, taking fully into consideration the objectives of the European Economic Community, would in practice take effect parallel with the Treaty of Rome.[8]

At the same time an intergovernmental committee at ministerial level with Reginald Maudling (the Maudling Committee) was established to carry out the detailed negotiations for a free trade area treaty. The Maudling Committee met nine times between November 1957 and November 1958, when negotiations abruptly ceased.[9] Despite diligent work by the committee, in April the negotiations had reached a stalemate from which they never recovered.

2.1 The Central Actors: the British and the French

Though technically it is easy to blame the French for the failure of the WFTA negotiations, in reality the British must carry the

---

[7]Miriam Camps, *Britain and the European Community, 1955-1963* (Princeton, N.J., 1964), pp. 122-3.

[8]Cmnd. 641, op. cit., p. 49.

[9]Meetings took place twice in November 1957, in January and February 1958, middle of March 1958, end of March 1958, July 1958, October 1958 and, 13 and 14 November 1958.

main blame. As Miriam Camps puts it,

> The suspicion that a strong, if not the primary, motive
> behind British proposals for a free trade area was a
> desire to undermine the Six took root very early in the
> negotiations, particularly among the Europeans and par-
> ticularly in France, and this suspicion persisted --
> with periods of comparative dormancy and periods of great
> virulence -- until the negotiations finally collapsed.
> The wave of suspicion in the early months of 1957 was
> nourished by the British attempts to persuade M. Spaak,
> and others, to keep the Six from agreeing on a system of
> tariff reduction and quota removal and on procedures for
> invoking escape clauses before they could be discussed
> within the wider group, and by the insistence with which
> the British argued the need for concerting the arrange-
> ments on these matters between the two groups. Similarly,
> the strong British opposition to the inclusion of the
> overseas territories appeared to some on the Continent
> as another attempt to side-track the Treaty of Rome.[10]

To this a number of additional mistakes on the part of the
British may be added. The fundamental error made by the British
Government was to miscalculate the strength of purpose among the
Six to move towards a common market during 1955-6. As Miriam
Camps points out in an analysis of the failure of the negotiations published in January 1959, "if ... the British Government
had thought that the Six would reach agreement on a common market
and that the agreement would, in fact, be ratified by the French
Assembly, it would, almost certainly, not have withdrawn from the
Brussels discussions -- with what result it is impossible to be
sure."[11] Undoubtedly, the cavalier withdrawal of the British
representative from the discussions after Messina, when the
discussions changed from a technical level to detailed consideration of the problems entailed in negotiating a concrete programme to be followed, made it clear to everyone that Britain was
simply not interested. It should also be recalled that this was
the second time in five years that the British had rejected
continental moves towards a common market, the first being the

---

[10]Camps, op. cit., p. 118.

[11]Miriam Camps, *The Free Trade Area Negotiations*, Policy
memorandum No. 18, Center of International Studies (Princeton
University, February 10, 1959), p. 30.

refusal by both the Labour and the Conservative governments in 1950-1 to join in the Schuman plan which resulted in the European Coal and Steel Community. Hence, it is not hard to accept the view that "many among the Six sincerely believed that only a belated recognition that they were determined to go ahead with a customs union brought the British Government to the point of suggesting that the possibility of a free trade area be studied."[12]

A second serious error made by the British was the publication of the White Paper of February 1957 on the European Free Trade Area. The problem with the Paper was not so much the substance as the way in which the argument was presented, which tended to substantiate the already negative suspicions of the continentals. Two matters, in particular, were offensive to the Europeans. The first was the apparent emphasis on simple removal of trade restrictions and the apparent slighting of the results of two years of intensive negotiation towards the integrated common market treaties. For example, paragraph 11 of the White Paper reads in part:

> The arrangements proposed for the Customs and Economic Union involve far-reaching provisions for economic integration and harmonisation of financial and social policies, and for mutual assistance in the financing of investment.... Her Majesty's Government envisage the Free Trade Area, on the other hand, as a concept related primarily to the removal of restrictions on trade such as tariffs and quotas. Nevertheless, Her Majesty's Government recognize that co-operation in the field of economic policy is of great and continuing importance. In practice an appreciable movement towards closer economic co-operation may be expected to take place among the members of the Free Trade Area over a period of years, either as a matter of deliberate policy or as a spontaneous development.[13]

The second offensive point was the simple position that agriculture must be excluded from the proposed Free Trade Area.

---

[12]Ibid., p. 30.

[13]United Kingdom Memorandum on the European Free Trade Area C(47), 27 of 7 February 1957 (White Paper), also cited in Camps, 1964, p. 114.

The flatly negative position taken on agriculture is a good
indication of the unrealistic "non-European" British view of
Europe, as well as an indication of a vast overestimation of
their own bargaining power. Although the United Kingdom was the
largest single importer of agricultural products in Europe,
discussions within Working Party No. 17 had made it clear that not
only the Six but most other members considered agricultural trade
and regulation to be central to the negotiations.

The third error was tactical. The retention of Reginald
Maudling as principal British spokesman after his appointment as
chairman of the intergovernmental negotiating committee was a
serious error because Britain took the initiative throughout the
WFTA discussions and negotiations, and was generally recognized
as the leader of the other eleven members of the OEEC, while the
French tended to act as spokesman for the Six. Hence, the Franco-
British cast to the WFTA negotiations.

A fourth "error" committed by the British that reinforced
continental doubts concerning the sincerity of Britain's interest in Europe was the misconceived proposal for a British-
Canadian free trade area which resulted from the election of John
Diefenbaker as Canadian Prime Minister in April 1957. At a
meeting of the Commonwealth prime ministers in London in the
summer of 1957, Mr. Diefenbaker suggested that an attempt be made
to achieve a 15% increase in their mutual trade in order to
lessen Canadian trade dependence on the United States. Mr.
Diefenbaker put the Canadian trade diversion proposal within a
general Commonwealth concept, urging that a new Commonwealth
trade conference be held to examine these possibilities: however,
when the Commonwealth finance ministers met subsequently at Mont
Tremblant the British privately suggested to the Canadians the
formation of a British-Canadian free trade area. Whatever the
merits of this scheme and whatever its tactical purposes, the
fact that it was widely publicized in the press strengthened the
"feeling in France, in particular, that free trade with the

United Kingdom would be an open door to the rest of the world."[14]

Of course, British "errors" and miscalculations do not fully explain the failure of the WFTA negotiations. Part of the explanation rests with the Six, principally the French. One of the major factors was the lack of a common position -- and indeed initially the lack of any position -- and a single spokesman for the Six. The Six continued to be represented at the meeting of the Maudling Committee individually even after February 1958 when Professor Hallstein, President of the Commission of the EEC, also attended the meetings -- without, however, having any authority to speak on behalf of the members of the Community; and this must also be taken as an indication of the relative lack of importance that the Six placed on the WFTA negotiations. The reason for this was the diversity of views among the Six - "ranging from those of Dr. Erhard, who would have been happy to accept the plan outlined in the British White Paper, to those who would have been satisfied only by a replica of the Treaty of Rome."[15] Hence a common position was difficult to achieve. Part of the cause was the little consideration that had been given to the implications of the WFTA proposal. Indeed it was not until late March 1958 that a committee of representatives from the Six under the chairmanship of Roger Ockrent, the head of the Belgian delegation to the OEEC, was set up to prepare a realistic common position for the Six. Though the Ockrent Committee was originally charged with presenting its report in time for the next session of the Maudling Committee, it was not until after two reports and three meetings of the Council of Ministers of the EEC that agreement was reached in Brussels on 7 and 8 October and the Community was able to present its memorandum (known as the Ockrent Report) to

---

[14]Camps, 1964, p. 129; see also the Ockrent Report (Memorandum from the European Economic Community of 20 October, 1958), Section III: Coordination of Trade Policies; and IV: Imperial Preference, in Cmnd. 641, op. cit., pp. 98-9; also discussed in Camps, pp. 159-60.

[15]Camps, 1964, p. 169.

the Maudling Committee on 17 October 1958. The main points of the report are summarized by Leon Lindberg:

> (1) The OEEC countries must accept the principle that the differences in treatment arising from the Treaty of Rome were valid and non-discriminatory; (2) there must be explicit recognition that any treaty of association could not impede the implementation of the Treaty of Rome; (3) the fact that there would be no common external tariff and no common trade policy would raise such problems as the deflection of trade and the transfer of activities, and these must be resolved not by general rules, but by means of sector studies of the main branches of economic activity; (4) the Member States of such a free trade area should coordinate their trade policies in regard to third countres (a common trade policy should not be regarded as an objective) so that competition between firms would not be distorted; and (5) if a Member State felt that the import system applied by another state to third countries would distort competition, the institutions would examine the system and make recommendations, the state that believed itself injured being permitted to have recourse to safeguard measures in the interim.[16]

But even the agreement in the Ockrent position was more apparent than real, as the French delegate to the Maudling Committee, M. Wormser, questioned both the principle of tariff autonomy implied in point 3 in the quotation above and the whole question of the extent to which a common commercial policy would be required.[17] This was confirmed a few weeks later when at the conclusion of the November 13-14 meeting of the Maudling Committee the French Minister of Information, Jacques Soustelle, announced that the French Cabinet had decided that "it is not possible to create the "Free Trade Area as wished by the British, that is with free trade between the Common Market and the rest of the OEEC but without a single external tariff barrier around the seventeen countries, and without harmonisation in the economic and social spheres."[18] The Soustelle statement was made without

---

[16]Lindberg, op. cit., pp. 142-3.

[17]Camps, 1964, p. 161.

[18]*Financial Times* (London, 15 November 1958), cited in Camps, *The Free Trade Area Negotiations* 1959, p. 20.

either prior notification or consultation with the other members of the EEC.[19] Though in the event the Soustelle statement became the "veto" that finished the WFTA -- mainly because it was interpreted as such, particularly by Mr. Maudling -- it should not have come as a surprise, being merely a restatement of what the French had been saying all along and in various contexts. What had changed during the Maudling Committee negotiations was that while the British had modified their position from the simple categorical White Paper of 1957 (having, for example, retreated from their White Paper position on agriculture in a memorandum of 6 January 1958 -- substantially, in their own eyes)[20] the French had become more and more intransigent and articulated their original position much more precisely.

Undoubtedly the French political situation throughout 1957 and 1958 had much to do with the development of the articulation of the French position as well as the interpretation placed on it by the United Kingdom and even the other Six, for it should be recalled that the last year of the Fourth Republic had seen unstable government in France, resulting in a succession of spokesmen participating in the WFTA negotiations; even the formation of the Fifth Republic and the installation of General de Gaulle as president on 1 June 1958 brought with it only the beginnings of stability and authority. It was unfortunate for the WFTA that the British misinterpreted not only the original French commitment to both the EEC and an EEC-type WFTA, but also the ability of General de Gaulle to keep Britain out. It is quite probable, had Mr. Maudling kept the negotiations going into 1959, that a compromise free trade area could have been worked out. As Miriam Camps concludes,

it is highly doubtful that the French Government would have held out in the end had they had to do so alone.

_____

[19]See also complete French text in Camps, 1964, footnote 49, p. 165.

[20]See Draft Outline of an Agreement on Agriculture and Fisheries. Submitted by the United Kingdom Government on 6 January 1958. Cmnd. 641, p. 190.

General de Gaulle's position in France and France's
position in the world were far weaker in the autumn of
1958 than they were in January 1963.[21]

2.2 The Peripherals: the Nordics

From the foregoing it is clear that the Nordic countries played a
peripheral role in the WFTA negotiations. Nevertheless, the
negotiations were crucial and proved to be the turning-point that
brought about a slowly dawning realization that eventual economic
integration with western Europe was both real and a problem.

It should be recalled that in 1956, when the WFTA question
arose, the Nordics were waiting for the completion of the Nordic
Economic Cooperation Committee report on the proposed Nordic
Common Market, and that Finland had just joined the Nordic
Council, adding representatives to the ministerial committee of
the Council and to the NECC.[22] Hence, the question of the WFTA
did not become a "Nordic" matter until the fifth session of the
Nordic Council in February 1957, although the Danes, Norwegians
and Swedes, in their capacity as members of the OEEC (Finland was
not a member and joined the OECD only in 1970), had to take a
position at the July 1956 meeting of the OEEC Council. The Danes
and Swedes, as members of the low tariff bloc, joined with
others and forced consideration of their long-standing plans for
tariff reductions. These were remitted to the OEEC's Steering
Board for Trade, but with the proviso that first the OEEC Council
would determine whether the report of Working Party No. 17 held
out "a prospect of substantial progress being achieved before the
end of 1957", before it would instruct the Steering Board to
complete the alternative (tariff reduction) plan for consideration by the full Council.[23]

Of the Nordic countries Denmark was the most active parti-

---

[21]Camps. 1964, p. 172.

[22]See Section 3, Chapter 4 above.

[23]Camps. 1964, p. 99; see also p. 137 above.

cipant in the WFTA negotiations. Beginning in February 1957 and
continuing for the two years of the WFTA question, Danish interest was shown by two market debates in the Folketing, plus
numerous parliamentary interpellations and extra-parliamentary
statements by ministers, farmers and other interest groups.[24]
In contrast, enthusiasm for the WFTA was much less in Norway and
Sweden where parliamentary interest was limited to information
being given to the foreign affairs committees and a few statements and interjections in House sittings. In the Swedish case
there was the parliamentary question of Mr. Antonson of the
Centre Party to the Minister of Commerce, why the Government had
not given Parliament sufficient information on the WFTA negotiations. The reply by Minister Lange was left to one of the last
days of the fall session of 1958[25] and led to a short debate in
the Second Chamber which showed that the four main parties (the
Communists did not participate) were in general agreement with
the Government's position -- which was one of disappointment over
the stalemate in the WFTA negotiations that had developed during
the fall session. Nevertheless, Lange suggested that "the main
interest in the current situation is therefore to create a basis
for continued negotiation and above all to avoid discrimination
in West Europe's common trade."[26] The Geneva negotiations among
the Outer Seven, in the minister's view, had been marked by
common understanding and had created a stronger basis for the
development of a common position.

The fact that the WFTA question arose in the final stages of
the Nordic Common Market discussions did not help the Nordic
countries to take positions; it rather served to confuse, as the
individual governments sought to establish priorities in the

---

[24]The first market debate took place on 6 February 1957 and
the second on 11 February 1958.

[25]Only a few days before the suspension of the WFTA negotiations which ended on December 11.

[26]*Nordisk Kontakt* 1958: 15, p. 816.

light of conflicting interests. The Danes, in particular, were
placed in an unenviable position: as the EEC plans began to move
forward rapidly and the British position on agriculture became
clear in the White Paper of 1957, the problem of the future of
Danish agricultural exports became acute and shifted Denmark from
its historic pan-Scandinavian orientation to an orientation
towards western Europe, and eventually -- by the end of 1958 --
towards the EEC. For the Norwegians the main conflict was the
internal one between the non-socialist parties' opposition to the
Nordic Common Market, and the socialist government party's general
support for it, while support for the WFTA, in contrast, appeared a foregone conclusion -- particularly since Norway's main
trading partner, the United Kingdom, was involved. Sweden found
itself, throughout, in a position of supporting both the Nordic
Common Market and the WFTA, and when the WFTA negotiations
faltered, attempted to reinvigorate the Nordic Common Market
issue. When the WFTA negotiations finally came to an end and the
Nordic Common Market matter seemed stalemated, the Swedes quickly
moved ahead to bring about the interim solution that became EFTA.
The Finns, from beginning to end, had the most straightforward
position of all: participation in any West European arrangement
was impossible but participation in a Nordic non-political
customs union was probable. In other words, the three Nordic
participants in the free trade and Nordic Common Market questions
operated on the basis of pragmatism, but a pragmatism based on
necessity, not preference.

2.2.1 The Danish Record

The search for priorities began with the first Danish market
debate on 6 February 1957. Prime Minister H.C. Hansen equivo-
cated about Denmark's relationship to the EEC, indicating that
there was not enough information yet about the plans of the Six
on "either the area of agriculture or on other matters", and
pointed out that "one thing is in the meantime certain: Denmark
cannot preserve its position as a low tariff country if we enter

the customs union of the Six." He continued, "Membership in the
union will also hinder our participation in a Nordic common
market...."[27] Nevertheless, in the very next sentence the Prime
Minister made it clear that "the Government places the greatest
emphasis on the position of agricultural goods." Similarly,
Minister of Economic Affairs J.O. Krag stressed the importance of
securing the inclusion of agriculture in the WFTA negotiations as
soon as possible. He pointed out that British willingness to consider this matter could become decisive for "our ultimate position and for our future external economic orientation". Minister
Krag also explained that he was of the opinion that "the agreement of the Six leaves the possibility open that outside countries can enter [the EEC]."[28]

Though there appeared to be no conflict between the speedy
establishment of the Nordic Common Market and participation in
European market developments,[29] and though Mr. Krag in his final
speech pointed out that the technical preparations for the Nordic
Common Market plan were far ahead of the European ones, and
consequently the former could be established "considerably faster
than the West European free trade area" and could be incorporated
as an integral part of the latter, the debate showed nonetheless
that West European developments had overtaken the internal Nordic
discussions and had shifted Danish interest from the north towards
the continent.[30]

In a general debate at the fifth session of the Nordic
Council held in Helsinki two weeks later on the relationship
between the Nordic and European market plans, it was agreed that
Denmark, Norway and Sweden would join the WFTA if it were esta-

[27]*Nordisk Kontakt* 1957: 2, p. 13: the market debate is
extensively reported on pp. 12 to 16 inclusive.

[28]Ibid., p. 14.

[29]The difference between a European Common Market and the
free trade area was not made precise in this debate.

[30]*Nordisk Kontakt* 1957: 2, p. 16.

blished. It was also agreed that the Nordic Common Market both
could and should be established. Nevertheless, final positions
could not be taken since views within the Nordic countries about
the relationship between the Nordic integration efforts and the
European plans varied considerably. Finally, it was decided to
postpone further consideration of the Nordic Common Market
question until the NECC report was presented in July 1957.

Shortly after it was presented, it became obvious that
European developments had upset the orderly process of the Nordic
Common Market deliberations. At a meeting of the Nordic Cooperation Ministers in Hamar, Norway, on 6-7 July 1957 it was
decided to postpone consideration of the Nordic Common Market
plan at the forthcoming session of the Nordic Council scheduled
for January-February 1958, apparently in order to permit completion of the WFTA plans which were not expected to reach completion before the late spring 1958. At the joint meeting of the
Nordic Cooperation Ministers, the NECC and the Nordic Council's
Economic Committee at Hindås, Sweden, on 9-10 November 1957, it
was decided to postpone both the Nordic Common Market discussion
and the Nordic Council session itself until late October 1958, in
the expectation that the WFTA plans would then be ready. A
contingency plan to call the Council into extraordinary session
for the purpose of considering both the Nordic Common Market and
the WFTA plans, should the latter be ready for political decision
earlier, was agreed on.[31]

In the meantime, Working Party No. 22 had been set up in
March 1957 and the initial round of consultations on the agricultural problem had already taken place both within the Council
of the OEEC and within the Working Party. At the Council Meeting
on February 12 and 13 the British White Paper position on agriculture was strongly opposed and the Council instructed the

---

[31]See *Nordisk Kontakt* 1957: 14, pp. 3 and 27; see also
discussion in Wendt, op. cit., pp. 206-16. Communique of Hindås
meeting reprinted in Royal Ministry for Foreign Affairs, *Documents on Swedish Foreign Policy 1957*, pp. 52-3.

second working party (in March to be numbered 22) to pay

> special attention to the objective of finding ways to
> ensure the expansion of trade in agricultural products on
> a non-discriminatory basis between all Member-countries
> of the Organization, and with a view to strengthening
> their agricultural economies and making them more
> competitive.[32]

When the preliminary WFTA negotiations began in March, the Danes,
closely supported by the Swedes, were very active in attempting
to bring the positions of Britain and the EEC on agriculture into
line. By the time that Working Party No. 22 reported to the
Council on 20 July 1957, little had been accomplished beyond
"that the diametrically opposite views represented at the start
by the United Kingdom and Denmark seemed to be at least partially
on the way towards reconciliation."[33] The Working Party report
came to the initial conclusion that nobody wanted completely free
trade in agriculture: "Progressive total liberalization of trade
in agricultural products is not at present acceptable to the
great majority of governments," and "the creation of a Free Trade
Area is inconceivable unless a special effort is made in the
agricultural sector as well, failing which the plan will be
unbalanced for most countries."[34] Nevertheless, the Danes did
not give up their campaign against the British position. In
fact, throughout the WFTA negotiations the Danes pursued an "open
door" policy toward the EEC. The purpose of this appears to have
been twofold: on the one hand to put pressure on the British,
and on the other to safeguard Denmark's agricultural exports to
the EEC in case the WFTA negotiations failed. In pursuit of the
latter, Minister Krag headed a Danish delegation on 16 and 17
April 1957 to negotiate with the Spaak Interim Committee in
Brussels, which received official confirmation that the EEC would
welcome Danish membership. Secondly, it discovered that the

---

[32]Cmnd. 641, op. cit., p. 9.

[33]The Swedish Royal Ministry for Foreign Affairs, *Negotiations for a European Free Trade Area, 1956-58* (Stockholm 1959), p. 41.

[34]Cmnd. 641, op. cit., p. 22.

views of the EEC and Denmark coincided on the inclusion of
agriculture in the WFTA. The third objective, to discover
whether or not special arrangements could be made to grant free
entry of Danish agricultural exports to the EEC (on a reciprocal
basis with Denmark granting free entry to the EEC's industrial
products), however, met with a rebuff, mainly because the EEC
Interim Committee found the Danes unduly hasty in attempting to
gain specific commitments before the Treaty of Rome was even
ratified.

But the Danes did not give up the pursuit of safeguarding
their agricultural exports. Another delegation negotiated with
the EEC Interim Committee in late July and with the West German
Government in early August 1957. The main purpose was to seek
participation in the EEC's agricultural conference scheduled for
the summer of 1958. This particular attempt met with a mixed
reaction. Though the German Government was reported to have
shown "an understanding" of Denmark's wish, the Dutch Government
on 20 September issued a statement in which it welcomed Danish
membership in the EEC, but only as a full member, and not through
some form of special agricultural association. If the Danes
insisted on the latter then the Dutch, the statement said, would
oppose Danish inclusion in the agricultural conference. Despite
this the Danes continued to seek admission to the conference
until May 1958, but failed.[35]

The "open door" policy towards the EEC, which stopped short
of proposing membership in the Six, was the result of internal
political-economic factors. These were three in number. First,
there was the problem of support in Parliament for a minority
government up till the election of 14 May 1957, and of a coalition of Social Democrats, Radical Liberals and the Georgist
Justice Party after that date; secondly, there were the interest
and pressure groups, with their parliamentary spokesmen ranging
from outspoken support for EEC membership to equally outspoken
opposition; and, finally there was the historic anti-continental,

---

[35]Nielsson, op. cit., pp. 442-44.

pro-Scandinavian and strongly nationalist Danish cultural ethos
which permeates Danish life, and has not been dissipated even by
the referendum of 5 October 1972. The first and second factors
forced both the minority and the successor coalition governments
of the Social Democrat H.C. Hansen, although he was supported by
the vocal anti-EEC and pro-Nordic labour movement, to pay careful
attention to the pro-EEC stand of the agricultural associations
and their parliamentary representation, the Liberal Party. The
fact that the Social Democrats lost four seats whereas the
Liberals picked up three in the 1957 elections added to the
authority of the economic policy demands of the latter party,
which moved from a cautious equivocating position on the WFTA-EEC
membership alternatives in 1957 to a firm stand in favour of EEC
membership by October 1958.[36]

Danish industry and commerce took a generally anti-EEC
position at this time. Industry's attitude was based on its
economic inefficiency. The Danish economic structure was the
reverse of the Swedish and of most continental economic structures which had efficient competitive manufacturing sectors and
highly protected inefficient agricultural sectors: in Denmark,
by contrast, the agricultural sectors, including basic production
and food manufacture, were highly efficient. Hence, the Danish
economy was a combination of a highly competitive agricultural
industry needing no tariff protection and a manufacturing industry hiding behind non-tariff barriers. Quota restrictions
covered 66% of Danish industrial production. Of all OEEC members
only Norwegian and French industry had as high protective walls
as Danish.[37] It was no wonder that Danish industry rejected the
EEC with its plan to remove all barriers to both industrial and
agricultural trade among its members.

What is more interesting is the gradual acceptance of the

---

[36]See Nielsson, op. cit., pp. 341-9; *Nordisk Kontakt* 1957:
9, pp. 7-12 on the election of 1957 and the formation of the
government.

[37]Nielsson, op. cit., p. 352.

WFTA, possibly encompassing a Nordic Common Market, as a solution to the challenge of the EEC. The reason for this is twofold: first, such an arrangement would permit a slow trade liberalization during which Danish industry could be structured to become more competitive, and secondly, since no common external tariff was required, a sizeable overseas market could be further developed to offset the intra-WFTA competition. The weakness of the competitive position of Danish industry and the consequent need to restructure it quickly was made clear in the report of the government commission appointed in 1957 to analyse the impact of both the EEC and the WFTA on Danish industry. It reported in July 1958:

A total of 39% of industrial production will thus be subjected to serious risks and production will decrease, unless a restructuring of production takes place in order to adapt it to the future conditions in a larger market. This restructuring is necessary immediately for over half of the industries involved.[38]

Note that the reference is not to the export industry but to total industry. The condition of Danish industry is further underlined in the conclusion to the first volume of the report:

Despite the strong growth in industrial export, developments in industrial production, employment and investments, etc., in the postwar years, however, cannot be characterized as satisfactory in relation to developments in other West European countries. While industrial production increased in all OEEC countries by over 50% from 1950 to 1957, industrial production in this country has risen by barely 15%, and while employment in industry in the OEEC countries has increased by 15% from 1950 to 1957, in this country it has increased only by 2 per cent.

Industrial investments have in the years 1950-7 rested on a plateau between 500 and 650 million kroner, corresponding to about 2% of Gross National Product, while industrial investment in the OEEC countries in total has been considerably larger.[39]

In the light of this kind of public analysis, it is not

[38]Udenrigsministeriet og Det Økonomiske Sekretariat, *Danmark og de Europaeiske Markedsplaner* (Copenhagen, 1958), Vol. I, p. 68.

[39]Ibid., p. 181.

surprising that Danish industry preferred the WFTA to the EEC.
The Nordic Common Market also began to look considerably more
attractive to industry -- which hitherto had been lukewarm
towards it -- particularly as a "training ground" for large-scale
industrial competitiveness.[40]

As far as the Conservative Party, the parliamentary partner
of industry, was concerned, its initial enthusiasm for the EEC --
the result of its close cooperation with the main opposition
party, the Liberals -- was considerably reduced by industry's
opposition to it. The parliamentary spokesman for the Conservatives, Ole Bjørn Kraft, took the position in the 1958 market
debate that

> The decision ought to be positive as a logical conse-
> quence of our acknowledgement that Western Europe is a
> unit. And if Denmark wishes to take advantage of ex-
> panded European cooperation we must also pay a price for
> that.... But naturally we must safeguard our own in-
> terests as effectively as possible. This concerns our
> agricultural export interests.... And it concerns our
> industries' interests.[41]

Kraft also made it clear that the Conservatives' preference
was that "the best solution for Scandinavia and for us would be a
Nordic Common Market as part of the Wide Free Trade Area which
includes both agriculture and industry."[42] He concluded that it
was essential to keep the door open to the EEC as a contingency
plan in case "the negotiations about the WFTA failed and bilateral arrangements were concluded between individual countries and
the EEC."[43]

Throughout the period of the Danish EEC "open door" policy,
the Norwegians and Swedes refrained from criticizing Danish
efforts, and sought instead to develop mutually supportive
positions in the WFTA negotiations. In this the three Nordic

---

[40]Nielsson, op. cit., p. 357.

[41]*Nordisk Kontakt* 1958: 3, p. 119.

[42]Nielsson, op. cit., p. 366.

[43]*Nordisk Kontakt* 1958: 3, p. 119.

countries were successful, as demonstrated by the joint memorandum of the three countries to the OEEC Council on 24 October 1948, which was a formal reaction to the EEC memorandum on agriculture of 25 June 1958. In it the Nordic countries found that they could support each other on the basic problem areas -- agriculture for Denmark, fisheries for Norway and forestry and metal industries for Sweden. Paragraph 2 of the memorandum reads:

> In order to be acceptable to the three governments, the plans for the progressive liberalization of the trade in industrial products by means of abolition of quantitative restrictions and customs duties must be matched by appropriate measures required to allow food-exporting countries adequate opportunities not only to maintain competitive exports of agricultural products, but also to increase such exports.

The Nordic countries further pointed out in their memorandum that they agreed with the EEC's proposal for the treatment of agriculture (including fisheries):

> The three governments are of the opinion that a multilateral agricultural arrangements based largely on the principles laid down in the Rome Treaty would be the best means of guaranteeing the food-exporting countries a reasonable degree of reciprocity, while taking into consideration the special social and economic conditions prevailing in agriculture in most of the member countries.... The proposals by the EEC seem to constitute a realistic basis for negotiations leading to such arrangements.[44]

2.2.2 The Norwegian Position

The agreement on the WFTA, expressed in the Scandinavian memorandum to the EEC Council, was possible because in Norway and Sweden, in contrast to Denmark, there was general agreement among the different sectors of the economy and among the political parties that joining the WFTA was necessary; however, joining the EEC was out of the question. For Norwegians the argument for joining the

---

[44]*Joint Memorandum from the Danish, Norwegian and Swedish Delegations on the Memorandum from the EEC Regarding Agriculture*, Cmnd. 641, op. cit., p. 204.

WFTA was simple: 'Whatever the United Kingdom does we must do as well, in order not to cut ourselves off from our important commercial links with it.' Even the National Union of Farmers (*Landbrukets Sentralforbund*) took the position in early 1957 that it would be "very difficult for Norway to keep itself outside if England joins a European free trade area."[45] This support is the more remarkable since Norwegian agriculture has always been marginal and in need of protection from external competition. Hence it is not surprising that the National Farmers Union also added a corollary to its support for joining the WFTA, asking that the Government show "caution and reserve during the negotiations and ... that serious attempts be made to keep agricultural goods outside."[46] In the light of the farmers' reservation, it is noteworthy that the Norwegians supported the Danes a year and a half later in their demand for inclusion of agriculture in the free trade area. The explanation for this is twofold. First, by the beginning of 1958 the British themselves had agreed to the inclusion of agriculture, and secondly, the argument by the summer of 1958 was over the method of including agriculture. In the Scandinavian memorandum a sectoral approach was recommended, including bilateral arrangements relating to both tariffs and import quotas which would facilitate the transitional period.[47]

By far the most important sector to be affected by European integration plans was that of the export industries. The Norwegian Export Council (*Norges Eksportråd*), in a statement at about the same time as the National Farmers Union pronouncement, took the position that "it was necessary and advantageous for Norway to participate in the plan about a free trade area on the most favourable terms and that Norway should actively support the

---

[45]*Nordisk Kontakt* 1957: 3, p. 35.

[46]Idem.

[47]*Joint Memorandum from the Danish, Norwegian and Swedish Delegations on the Memorandum from EEC Regarding Agriculture*, Cmnd. 641, op. cit., pp. 204-5.

work to make the plan a reality." The Export Council regarded the WFTA as a necessary defensive mechanism to safeguard the Norwegian markets in the EEC. As they put it, "if the free trade area with participation of most western European countries does not become a reality, then one can count on a common market between France, West Germany, Italy and the Benelux ... [which] will develop into a mighty economic factor."[48] In the light of such fears it is not hard to see Norway joining Sweden in supporting Denmark to strengthen its hand in pushing the negotiations forward toward a conclusion.

It may also be added, as a corollary, that the Nordic practice of showing a united front towards the outside world made a joint communiqué taking a common position almost a necessity, particularly in a situation when agreement was dictated by external factors anyway.

2.2.3 The Swedish Position

In Sweden there was unanimous agreement among the political parties and the economic sectors and interest groups that joining the EEC was unacceptable because of its aim of political integration and economic union with powerful supranational institutions. Furthermore, the high tariff walls of the EEC were unacceptable to Sweden because of its long tradition of low tariffs and its commitment to free trade. Although no parliamentary debates were arranged to discuss either the WFTA or the EEC, a statement was read to the Riksdag on 20 March 1957 by the Prime Minister in the First Chamber and by the Foreign Minister in the Second Chamber, in which the Government pointed out:

> In view of the fact that a very considerable part of
> Sweden's external trade is with the United Kingdom and
> countries on the European Continent, it is clear that for
> Sweden too it is important not to stand outside a free
> trade area comprising most of the member-states of the
> OEEC.... The creation of a free trade area is in line
> with the efforts which traditionally have been one of the

---

[48] *Nordisk Kontakt* 1957: 3, p. 35.

main aims of Swedish commercial policy.[49]

At a series of meetings held during the fall of 1958 at Harpsund, the Swedish prime ministerial country residence, between the Government and representatives of various branches of the economy, including the trade unions, it was reported that "total unity was reached on the question of the European market among the different groups." Prime Minister Erlander explained after the meeting that it was "certainly the most thorough discussion that we have had with the business community about free trade...." The Government, the business community and the trade union movement were fully agreed that everything possible ought to be done in order to get the WFTA established, and to "counteract all the attempts at discrimination which it is feared will arise beginning with the first of January when the Six power treaty enters into force."[50]

2.2.4 External Unity, Internal Disunity

The agreement between Denmark, Norway and Sweden on the WFTA position is all the more remarkable since the three could not reach a similar degree of unity on the Nordic Common Market question which was being negotiated simultaneously with the WFTA. Indeed the Nordic Economic Cooperation Committee held seventeen meetings during the WFTA negotiations of 1957 and 1958, the Secretariat of the Nordic Council held thirty meetings, while twenty-four special committees gathered for sixty-five additional meetings.[51] The staff for these meetings included approximately

---

[49]The Royal Ministry for Foreign Affairs, *Documents on Swedish Foreign Policy 1957*, pp. 23-4.

[50]*Nordisk Kontakt* 1958: 14, pp. 772-3. It should be noted that the interpellation debate at the end of the session in 1958 in December revolved around the "jealousy" of the opposition parties over having been left out of the informal Harpsund discussions. There were no criticisms of the positions reached at Harpsund.

[51]Anderson, op. cit., p. 155, see also the 1958 Record of the Nordic Council, p. 1255.

twenty Norwegian civil servants, over forty Danish and more than
forty Swedish civil servants and consultants, and about sixty-
five Finnish government officials and experts.[52] Despite the
prodigious activity of all these experts which resulted in over
1,800 pages of reports supporting the formation of a Nordic
common market, the three countries could not agree politically.
Although the Danes lost interest in the Nordic Common Market in
early 1957, it should not be forgotten that all four countries
involved, including Finland, agreed at the top level meeting at
Hindås in early November 1957 to postpone the Nordic Common
Market discussions until October-November 1958 in the expectation
that the WFTA plans would then be ready.

In the summer of 1958, during the lull in the WFTA negotiations resulting from the metamorphosis in France of the Fourth
into the Fifth Republic, the Swedish Government seized the
initiative for pressing for decisive action on the Nordic Common
Market at the forthcoming Nordic Council session. The Danish
Government also showed renewed interest in establishing the
Nordic Common Market before the conclusion of the European
negotiations, because the common external tariff of the Nordic
Common Market would mean that the Danish import tariffs would be
increased to the common Nordic level, and would put Danish
industry in a better position from which to negotiate mutual
tariff reductions with the EEC and other European states. It was
also felt that should the WFTA negotiations fail, then the Nordic
Common Market would be in a better position than individual
countries to negotiate a tariff agreement with the EEC.

Another top-level meeting of the Nordic Cooperation Ministers, the NECC, the Nordic Council's Presidium and its economic
committee was held on September 22 and 23 at Saltsjöbaden in
Sweden where the final report of the NECC, covering the last 20%
of intra-Nordic trade (except agriculture), was discussed. At
the meeting Gunnar Lange, the Swedish Minister of Commerce,

---

[52]Anderson, ibid., p. 116.

proposed that the Nordic Common Market should be instituted immediately for a limited range of commodities, to be followed by a political decision to expand this to a full common market within two years. The proposal was rejected out of hand by both the Danish and the Norwegian representatives. In fact, the Danes favoured another postponement of the Nordic Council's annual session to January 1959, whereas the Norwegian representatives took the position that a Nordic customs union should not be formed if the WFTA negotiations led to a successful conclusion. However, if they failed, a "British-oriented" Nordic cooperative structure should then be established. The only agreement at the Saltsjöbaden meeting was to postpone the Nordic Council session for two weeks in the hope that the October session of the Maudling Committee would clear up the confused WFTA situation, for the meeting felt that the Nordic governments could not be expected to take a stand on the Nordic Common Market until the future of the West European free trade area was more predictable.[53]

It was against the background of the threat of collapse of the WFTA negotations, which had become very real in the three weeks since the Saltsjöbaden meeting, that the Nordic Council's sixth session was held at Oslo on November 9-15. The discussions of economic cooperation were dominated entirely by the pessimistic outlook of the WFTA negotiations and led to an unusual step being taken: the Council passed a resolution in which the governments of Denmark, Iceland, Norway and Sweden were urged to inform the other parties to the negotiations in the OEEC of the strong support of the Nordic countries for the WFTA and "to join forces during the OEEC negotiations to obtain a solution which would safeguard and strengthen economic cooperation in Europe through the formation of a free trade area."[54]   In addition,

---

[53]See Nielsson, op. cit., pp. 426-7; Wendt, op. cit., pp. 222-3; Anderson, op. cit., p. 133; *Nordisk Kontakt* 1958:   12, p. 601.

[54]*Nordisk Kontakt* 1958:   13, p. 661.

Swedish Prime Minister Tage Erlander, in his opening statement to
the Council on November 9, issued a warning that

it is also of joint Nordic interest that such a solution
be found as quickly as possible. By their own treaty,
the Six continental countries are to begin to remove
barriers to mutual trade on 1 January 1959. In this way
there is a danger that our countries up here in the North
will be subject to discrimination by the Six Powers which
is irreconcilable with a close Western European association, and that is something which we could not accept
without protest.

After pointing to the importance to the Nordic countries of
continuing to stick together at the WFTA negotiations, since "we
are by no means insignificant as negotiating partners" in view of
providing a sizeable market for the EEC, he was nevertheless pessimistic about the possibilities of success and came to this
conclusion:

What is clear, however, is that we should then be faced
with a new situation and this new situation would perhaps
make it even more essential for the Nordic Market to be a
living reality.[55]

Unfortunately, the Danes had reversed their recent enthusiasm for the Nordic Common Market and took the position, in the
words of Minister of Finance Viggo Kampmann, that the Danish
Government "hopes that the currently ongoing negotiations about
the European market plans in the near future will develop in such
a way that there will be a basis to take a favourable position on
the Nordic plans."[56] Clearly, it was not possible to come to any
conclusion on the question of the Nordic Common Market, and the
Council simply agreed unanimously that it now considered its work
on the common market finished. Ironically, the final resolution
recommended that the four governments "take up negotiations on a
draft convention for Nordic economic cooperation to be presented
to the parliaments when the preconditions for final ratification
are considered present."[57] In other words, nothing had changed

---

[55]*Documents on Swedish Foreign Policy*, 1958, p. 37.

[56]*Nordisk Kontakt* 1958: 13, p. 662.

[57]Recommendation 26/1958, see *Nordisk Kontakt* 1958: 13, p.
661.

since the beginning of common market discussions in 1948. In the light of direct government involvement in the Nordic Economic Cooperation Committee's researches, preparations and negotiations, the final resolution of the Council can only be taken as an empty gesture meant to keep the Nordic Common Market idea alive, as it had been kept alive for ten years. The Nordic countries simply did not want to overcome their individual differences unless forced to do so by external factors beyond their control.

CHAPTER 6. EFTA -- THE PRAGMATIC EPILOGUE

After the collapse of the WFTA and the Nordic Common Market negotiations, Sweden quickly mobilized the unanimity of views that
had developed among the Other Six at the OEEC negotiations in
Paris, and proposed the formation of a rump free trade area to
counteract the economic power of the Six. The Swedish initiative
was possible because of three factors: first, the habit of
economic consultation between the United Kingdom and the three
Scandinavian countries which had been formalized through the
establishment of UNISCAN in 1949; secondly, during the Maudling
Committee negotiations the Scandinavians and the United Kingdom,
joined by Switzerland and Austria, had found themselves generally
agreeing on the key issues, with the result that they became
known as the Other Six; and thirdly, the Other Six were generally
agreed -- though with differing degrees of enthusiasm -- on a
preference for a free trade area as opposed to a customs union.
Nonetheless, despite their history of consultation, they formed a
disparate group and united around the concept of free trade only
because it was the sole alternative to the two other choices:
political integration implied by the EEC, or isolation implied by
rejection of both the EEC and the free trade area concept. For
the three neutrals -- Sweden, Switzerland and Austria -- a

customs union requiring a common tariff and a common commercial
policy would have raised political problems inconsistent with the
requirements of neutrality. For Britain the whole idea of supranational arrangements implied by a customs union was repugnant
both in principle and on the basis of its estimation of its own
position in the international system. And Norway simply did not
want to become caught up in any economic movement which might
lead to political integration. Of the six, Denmark was the only
one which did not have a preponderantly anti-integrationist
position. Denmark's great fear was to be isolated from the other
Nordic countries and from the United Kingdom on both the political
and economic levels.

From the strictly economic point of view the Other Six
formed yet another mix. The United Kingdom, Switzerland and
Sweden were three traditionally low tariff countries with industrial structures based on the assumption that they could import
most raw materials and semi-manufactures either tariff-free, or
at very low tariff rates, and were therefore strongly opposed to
the raising of their own tariffs which harmonization with the
common tariff in a customs union with the Six would require. The
Danes and Norwegians -- also relatively low tariff countries,
though with high non-tariffs barriers against selected manufactures -- were also opposed to any arrangement which would neces-
sitate the raising of tariffs. In contrast the Austrians,
already the possessors of high tariff barriers, were not con-
cerened at all about the economic consequences of harmonization
of tariff barriers, but were deeply troubled by the political
consequences of opening their borders to the economic might of
their neighbour West Germany.

In addition to the diverse economic positions, Denmark
presented a case of economic schizophrenia. On the one hand, it
wished to preserve its sizeable, though declining, agricultural
market in the United Kingdom, while on the other hand, it des-
perately wished to safeguard and secure the expansion of its
sizeable markets within the EEC, particularly in West Germany.
The composition and direction of Danish trade shows that agri-

cultural exports were of such overwhelming importance to Denmark
in the 1950s that the economic dislocations that the manufacturing industry would suffer would have been overshadowed by the
advantages of membership of the EEC, had that not been politically distasteful to the Danes. As it was, Denmark might very well
have joined the EEC in 1959 had EFTA not been formed and had
Britain not made membership in the EFTA palatable through special
agricultural concessions. Even so, throughout the existence of
EFTA, Denmark was its most restless member and was keenly interested in every opportunity to join the EEC.

Given the disparate political and economic interests and
positions of the Other Six, it is probably a fair assessment that
the main reason for the Swedish initiative getting off the ground
was the great fear among them that if they did not unite in some
minimal form for at least some temporary period to counteract the
unity of purpose of the Six, they would all be in a highly
disadvantageous position in attempting to reach bilateral trade
agreements with the Six.

The negotiations leading to the signing of the European Free
Trade Association may be divided into two phases. In the first,
lasting from December 1958 to March 1959, private discussions and
consultations took place at both the official and non-official
levels. The second phase, which lasted a scant half year (May -
November 1959), saw continual negotiations carried on among the
"Outer Seven" (the Other Six were now joined by Portugal) on the
basis of a firm draft convention drawn up by Sweden.

The first phase began only two days after Maudling suspended
the WFTA negotiations. On 18 November 1958 the Swedish Government invited representatives from the Other Six to a meeting at
Stockholm to discuss the coordination of future trade policies.
This, however, was considered premature, and the invitation was
withdrawn the very next day. The industrialists evidently did
not think so, as was demonstrated by the statement issued on 17
December 1958 by representatives of the Federation of British
Industries (later renamed the Confederation of British Industries)
and the Swedish Federation of Industries which called for the

immediate establishment of a trading association among the Other
Six. This was followed by an extensive series of discussions
among the industrial federations of the Other Six carried on with
"the knowledge and tacit approval, if not open support", of the
governments.[1]

At the bureaucratic level, the move from WFTA negotiations
to EFTA discussions was a natural progression resulting from the
abrupt collapse of the Paris talks. High government officials
from the Outer Seven met in Geneva on 1 and 2 December 1958 to
discuss the problem of tariff discrimination which would begin on
1 January 1959, the effective date of the Rome Treaty. At this
meeting there was general agreement that, whatever happened in
the short run, the long term solution should be built on cooperation within the OEEC, and that negotiations to this end
should be continued within the framework of the OEEC. One
hopeful sign was the mandate given by the ministerial Council of
the EEC to its operative arm, the Commission, to work out a new
proposal to produce a multilateral solution to the problem of
tariff discrimination between the EEC and the rest of OEEC, to be
presented by 1 March 1959. Early in the new year, however, it
became clear that the Commission was not going to produce a
proposal which would satisfy the interests of the rest of the
OEEC. This led to another meeting of senior officials of the
Outer Seven at Oslo on 21 February 1959. The discussions now revolved around possible long-term solutions, rather than immediate
problems of discrimination. Although it was agreed to await the
report of the EEC Commission, the generally pessimistic outlook
for any OEEC-wide solution led to the idea of establishing closer
economic cooperation among the Seven in order to prepare for a
later Europe-wide solution. It was agreed to study the possibilities of such cooperation while awaiting the Commission's
report.

In the event, the pessimism about the report was well justified. It proved to be little more than a collection of views and

---

[1]Camps, op. cit., 1964, p. 213.

assessments of possible future trade developments rather than concrete proposals for their solution. The Commission took the position that long-term solutions could not be found within the limited European framework but had to be sought on a worldwide basis. Consequently, the Six could not consider the OEEC countries in isolation from the rest of the world. A European solution could perhaps take place, but not in the immediate future. According to the Commission, those European countries which wished to reach closer economic cooperation with the Six in the meantime could do so either on the basis of Article 237, which provided for full membership, or Article 238, which provided for association with the EEC.[2]

The report, presented at the beginning of March, had an immediate and decisive effect on the Outer Seven. A meeting of senior officials was called for March 17-18 in Stockholm, at which a decision was made actively to pursue the formation of a free trade area apart from the Six, but still within the framework of the OEEC, and with the long-term objective of including all the members. In the meantime it was agreed that the Seven should not make separate agreements with the EEC countries without prior consultation with each other.

At the Stockholm meeting the leader of the Swedish delegation, Hubert de Besche, Assistant Under-Secretary in the Swedish Department of Foreign Affairs, was appointed coordinator of the negotiations and was given the task of drawing up a proposal outlining a plan for the Outer Seven free trade area. During the next month, de Besche toured the capitals of the seven prospective free trade area members, discussed the problems involved and lined up support for the project. As a result of these informal discussions, de Besche and S. Chr. Sommerfelt, the Norwegian representative at the Stockholm meeting, reported of the informal consultations that all were agreed on the plan for a free trade area but that there were two main problem areas where the members

---

[2]See Norway, Utenriksdepartementet, Stortings proposition nr. 75 (1959-60).

of the group had differing views. The first concerned the form
of the transitional period. Two views were presented. The one
preferred an immediate removal of import barriers -- excepting
a limited amount, about 15%, where barriers could be reduced over
a period of ten years. The alternative view was that there
should be a gradual reduction in barriers to imports over a
period of ten years, which would coincide with the EEC's transitional period of twelve years, since it would take at least two
years for the free trade area to come into operation. In order
to bring the latter into step with the EEC, the initial tariff
reduction -- to go into effect on 1 July 1960 -- should be 20% of
the existing rate. The informal consultations by de Besche had
shown that the majority of the Outer Seven were in favour of the
longer transitional period, not least because the former was
regarded as an attack on the EEC, whereas the latter appeared to
be directed towards the original OEEC idea of solving the problems of trade on a Europe-wide basis.

The second main problem concerned agriculture and fisheries.
The British, in particular, were unwilling to apply the general
rules of trade liberalization to these two areas, but they did
indicate that they were willing to make special concessions to
particular countries and in particular commodity sectors. Apart
from these two areas of disagreement there was general consensus
as there had been during the Paris negotiations where the Outer
Six had taken very similar positions on the details of trade
liberalization.

The second, or political phase, of the EFTA negotiations was
inaugurated at a meeting at Saltsjöbaden called by the Swedish
Government for the beginning of June. The meeting, which took
place on 7-13 June, involved forty government officials from the
seven countries and had as its mandate the preparation of a draft
European Free Trade Area convention which could then be presented
to the respective governments for political decision. The
conference took as its point of departure de Besche's report,
and quickly came to the conclusion that a longer rather than a
shorter transitional period was required. As expected by now,

discussions about agriculture and fisheries took up a great deal
of time without much agreement, but at least the main problem
areas were detailed. Discussion relating to other problems, such
as the problem of origin which the establishment of the Free
Trade Area would raise, followed in large measure the positions
taken by the Other Six at the Paris negotiations. Two reservations were raised by the Danes and the Portuguese. The Danish
representatives emphasized that the final Danish position with
respect to joining or not joining EFTA would be taken on the
basis of a calculation of the advantages for the export of Danish
agricultural products. The Portuguese took the position that
Portugal required a longer transitional period than the others
because of its less developed industrial status. Indeed, this
was the reason why Portugal had belonged to the "forgotten five"
rather than the Other Six at the Paris negotiations.

In the meantime, while the senior officials of the Seven had
been busy consulting, discussing and negotiating for about half a
year, the Nordic Common Market proposal had been revitalized. On
24 and 25 January 1959 a prime ministerial meeting of the four
Nordic countries involved in the Nordic Common Market was held in
Oslo, with seventeen other cabinet ministers attending, to
discuss future possible common action in the light of the breakdown of the WFTA negotiations. The Norwegians and the Finns led
off the discussion with a reversion to the earlier idea of
initiating a gradual Nordic Common Market process, but with a new
twist: for some commodities, the common market should go into
operation according to the NECC draft plan, but for other commodities a "declared customs union" with gradual harmonization of
external tariffs and reduction of internal tariffs should apply.
The Swedes and the Danes objected to the proposal, but it was
agreed that the cooperation committee should look into the
possibility of modifying the original plan. It was also agreed,
for the first time in the ten years of common market discussions,
that agriculture and fisheries ought to be included in the Nordic
Common Market. Denmark, Norway and Sweden also had a discussion
about the current confused state of economic cooperative posi-

tions on the European front. Finally, at the insistence of
Denmark, it was agreed that future prime ministerial meetings
relating to the Nordic Common Market should be suspended until
the Commission of the EEC made its report on resolving the
dilemma between the EEC and the Other Six.

The upshot of the Oslo meeting was the immediate institution
of two series of meetings, one at the ministerial level at which
agriculture and fisheries were negotiated bilaterally, and one
involving the Nordic Cooperation Ministers and the NECC which
discussed the Norwegian-Finnish proposal and alternatives to it.
At first, good progress was made in both series of negotiations,
but between March and June it became clear that Sweden, Norway
and Denmark were all more interested in the wider EFTA solution
than in the Nordic solution. The foreign affairs debate in the
Swedish Second Chamber in March 1959 showed a general preference
for an EFTA which should, however, include a Nordic Common
Market.[3] Similarly, in May in a joint letter to the Prime
Minister, the Norwegian Union of Banks, the Federation of Industries, the Federation of Craft Unions, and the Federation of Ship
Owners expressed a very strong opposition to the Nordic Common
Market, on the grounds that a Nordic Customs Union would weaken
the Norwegian terms of trade by isolating Norway from its West
European trade partners.[4]

Denmark, still working for a compromise solution with the
EEC in which the EFTA and the Nordic proposals could be fitted,
was finally forced to make up its mind by the failure of the
"bridge-building" attempt between the EEC and the Outer Seven in
late May 1959, which demonstrated to the Danes that any West
European Free Trade Agreement including the Six was impossible
and that the choice was to join either the EEC or EFTA. And once
the decision to join EFTA -- as the lesser of two evils -- was
made, the attraction of the Nordic Common Market also lessened.

---

[3]*Nordisk Kontakt* 1959: 5, pp. 245-9.

[4]*Nordisk Kontakt* 1959: 9, p. 439.

In any case, the Nordic Common Market had never proved particularly attractive to Danish agricultural interests.[5] The Danes were also under considerable pressure from the other Nordics to join in the EFTA plan.[6] Once the Danes had made the decision to join EFTA, they immediately began to explore the possibilities of securing their agricultural exports in their traditional markets within the Outer Seven, as the Danish representatives to the Saltsjöbaden officials' meeting had promised. These explorations resulted very quickly in a British-Danish bilateral agreement in which the United Kingdom agreed to eliminate its 10% *ad valorem* tariff on bacon imports from Denmark (and from the other countries within EFTA) in two stages. A 50% reduction in the tariff was to be made on 1 July 1960, with complete elimination a year later. It was also agreed to eliminate a few less important tariff items, including canned pork luncheon meat, canned cream and blue-veined cheese.[7] A similar bilateral agreement was also concluded between Denmark and Sweden. As the result, at an extraordinary meeting on July 15, the Danish Parliament quickly gave its approval to the Government's participation in the EFTA negotiations.

Despite all these activities reflecting attitudes inimical to the Nordic Common Market, the negotiations authorized by the Nordic prime ministerial meeting in January 1959 were carried to conclusion. A prime ministerial meeting held at Kungälv on July 11 and 12 received the report and promptly buried it because "the plans for a Free Trade area between the Seven and the possible consequences of such an area have created a new situation." Therefore,

> the Nordic plans for collaboration should be adapted to the proposed Free Trade Agreement between the Seven. The Nordic Countries will continue their deliberations on

---

[5]See the third market debate in Denmark on 17, 19 and 20 February, reported in *Nordisk Kontakt* 1959: 3, pp. 112-7.

[6]See the fourth market debate held in June, reported in *Nordisk Kontakt* 1959: 10, pp. 471-3.

[7]Camps, 1964, op. cit., p. 221.

questions concerning economic cooperation between them and
the shape it will take in the light of the changed conditions.[8]

With that, although the question of the Nordic Common Market
was still to be discussed at the seventh session of the Nordic
Council in November, it was effectively buried until its resur-
rection under the title Nordek in 1968.

The only thing of value to come out of Kungälv was the Finnish Prime Minister's expression of interest in the plans for the
establishment of EFTA. This was a major departure for Finland,
which had hitherto carefully kept itself apart from the OEEC
discussions, and the EFTA aftermath, as a result of its interpretation of Soviet displeasure with these activities. Now,
however, Finland took the first hesitant step, believing that a
free trade area which included both Austria and Switzerland would
be sufficiently non-political to permit Finnish participation of
some kind which would not irritate the Soviet Union. This step
was a logical progression in Finnish participation in the Nordic
Council and the Nordic Common Market negotiations, and culminated
in its declaration of willingness to participate in the latter at
the January 1959 meeting of the Nordic prime ministers.

The Finnish initiative was followed up at a meeting of the
Nordic Ministers of Cooperation held during the subsequent
ministerial meeting of the Outer Seven at Saltsjöbaden on 20-21
July 1959. The result of the Nordic meeting was the arranging of
a meeting between the Finnish delegation and the Outer Seven at
which Ahti Karjalainen, the Finnish Minister for Trade and
Industry, explained his Government's attitude to the plan for
EFTA. Mr. Karjalainen referred to Finland's participation in
the Nordic Common Market negotiations, and drew attention to the
economic significance and interest of the EFTA plan for Finland.
He pointed out, however, that

Finland would only in this connection make agreements on
tariffs and trade in a way consistent with its declared

---

[8]Communiqué from the meeting at Kungälv reproduced in *Documents on Swedish Foreign Policy, 1959*, pp. 70-1.

foreign policy based on existing international agreements and with the traditional trade relations, including trade based on bilateral agreements.[9]

Unfortunately, since Finland had not thus far been able to follow the discussions on the EFTA plan, and since the Finnish Parliament had not had an opportunity to consider the question, it was not possible at that time to define the final position on EFTA. However, the Finnish Government hoped to be "provided with facilities to follow further discussions" among the Outer Seven more closely. The press release of the Saltsjöbaden ministerial meeting notes laconically: "Ministers of the seven countries took note of the Finnish statement and agreed that Finland, as a member of the Nordic Group, should be afforded such facilities." In the event, it took Finland two years of internal considerations and negotiations with the Soviet Union, particularly about the problem of extending most favoured nation treatment to the other EFTA members without discriminating against the bilateral trade agreements with the Soviet Union, before it found the solution to be the creation of yet another association, FINEFTA.[10]

Apart from the Finnish interlude, the July ministerial meeting at Saltsjöbaden carried on the squabble about fisheries begun at the previous month's officials' meeting, considered the draft plan drawn up by the officials, agreed to recommend to their governments that a Euorpean Free Trade Association among the seven countries be established, and instructed the senior officials to draft a convention to be presented for submission to the ministers by 31 October.

The draft convention was subsequently prepared over a series of four meetings at Stockholm between 8 September and 18 November 1959. On November 20, the convention establishing EFTA was initialled at Stockholm at a ministerial meeting of the Outer Seven. It was to be ratified by 31 March 1960 and to go into

[9]Ibid., Press Release of the Meeting of Ministers of the Seven at Saltsjöbaden, pp. 99-101.

[10]See Max Jakobson, *Finnish Neutrality*, pp. 59-68.

effect on 1 July 1960.

In general, the Stockholm Convention, as the EFTA document is generally called, provided for a ten-year period of trade liberalization in parallel with the progress of the EEC's internal tariff reductions. To ensure parallelism with the latter and to permit variations, provision was also made for accelerating the tariff cuts. Special provisions covered agricultural and fish products, including bilateral agreements promoting the expansion of trade and ensuring reciprocity to the countries whose major exports were agricultural and fisheries products.

Finally, the Convention itself, and the final ministerial meeting at which the Convention was signed, make clear that EFTA was considered a transitional arrangement. The Convention permits any member to withdraw on twelve months' notice. In this respect it is quite different from the Rome Treaty, which is a permanent contractual arrangement from which there can be no withdrawal on the logical ground that once the integration process begins, then the members are no longer free agents. The ministerial meeting also adopted a resolution on relations with the Six, which is clearly an attempt at bridge-building.[11] But, at the same time, the Outer Seven were sufficiently miffed at the March report of the EEC Commission, and the general attitude of the EEC, proclaiming the Community a conscientious trade liberator, to issue the following press release:

As world trading nations, the countries of the European Free Trade Association are particularly conscious of Europe's links with the rest of the world. They have therefore chosen a form of economic cooperation which, while strengthening Europe, enables them to take full account of the interests of other trading countries throughout the world, including those facing special problems of development. The Association is a further expression of the post-war drive towards lower trade barriers, and reflects the principles which have been established by the General Agreement on Tariffs and Trade (GATT). The individual freedom of action of EFTA Members in their external tariffs will allow each of them to

---

[11]See Appendix II.

participate actively in GATT negotiations for tariff
reductions.[12]

---

[12]*Documents on Swedish Foreign Policy*, 1959, p. 102, Press
Release, 20 November 1959.

CHAPTER 7. DENMARK: THE ANXIOUS EUROPEAN

1. Foreign Policy[1]

There have been two major "crises" -- crises in the sense that
widely diverging avenues of policy decision existed in Denmark's
foreign policy in the period since the Second World War. The
first, about the basic security of the nation, was decided within
the period of one year in the late 1940s. The second, about
economic growth and wellbeing, arose a decade later and was not
settled for yet another decade. Despite differences in time and
in conditions of the international system similar attitudes were
involved. These were the attitudes of two groups, the establishment and the opposition, toward the value of sovereignty which we
characterized in the Introduction as "the viability of the Danish
way of life".

It is because the arguments about the EEC and economic well
being were similar to those about national security, and because

---

[1]The analysis in this section is partially based on Peter
Hansen, "The Formulation of Danish European Policy", English
manuscript, December 1972, published later in German as "Die
Formulierung der dänischen Europapolitik", Österreichische
Zeitschrift für Aussenpolitik, Vol. 13, No. 1, 1973. All
references are to the English manuscript.

both were argued partly on a cultural value basis, that it is useful to discuss the economic decision within the broader context of Danish foreign policy in general.

During the past three decades Danish foreign policy may be said to have had three objectives and four orientations. Though the objectives are generally agreed as underlying the main value of sovereignty, and though there is some overlapping of support among the proponents of the four orientations, a deep cleavage continues to exist between the "establishment" and "opposition" assessments of the effects of these orientations on the "viability of the Danish way of life". The three objectives which underpin the ultimate value are the security, the economic and the cultural, and the four orientations through which these are pursued may be labelled the Atlantic, the European, the Nordic and the Universalist. These provide the "four cornerstones of Danish foreign relations".[2] Although there is consensus about the three objectives there is conflict over the orientations through which these objectives ought to be pursued. The conflict has been remarkably stable over the post-war period, and takes the form of two distinct sets of approach as shown in Figure 1(a) and (b). The foreign policy "establishment" includes the Social Democratic Party (the largest in the country since 1924), the Liberal and Conservative parties (the second and third largest parties) and the Radical Party.

The foreign policy "opposition" presents a much more confusing picture in its composition. Its main parliamentary representation is the Socialist People's Party, which was established in 1958 by the renegade Communist leader, Aksel Larsen, as a "real mass-party and not a 'steel-hard' militant sect.... Its language shall be the Danish people's language, its policy immediately understandable ... so that it can catch fire in the working masses, stir up, activize and win them."[3] In the foreign policy

---

[2]Former Foreign Minister Per Haekkerup, cited in Hansen, 1972, op. cit., p. 4.

[3]Kenneth E. Miller, *Government and Politics in Denmark*

Figure 1.   Approaches to Danish Foreign Policy
(a) Foreign Policy Establishment

		ORIENTATION			
		ATLANTIC	EUROPEAN	NORDIC	UNIVERSALIST
O B J E C T I V E S	SECURITY	primary preference	complements Atlantic	reject	complements Atlantic
	ECONOMIC	complements Europe	primary preference	complements Europe	complements Europe
	CULTURAL	complements Nordic	complements Nordic	primary preference	complements Nordic

(b) Foreign Policy Opposition

		ORIENTATION			
		ATLANTIC	EUROPEAN	NORDIC	UNIVERSALIST
O B J E C T I V E S	SECURITY	reject	reject	desired alternative to universalist	ultimate preference
	ECONOMIC	reject	reject	desired in conjunction with universalist	ultimate preference
	CULTURAL	reject	reject	primary preference	ultimate preference

field this party took over the Radical Party's former traditional
neutralist attitude, and formed the parliamentary focus for the
opposition foreign policy attitudes among a considerable segment
of supporters of the Radical and Social Democratic parties. As a
result, the Socialist People's Party has been able to exert

(Boston, 1968), p. 89, citing Aksel Larsen, *Den Levende Vej*
(Copenhagen, 1968), p. 345.

considerable pressure on the Social Democratic Party particularly since the Social Democratic governments of 1964-8 and 1971-3, had to rely on the Socialist People's Party for parliamentary support. This has become even more important since the Radical Party (the Social Democrats' traditional coalition partner) moved closer to the bourgeois parties and formed a government coalition with them in 1968-71. The conflict between the establishment and opposition foreign policy orientations was formally expressed in the third EEC application campaign by the oppositions within the Social Democratic and Radical parties forming independent organizations to combat the official party positions. The foreign policy opposition is further supported by the small Communist Party, the even smaller Justice Party and a number of extra-parliamentary groups such as parts of the trades union movement, a number of interest groups and some very small left-socialist splinter groups, which at times receive some parliamentary representation.[4]

The basic difference between the establishment and opposition approaches is perhaps best expressed, respectively, by the terms "realist" and "idealist". The "realist" view is well expressed in a much cited passage by Eric Scavenius (Foreign Minister 1913-20 and 1940-3):

> It is a widely held view in this country that the foreign policy of Denmark is determined by the Danish Government and Parliament. This, however, is correct only insofar as the formal decisions through which this policy is given expression appear as decisions of these organs. In reality, Danish foreign policy is determined by factors on which the Danish Government has little influence. The main task of Danish foreign policy, therefore, is to keep informed about these factors and their interplay and in this connection to form an opinion of the right moment to exploit the prevailing situation to further Denmark's interests. Decisive among the factors whose interplay determines Danish foreign policy are the actual power relations in the world around us, especially the power balance between the Great Powers next to us.[5]

---

[4]See Miller, op. cit., Chapter 3 on political parties.

[5]Eric Scavenius, *Forhandlingspolitikken under Besaettelsen*

It should be noted that the realist position does not exclude an appreciation, and even an emotional preference for, the idealist position. The reverse, however, does not hold true: the idealist tends consistently to damn the realist. This cleavage is illustrated by Figure 1(a) and (b). Whereas the establishment considers all four orientations through which the external objectives are pursued to be complementary to a primary preferred position, the opposition, on the contrary, considers the Atlantic and European orientations to be incompatable with the preferred Nordic and Universalist orientations. While the establishment considers certain orientations more "realistic" for achieving specific goals than other orientations, other orientations are not excluded, and all are considered mutually supportive.

The foreign policy opposition, on the other hand, denies compatibility between the preferred and the conflicting orientations. The opposition has, with a rare degree of consistency, rejected the Atlantic and European orientations *in toto*, considering them instruments of great power *Machtpolitik* which ill suits little Denmark's position in the world and the opposition's views of the basic value of "the Danish way of life". Support for the Atlantic and European orientations is regarded as compromising the values of Danish culture, and the integrity and security of the Danish state, by bringing it within the ambit of the foreign interests and values of the great powers. As Hansen puts it,

> The striking, almost simplistic, reflection of the basic oppositional pattern of the foreign policy orientations was the proposition forwarded as an alternative to EEC membership during the market debate in the early sixties. According to this proposition Denmark should join the other Nordic countries in a universal policy, in the economic field through a unilateral dismantling of trade barriers as an example for the rest of the world and in the security field by leaving NATO and putting the armed

(Copenhagen, 1948), p. 9, as quoted in Hansen, 1973, op. cit., p. 1.

forces at the disposal of the UN.[6]

2. The Course of Market Policy

The beginnings of Denmark's European market policy may be traced to September 1957 when the Government decided to establish a committee to study the relative effects on the Danish economy of the three then current proposals for trade and economic cooperation: the Nordic Common Market, the Wide Free Trade Area, and the European Economic Community. The latter had already been established by the Treaty of Rome on 25 March 1957, and was the immediate cause of the Government's decision to study the situation. The committee report, in five volumes totalling 567 pages, covered the various sectors of the economy and produced a double shock for the Danes.[7] Volume I, analyzing the impact of both the EEC and the WFTA on Danish industry, concluded that a total of 39% of industrial production would be subjected to "serious risks" and production would decrease, thus requiring an immediate structural transformation of more than half of the affected industries.[8] Volume II, in a similar analysis of the agricultural industry, concluded that "the production of animal products [in the EEC] must be expected in the immediate future to increase at a rate which will closely correspond to the increase in consumption."[9] This was a direct refutation of the farmers' contention that the EEC provided a future potential market for Danish agricultural produce. According to the report, the current agricultural trade would continue, but would be affected by any policy changes within the EEC. These would depend on whether the "free trade" industrialist interests or the protec-

---

[6]Hansen, 1973, op. cit., p. 6.

[7]Udenrigsministeriet og Det Økonomiske Sekretariat, *Danmark og De Europaeiske Markedsplaner* (Copenhagen, 1958), Vol. 1-5.

[8]Ibid., Vol. I, p. 68.

[9]Ibid., Vol. II, pp. 150-9.

tionist agricultural interests would prevail. In contrast, the
report concluded that in the long run the WFTA presented a
greater potential for expansion of agricultural trade because of
a lower degree of self-sufficiency than in the EEC countries.
Both the British market and the overseas market, it was emphasized, represented potentially larger long-term gains than did
the EEC.

The effect of the report was twofold. On the one hand, it
forced government and industry to take stock of the condition of
the industrial sector and to begin preparations for its restructuring. On the other hand, the report gave the Government, and
the establishment in general, additional enthusiasm for sustain-
ing its politically and psychologically preferred "ideal solution", which was actively to pursue the economically and politically less restraining Wide Free Trade Area in which a Nordic
industrial common market could perhaps play its part. Nevertheless, the larger farmers and the industrialists -- and their
parliamentary representatives, the Liberals and the Conservatives
-- kept insisting throughout 1958 on keeping open the option of
membership in the EEC as an alternative in case of a collapse of
the WFTA negotiations. The argument was sound from an economic
point of view, since the proposed Nordic Common Market could not
be a realistic alternative to either the WFTA or the EEC. It
was, after all, to be an industrial arrangement only, and to offer
small possibilities for Danish industry to expand its exports.
But politically and emotionally, Denmark was not yet ready in 1958
to join a political, social and economic pact with such former
enemies as the Germans and such politically unstable Latins as
the Italians and the French. In contrast, a free trade area was
an entirely different proposition: it was to be a straight
commercial contract, leaving every member free to conduct its own
internal economic and social affairs. Indeed Denmark was not
ready till 1960 to make the political and psychological switch to
Europe. Hence the insistence on bridge-building, a euphemism for
some form of free trade area.

However, the crux of the matter, despite the political and

emotional considerations and attachments, was to secure access
for Danish agricultural exports to the markets of the Six and
"without discrimination".[10] It was this economic reality which,
because of agriculture's heavy share in Denmark's GDP and even
heavier share in exports in the late 1950s and early 1960s,
forced the Danish Government and establishment to come to terms
with the reality of the EEC. Of course, it took another decade
to come to terms with the EEC itself -- on the EEC's terms. The
first part -- that of realizing that there was no alternative to
the EEC -- was not particularly difficult for Denmark, for it was
mainly an economic decision, forced on Denmark by the failure of
the WFTA negotiations and the non-solution of EFTA, as well as
the re-formation of the OEEC into the OECD.

The failure of the WFTA negotiations was a heavy blow for
the Danish Government, which, despite the persistence of the
Liberal-Conservative opposition for "an open door policy", had
not considered applying for membership in the EEC. As the Prime
Minister put it at the time, "for Danes there is no satisfactory
alternative to an all-European solution."[11] EFTA was a non-
solution for Denmark's agricultural export problems because it
would, in the opinion of the Government, "draw an economic iron
curtain between our main customers"[12] and might easily touch off
a European trade bloc war. If Denmark joined one of these blocs,
it was argued, it would run the risk of retaliation from the
other bloc against its agricultural exports. In the end, Denmark
joined EFTA, but only to avoid economic isolation, and because,
in terms of internal politics, it was the only immediate action
that the Government could take. There was no illusion, as there
was in Sweden and Norway, that it would be a long-term solution.
The correctness of this view was supported by the subsequent

---

[10]Minister of Foreign Economic Affairs, cited in Hansen,
1969, op. cit., p. 39.

[11]Hansen, ibid., p. 39.

[12]Idem., p. 39.

trade statistics.[13] For Denmark, EFTA was strictly a half-way
house, regarded in 1959-60 as a step, albeit unsatisfactory,
towards a pan-European solution. Throughout EFTA's existence,
Denmark was the most vocal adherent of the view that the purpose
of EFTA was to negotiate reconciliation with the EEC, and not to
retaliate against it.

Indeed, membership of EFTA was considered of little economic
advantage to Denmark since agricultural commodities were not
included in the multilateral trade liberalization programme. It
is interesting to note that Danish accession to EFTA came only
after the British and Swedish bribes to permit easier access of
Danish agricultural produce to their markets,[14] and after a
German assurance that joining EFTA would not be considered an
unfriendly act. The Foreign Minister's explanation of Danish
membership, that "accession to the Seven was the least risky
possibility, less risky than accession to the Six would have
been, especially considerably less risky than a decision that
Denmark should be standing outside, isolated",[15] is a clear
illustration of the confusion in 1959 in Danish government
circles. It should be noted that throughout this period the EEC
apparently still welcomed Denmark's application for full membership. However, Denmark was not able to take advantage of this
because of the internal political cleavage, which was based on
the continuing psychological distrust of the continent, strongly
supported by pro-Scandinavian and pro-British attitudes and
emotions.

With the failure of the restructuring of the OEEC resulting
in the establishment of the OECD, however, Danes began to realize
the futility of the bridge-building objective. But it was the
EEC itself which, in reaching agreement on the fundamentals of a
Common Agricultural Policy during 1961-2, brought an abrupt end

---

[13]See statistical tables in Appendix I.

[14]See Chapter 6, p. 151, above.

[15]Hansen, 1969, op. cit., p. 40.

to vacillation. The transformation of Danish market policy from free trade to "Community" was also greatly aided and abetted by the reversal in British policy. The progress of British moves of raprochement with the Six was carefully watched and hailed by Danish politicians. The reason for this was that it satisfied both the economic and the psychological requirements for solution: the essential elements of the ideal solution were to have Germany and Britain -- the two major customers -- together in a trade bloc of any kind, as long as it included agricultural products; and psychologically, any arrangement entered into by the Mother of Parliaments would provide ample safeguards for democracy and political stability.

But despite the applause at Britain's moves towards the EEC, and despite consultations between Anthony Barber, Economic Secretary to the British Treasury, and the Danish Government during a visit to Copenhagen in January 1961, the Danes were not prepared for the rapid change of British policy during the spring of 1961. At the ninth session of the Nordic Council at Copenhagen in February 1961, the Danish Foreign Minister, Jens Otto Krag, made a pessimistic evaluation of the prospects for rapid reconciliation of the Six and the Seven. He welcomed the re-establishment of contact between British and French government officials but warned against too optimistic expectations. The Foreign Minister counselled patience, though he believed that time was running out on the possibility of reaching compromise between the EEC and EFTA, and suggested that in a year or two the vested interests in the continuation of the economic division in Europe would become too intensive to permit a "broad solution". Unfortunately, the Nordics could do little to assist in the coming together of the Six and the Seven but, during the period of patient waiting on the sidelines while the larger states in Europe manoeuvred into hopefully more conciliatory positions, the Nordic countries should consolidate their cooperation in EFTA and "... in every way strengthen Nordic co-operation in order that our position and our influence can be the best possible [for the reopened negotiations]".[16]

2.1 The Decision to Apply for Membership of the EEC

After Prime Minister Macmillan's April commitment to apply for
membership of the EEC, the Danish Government went into feverish
activity: a diplomatic note was sent to the United Kingdom on
April 17 asking to be informed of the status of the British
position on the EEC, and a series of ministerial visits was made to
Rome, Paris and Bonn. On 2 May 1961 the government committee
which had prepared the 1958 reports on Denmark's position on the
European market plans was reactiviated and given the task of
studying the impact of EEC membership on Danish economic life.
On May 9, at the NATO Council meeting in Oslo, Foreign Minister
Krag made the official declaration of Denmark's position on the
EEC:

> Denmark would heartily welcome a decision by the British
> Government to begin negotiations with the EEC for the
> purpose of joining the Rome Treaty. If the United
> Kingdom should do so, the Danish Government would also
> want to initiate such negotiations with the EEC.[17]

The Danish eagerness to follow the British lead towards
the continent brought about an angry reaction on the part of the
Swedes, in which they criticized the Danes' abrupt *volte face* as
disruptive of Nordic harmony and an erosion of EFTA's negotiating
strength even before negotiations had begun.[18] The Swedish
position was understandable enough: it was based on their fear
that if Denmark and Norway -- which had indicated that it too
would follow the British lead -- joined the EEC, Sweden -- along
with Finland -- would be left in an exposed and isolated position. Hence the Swedes insisted that the association approach to
negotiations with the EEC be maintained and that EFTA negotiate

---

[16]Cited in Nielsson, op. cit., p. 526.

[17]As reported in *Berlingske Tidende*, 10 May 1961, cited in
Nielsson, op. cit., p. 528.

[18]Nordic Cooperation Ministers meeting in Oslo on 15 May 1961.

as a unit. This was rejected by Danish Foreign Minister Krag on the grounds that it was no longer a feasible policy since the EEC had rejected it. Krag's response indicates the extent of the transformation of Danish policy and its reason:

> For Denmark, the question of timing plays a significant role in our integration policy. Danish exporters -- especially of agricultural products -- are already feeling the impact of discrimination. Instead of continuing the old negotiation methods, which have so far shown no results, we are much more interested in the new thinking shown by the United Kingdom.[19]

So much for the traditional protestations of Nordic solidarity. But it was the Swedish criticism of the imminent Danish, Norwegian and British desertion of EFTA that led to the London Agreement of June 1961, in which the states on the verge of seeking membership of the EEC committed themselves to maintain solidarity with EFTA during the negotiations, and pledged that they would not enter the Common Market until a solution for all EFTA members was found.

However, opposition to the Danish Government's new-found enthusiasm for the Common Market was not encountered only from Sweden. The government party, the Social Democratic Party, was itself split internally, with the labour movement -- the party's main source of support -- strongly against the policy of full membership of the EEC. At the annual party conference, Hans Rasmussen, leader of the second largest trade union in Denmark, was elected vice-chairman of the Social Democratic Party and delivered a major attack on the Government's policy. According to him, the policy had been adopted too rapidly and without sufficient study. It was not only agricultural interests that deserved consideration, but also industrial and labour interests. Hence he urged the Government to coordinate its policy with the other Nordic countries before proceeding too far on the road towards union with the Six. He concluded his criticism with an

---

[19]Reported in *Politiken*, 16 and 17 May 1961, as cited in Nielsson, op. cit., p. 530.

emotional attack on Germany which was later to become the heart
of the anti-EEC movement. He said:

> Within the Six, Germany will occupy an overshadowing
> position of dominance. Even if time does heal many
> wounds, it should be remembered that it is with Germany
> that Denmark has had so many great troubles throughout
> its history. We cannot grant to German ministers the
> right to decide the level of unemployment in this
> country.[20]

Four days later Foreign Minister Krag replied on behalf of
the Government. In his address to the party conference he considered membership of the EEC, along with the United Kingdom,
as a continuation of the past policy of seeking a broad European
solution. This objective had not changed, but only the format of
the solution. In support of the argument for joining the EEC he
stressed the economic necessity, not only for Denmark but for all
of EFTA. He concluded by making it clear that Danish entry in
isolation was unthinkable and that the securing of a satisfactory
solution for both Sweden and Finland was also an important part
of Danish policy. Nielsson concluded:

> The two major issues for the Labour Movement were thus
> defined immediately. British membership was considered
> an absolute prerequisite for Danish membership and every
> precaution should be taken to maintain close Scandinavian
> relations.[21]

The external Swedish pressure and the internal political
cleavage -- especially within the Social Democratic Party -- led
to a typically Nordic compromise resolution in Parliament authorizing the Government to initiate negotiations with the EEC. The
Folketing resolution contained three basic guidelines for the
negotiations: first, Denmark was to seek membership together
with the United Kingdom; secondly, throughout the negotations
full consideration should be taken of the interests of the other
EFTA members; and thirdly, Nordic cooperation should be continued

---

[20]*Politiken*, 14 June 1961, as cited in Nielsson, op. cit., p.
532.

[21]Ibid., p. 533.

and increased.[22] During the market debate, which took place at a special session on 3 and 4 August 1961, it became clear that the requirement to keep in step with the British was not merely a Social Democratic requirement but was shared by the Radical Party -- the Social Democrat's coalition partner -- and the Conservative Party. The second requirement was clearly a reiteration of the London Agreement, and the third was an attempt to satisfy both the Swedes and the internal pan-Nordic movement. It could also be described as a Danish attempt to balance the economic attraction of the continent with the emotional attachment to *Norden*.

Although there were numerous protestations of Nordic solidarity, the emotional attachment to the North could not compete with the economic attractions of the EEC. According to Peter Hansen, "... the Government made it clear that it did not intend to let its freedom of manoeuvre in relation to the EEC be reduced by any strengthening of Nordic ties."[23] Hence, when the Swedish-inspired proposal for a Nordic treaty codifying the juridical, cultural, social, economic and other forms of cooperation among the Nordic countries came up for discussion in the Nordic Council in August 1961, the Danish response was cool, and it was largely due to Danish reluctance to increase its responsibilities in the Nordic area that the Helsinki Convention of 1962 was a much watered-down version of the original proposal.[24]

During the August 1961 market debate, it also became clear why the Danish Government found it so important to synchronize its EEC negotiations with the British. It was "... clearly ... the fear that absence from the negotiations, where questions of

---

[22]Hansen, 1969, op. cit., p. 41.

[23]Idem., p. 41.

[24]See Treaty of Cooperation between Denmark, Finland, Iceland, Norway and Sweden reproduced in Anderson, op. cit., Appendix D, pp. 174-81; see also *Nordisk Kontakt*: 1961: 4, pp. 184-91 on Council session debate.

agricultural trade could be expected to become a central issue
immediately, might very easily lead to agreements detrimental to
Danish interests. What the Government wanted to prevent was a
possible British-French deal on agriculture at the expense of
Denmark."[25]

Hence, Denmark submitted its formal application to the EEC
on 10 August 1961, on the same day as the British made their
application. The EEC Council accepted the Danish application on
September 27 and fixed October 26 as the date for the first
hearing of the Danish case. The presentation by Foreign Minister
Krag followed in general the earlier statement by Britain's
Edward Heath on October 10 in Paris. Denmark applied for full
membership according to Article 237 of the Treaty of Rome, and
accepted without reservations both the goals of the Economic
Community and the letter of the Rome Treaty. Moreover, Krag
declared, Denmark was ready and willing to participate actively
in establishing close political cooperation in the EEC on the
basis of the Bonn Declaration of July 1961. Although he assured
the ministers that Danish membership of the EEC would not entail
any changes in the Treaty of Rome, Mr. Krag did state that
accommodation of all the EFTA members in one form or another
within an enlarged EEC, and the maintenance of Denmark's special
relations with the Nordic countries, were fundamental conditions
to be satisfied before negotiations could be concluded. The
Foreign Minister then launched into a detailed presentation of a
number of special problems which EEC membership entailed for
Denmark. The most important of these were five: a different
base year for the calculation of the gradual reduction of tariffs; decalage -- i.e. a slower rate of removal of trade restrictions -- for 10% to 15% of industrial imports from the EEC; the
maintenance of the Nordic Common Labour Market; special treatment
for capital transfers and harmonization of social policies; and

---

[25]Hansen, 1969, op. cit., pp. 40-51.

special treatment in regard to agriculture.[26]

2.2 The Negotiations

The ensuing negotations, carried on in parallel with the British, consisted of six meetings at ministerial level and five with officials, and lasted from the end of November 1961 to December 1962. As in the British case, the negotiations were largely technical and revolved around the detailed "special problems" of transition to membership. To the Danes the last of the five special problems outlined by Foreign Minister Krag, that of agriculture, was the most important. Here the Danes attempted to get three different concessions from the Six during the negotiations, and were rebuffed on every one. The first request was to participate in the process of formulation of the Common Agricultural Policy along with the Six, on the two grounds that by engaging in negotiations for membership Denmark could no longer be regarded as an outsider, and that Danish agriculture was of significant size and hence of special importance to the EEC. The second rebuff came on the proposal that negotiations on agriculture between Britain and the Six, and between Denmark and the Six, be carried on a tripartite basis on the grounds that Denmark had a vital interest in both the British and the EEC markets in pig meat and dairy products. This, like the previous request, was rejected by the EEC on grounds of principle, and by the British because the Danish position on subsidies in agriculture was that of the Six, and differed significantly from the British position. The third special agricultural request consisted of a proposal to maintain Danish agricultural exports to the Community during the negotiations by means of special bilateral agreements with the individual member-states, and amounted to an attempt by the Danes to escape the effects of the Common Agricultural Policy, which they

---

[26]Foreign Minister Krag's presentation of the Danish case is published in *Folketingets Markedsudvalg, Beretning No. 1*, pp. 2-8. It is also reported extensively in *Nordisk Kontakt*, 1961: 12, pp. 655-7.

argued would be immediate and disastrous to Denmark. Needless to say, this was rejected by the EEC on the principle that bilateral solutions were incompatable with the principles of CAP.

The Danes were somehwat more successful when the negotiations turned to the industrial problems of adjustment to the customs union. The first request was an attempt to move the base year forward from the date used by the Six, 1 January 1957, to 1960, for the application of the Common Market timetable on the reduction of tariffs. The Danish justification for this request was based on the 1960 reform of their tariff structure, which until then had been largely based on non-tariff barriers such as quotas and licenses. This the EEC negotiators appeared to be ready to accept. But then the Danes went further and attempted to move the base year further forward, to 1962, on the grounds that the 1960 reform covered industrial goods only with agricultural goods scheduled to be included by 1962. This the EEC representatives rejected out of hand on the principle that consideration of a base year to be established after the negotations had begun would produce a precedent which would be difficult to ignore in any other negotiations.

The common external tariff problem was tackled by the Danes with an either/or request: either a reduction of the common external tariff, or a special quota provision for duty-free import of a specific list of raw materials from third countries. In the EEC's opinion most of the listed raw materials were available from within the EEC and such a provision would consequently be discriminatory to other members. However, since the British had presented a similar request, the Danish one was postponed until negotiations with the British had been completed.

The request for decalage for a group of industrial products equivalent to 10% of Danish imports from the EEC, to secure a transitional period of protection for about 15% of Danish industry, which would be seriously hurt if intra-EEC barriers were reduced too rapidly, was greeted with reservations by the EEC negotiators; the Danes were asked to show more confidence in the EEC machinery which provided for exemptions on the basis of escape clauses for seriously affected industries as per Articles 92-94 and Article 226 of the Treaty of Rome. Although the Danish negotiators subsequently reduced the industries to be covered to about 6%, the issue was not resolved by the time the negotiations broke off. But the decalage issue was not merely an economic problem; it was also a political problem. It was a promise that the Danish Government had made to the labour unions, which feared that sudden competition from the EEC countries would lead to the closure of industries employing about 20,000 people. This the Danish negotiators were careful to spell out at the negotiations, pointing to the need for some form of special treatment in this area in order to ensure the five-sixths majority in the Folketing in the ratification stage of the accession process.

The three remaining problems of adjustment to the economic union provisions of the Treaty of Rome, the common labour market, the provision for free transfer of capital, and the stipulation of harmonization of social policies, were all of significance to Denmark but were all rejected by the EEC negotiators. It is interesting to note that in the third application negotiations, these three became the major bones of contention, the former having largely disappeared as a result of internal economic growth and restructuring. In the early 1960s all three could have become serious political liabilities -- and they were soon picked up by the anti-EEC movement -- had negotiations proceeded to conclusion. In the event, negotiations were broken off before serious discussion could take place.

The first of the three, the common labour market, was chiefly a Nordic issue in that since 1954 the Nordic countries had had free labour movement among their citizens. This would be disrupted by the EEC requirement that members of the EEC grant each other's citizens preferential job opportunities. If the other Nordic countries did not join the EEC, this could create a considerable strain on both Denmark and the EEC, unless Denmark were to abrogate its prior Nordic commitments. In the third application negotiations, the strain did develop but was solved by a special provision granting a double preference system for

Denmark to include both the EEC and the the Nordic labour market.
It is doubtful that this possibility existed in the early 1960s,
since the EEC itself was in an early formative stage and therefore unwilling to make special arrangements which could set
precedents for future negotiations.

The common capital market question was really a non-issue
based on Danish fears that "hot money" chasing after the very
high Danish interest rates would flood the Danish capital market
and thus severely disrupt it.[27] It was a non-issue because the
EEC pointed out that it had ample provisions in its regulations
to govern the movement of "hot money". Though the negotiators
dropped the question, the anti-marketeers did not and it remained
a public issue during the third application negotiations.

The question regarding harmonization of social policies was
a serious one for the Danes for the simple reason that the Danish
system of social security was funded by employer contributions.[28]
Although in 1961 the EEC had not yet proceeded to implement
harmonization in this area, it nonetheless insisted that all
members had to abide by the same regulations. This provided yet
another argument for the anti-marketeers, namely that joining the
Common Market meant the abrogation of Danish social, economic and
political independence in favour of domination by the continentals. It was to become an issue that in the early 1970s found an
echo of sympathy among almost all Danes, including the strong
supporters of union. Despite this, the Danes were unsuccessful
in obtaining major concessions either in 1961 or ten years later.

In September 1962 an incident took place which was to have
far-reaching consequences for Denmark's future EEC policy. As is
evident from the foregoing, the Danes had been concerned primarily with a commercial arrangement, although the Foreign Minister

---

[27]The Danish central bank discount rate was and has remained
high because monetary policy has been used by Denmark, and the
other Nordic countries, as a central means of controlling the
economy.

[28]In contrast, the social security systems of the EEC
members are based on employer and employee contributions.

had paid lip service to the political unification idea in his opening statement to the EEC Council. And it must be said that although the British application was made on a political basis, the British-EEC negotiations throughout concerned themselves with details of economics. In the meantime, the EEC, apart from its concern with CAP, had also been involved with discussions, arguments and negotiations for political unification, carried on among heads of government, foreign and other ministers and by the Fouchet committee. The apparent commercial concerns of the Danes and the British during the negotiations and the continuation of consultations within EFTA led many Europeanists in the EEC to doubt the commitment of the British, the Danes and the other EFTA applicants to political unification. The upshot was a proposal, contained in a position paper written at the initiative of a member of the EEC Commission, Jean Rey, in which it was proposed that the United Kingdom be granted immediate membership but that the other applicants be given associate status for a three year transition period. The purpose of this would be to isolate the British from the other applicants and to "Europeanize" them without the threat of Anglo-Nordic bloc behaviour, against which the EEC had no safety mechanisms in any of its institutions.[29]

This leaked report gave Prime Minister Krag (who assumed office on 3 September 1962, following the resignation of the previous Prime Minister, Viggo Kampmann, due to ill-health) an opportunity to begin an internal campaign for full support for the political integration of Europe. In the opening address to the fall session of the Folketing on 2 October 1962, he said:

> The decision to open negotiations concerning Danish membership in the EEC was at first based primarily on economic reasons. However, it is the Government's conviction, on the basis of other considerations and attitudes, that it will be in Denmark's interest to participate actively and on an equal footing with other European states in the attempts to unify Europe which are now taking place. The Rome Treaty opens up possibilities for significant efforts in co-operating in the

---

[29] See *Nordisk Kontakt* 1962: 12, p. 703.

establishment of common policies in such spheres as
social welfare, labour markets, right of establishment,
traffic and finance.... Danish membership in an expanded EEC in the near future will open the possibility
for participation in the negotiations concerning the
framework for future political co-operation.[30]

At the time of the breakdown of the British-EEC negotiations
in January 1963 a curious incident took place. During an official visit by Prime Minister Krag to Paris on 26-29 January,
President de Gaulle offered the Danes either isolated full
membership in the EEC or an associate membership. Instead of
commenting unilaterally on the offer, Krag in an immediate press
conference declared his intention of discussing the matter with
the British. The upshot of a two-day meeting with Prime Minister
Macmillan was a strong declaration of solidarity with Britain and
EFTA: "An isolated Danish entry is of no interest for us at the
present time. Such negotiations will not take place. A split in
EFTA will not come about."[31]

Whether de Gaulle's offer was genuine or not or whether it
was merely an attempt to split EFTA is immaterial. The point is
that the Danish Prime Minister was unable to think in terms of
independent entry and decided to consult the British even before
consulting his principals at home. It was undoubtedly the
correct procedure, because by this time the Danish Government's
negotiating base at home was firmly established on simultaneous
British entry into the EEC. It would have been impossible, in
the light of both the parliamentary commitments and the strength
of the anti-marketeers' campaign, to change political course in a
short enough time to take advantage of de Gaulle's offer without
major political upheavals at home.

2.3 The Intermission: Diversions

As in the British case, the period of the first application nego-

---

[30]*Folketingstidende*, 114 Aargang: 1962-3, columns 5-6, as
quoted by Nielsson, op. cit., pp. 587-8.

[31]*Politiken*, 1 February 1963, as quoted by Nielsson, op.
cit., p. 593.

tiations saw the establishment of the parameters for entry into the EEC. The only difference was that the British considered the political ramifications first and made their decision on that basis; the economic considerations were left to the period of negotiation. The Danish process was the reverse: the economic considerations determined the original application, and were followed by political considerations. For both Britain and Denmark the first negotiations outlined the framework which was followed and implemented during the third application negotiations.

During the period between the breakdown of negotiations in January 1963 and the beginning of the successful negotiations in 1970, Danish market policy did not change significantly. There were, of course, a number of diversions conditioned by political and economical considerations, all important at the time but insignificant in the context of the inexorable march towards membership of the EEC.

One of the diversions was the renewed enthusiasm for EFTA immediately after the breakdown of January 1963, along with another Danish emphasis on preparations for a new round of "bridge-building". Another was the replacement of the 1961 three-point market policy by one accepted by the Folketing in October 1964, which authorized the Government to "seek new ways, which can lead to the realization of the goal of Danish market policy: a comprehensive European Community."[32] This was the result of a fit of pique at the British imposition of a 15% surcharge on imports in 1964. Although the dropping of the British entry precondition led to widespread speculation that Denmark was preparing for a change of policy leading to isolated membership of the EEC, and although the speculation was supported by the worsening of the British economy in the mid-1960s, and by increasing Danish trade with the EEC, the internal political alignments patently prevented any such possibility.

---

[32]Hansen, 1969, op. cit., p. 42.

The diversion in market policy was rectified in 1967 when Denmark immediately followed the British in renewing its application for EEC membership. The parliamentary mandate authorizing the Government to proceed with the negotiations returned to the formula of 1961, and again stressed the importance of entering the EEC jointly with the United Kingdom.

The whole formula, however, was not a repetition of the 1961 mandate. The EFTA point was dropped, for the simple reasons that EFTA as a negotiating body had never been taken seriously by the EEC, and its economic importance to Denmark was limited to the British and Nordic markets. Hence the emphasis on the British and on the Nordic aspects, which was phrased in stronger terms than in 1961. The reason for the Nordic emphasis was simply that trade liberalization within EFTA had brought about a strong surge in Danish industrial exports to the Nordic countries, to the extent where these now formed by far the most important export markets for Danish industry.[33]

The renewed French veto against British entry in 1967 led to another Danish diversion. This time Denmark, having given up on EFTA, turned northwards and proposed the reactivation of the Nordic Common Market plans. The purpose of this action was twofold: first, because of the importance of the Nordic market, a strengthening of the economic relations within it would be to Denmark's advantage, at least while it awaited the greater opportunities of EEC membership; however, the latter was uncertain since it depended on the demise of General de Gaulle, secondly, a strong Nordic Economic Community would strengthen the bargaining positions of both Denmark and the whole Nordic area vis-à-vis the EEC, and lead toward a kind of "broad solution", though more in the shape of two "communities" coming together than of a Europe-wide free trade area being formed. It was, of course, the latter objective which forced the Finns to reject Nordek and to abort the whole proposal.

---

[33]See tables in Appendix I.

For the Danes the failure of Nordek, when it came in 1970, was relatively unimportant in the overall market perspective, because the EEC Council had already decided at the end of 1969 to reopen negotiations with Britain, Denmark and the other applicants of 1967.

It became even clearer that Denmark had set its eyes firmly on the goal of EEC membership, and that the Nordek experiment was merely a tactical attempt in this direction with the re-establishment on 9 March 1966 of the committee which had produced the market reports of 1958 and 1961. This time the committee was given the authority to produce not only an updated report, but annual supplements to it. The committee produced the 1,100-page report *Danmark og de Europaeiske Faelleskaber* in 1968 in two volumes, and annual volumes of 400-500 pages for each of the years 1968-72 inclusive, in which the previous year's developments in the Danish economy, the developments in the EEC, and the relative positions of the Danish economy and those of the EEC were analyzed in detail. By the time it made its opening statement at the EEC's negotiating meeting on 30 June 1970, the Danish Government was thoroughly prepared.

2.4 The Final Round

In his opening statement, the Minister of Economics and Market Relations, P. Nyboe Andersen, began with a reiteration of the two points in the May 1967 parliamentary authorization to reopen negotiations: accession to the Rome Treaty parallel with the United Kingdom, and "the expectation that the other Nordic countries would find satisfactory solutions for their relations with the European Communities". He then proceeded to deal with the three main conditions for membership as determined by the EEC: the acceptance of the two Rome treaties (the EEC treaty and the Euratom treaty), and the Treaty of Paris, together with the rules and regulations developed since; the acceptance of the plans for the further development of the Community; and the acceptance by the applicants of the political objectives of the three treaties. Denmark, the Minister said, was ready to accept the first condition, because he found "first, that the deciding principles are the right ones, and secondly because we wish the coming negotiations to lead to a positive conclusion." However, he added that Denmark hoped the Communities would take into account the special transitional problems that the accession process would create for Denmark.

On the second and third conditions Minister Andersen was much more positive, and repeated, almost word for word, the statement made by the former Prime Minister, Krag, at the opening of the fall session of the Folketing in 1962. "Denmark," he said, "is ... prepared to accept the plans for the further development of the Communities which, we understand, will maintain the dynamic character of European integration. A further development of cooperation in monetary, economic, industrial and technological areas will, according to Danish understanding, be essential elements thereof." After declaring Denmark's acceptance of the political goals of the Communities, the Minister added:

We have noted that this cooperation will be carried out outside the institutions of the Community. We regard such political cooperation as the natural and essential consequence of the ongoing integration, which has already been carried out or planned for within the framework of the treaties.[34]

In the course of his presentation, Minister Andersen made a statement which clearly showed Danish anxiety to enter the Common Market. He said: "The Danish Government has indicated that from an overall point of view we do not wish any transition period and are ready to accept the full obligations of membership soon after the ratification of the treaties of expansion."[35] The reason for this was simply that Denmark had been restructuring its economy towards greater industrialization since the "shock-report" in

---

[34]*Supplerende Redegørelse, Udviklingen i 1970*, Appendix I/1, p. 352.

[35]Idem., p. 353.

1958, and had furthermore been preparing ever since for membership by restructuring its economic regulations to harmonize with those of the EEC.

The Minister, however, recognized that a quick transition was not possible because of the requirements of the other applicants for longer transitional periods, and the requirement that all transitional periods be applicable to all the new entrants simultaneously. Hence he requested that the transitional periods be as short as possible, and refrained from a detailed listing of the specific technical problems which would have to be negotiated in order to permit Danish accession. The latter were presented on the same date in a short memorandum of six pages and took up the questions of the customs union; the Common Agricultural Policy, including the raising of Danish agricultural prices to the level of the Community's; Denmark's contribution to the budget of the Communities; the wish to participate in the development of the economic and monetary policies during the period of the accession negotiations; the special positions of the Faroes and Greenland; Euratom and CECA; the institutions of the Common Market; and other questions, such as the Nordic Common Labour Market, and social services for temporary foreign workers under the Community's common labour market regulations. On many of the listed questions, Denmark either indicated complete agreement with the current regulations, made minor comments or requested clarifications for the purpose of making changes in extant Danish laws to conform with the Community's rules and regulations.[36]

As the negotiations progressed, it became evident that there were indeed no political problems between the EEC and Denmark and that on the technical problems of accession, as well as transition, the Danish and the Community's views coincided on almost all points. Had it not been for the British and, to a lesser extent, the Norwegians -- who found it very difficult to accept

---

[36]Ibid., Appendix I/2, pp. 359-65.

the opening of their fishing waters to other members -- the negotiations could have been concluded within a few months of June 1970. As it was, they dragged on until an agreement was reached on January 14 on the Faroes and Greenland, and it was 22 January 1972 before the four applicants and the Six members were ready to sign the Treaty of Accession. All that remained now for the Danish Government to achieve success in the referendum, and to ratify the Treaty of Accession in Parliament. Although the latter was almost assured -- although the outcome depended on the referendum -- the former was an entirely different matter.

3. The Clash of Interests

The difficulties of ratification that the Danish Government faced during the summer of 1972 had sources in four antecedents: in the Constitution, in class-partisan interests, in emotional nationalism-Scandinavianism and in the partisan-political structure of Denmark. The constitutional sources were twofold, one direct and the other indirect. The direct source was the requirement of Section 20 of the Constitution Act of 1953, which permits "powers vested in the authorities of the realm ... [to be] delegated to international authorities...." But "for the passing of a Bill dealing with the above, a majority of five-sixths of the Members of the Folketing shall be required," and if this cannot be obtained a referendum shall decide the matter.[37] The indirect source was the reversion of the Social Democratic Party in May 1971 to its long dormant support of direct democracy through referenda. Along with the Radical Party, it had originally proposed the use of referenda on laws in its proposals for constitutional reform in 1937,[38] and had succeeded in including a formula in the 1953 Constitution whereby a Bill passed by the Folketing might be submitted for referendum by one-third of

---

[37] The Constitution of Denmark, para. 20.

[38] See *Betaenkning afgivet af Forfatningskommissionen af 1937* (Copenhagen, 1938); and Miller, op. cit., p. 38.

the members.[39] Although the procedure had been used only once
before, in 1963, with disastrous results for the then Social
Democratic Government,[40] the die was cast when the Social Democratic Party in 1971 made it its official policy that the question of membership in the EEC should in any case be subjected to
a referendum, since the party held sixty-two seats in Parliament,
or 34.6% -- enough to force a referendum. Since there was little
likelihood of averting a referendum, the other major parties
reluctantly accepted the idea in order to maintain the tenuous
multi-party consensus on market policy. After much debate as to
whether to hold the referendum before, during or after the
consultative Norwegian referendum, it was decided to hold it one
week after, on 2 October 1972.

The Social Democratic Party's decision in May 1971 began as
a political manoeuvre to prevent the EEC question from becoming
an issue at the forthcoming elections scheduled for 21 September
1971. The objective was to minimize the risk of losing traditionally socialist but anti-market votes to the strongly anti-EEC
Socialist People's Party. It also hoped to gain additional time
to undermine the anti-market campaign and to bring the disaf-
fected party voters back to supporting the consistently pro-
market stand of the Social Democratic Party and governments
during the 1960s. In the event the Social Democratic Party was
only partly successful. It did "win" the election by increasing
its share of the popular vote from 34.2% in 1968 to 37.3% in

---

[39]The Constitution of Denmark, Section 42, para. 1; Section
42, para. 5 reads: "For the Bill to be rejected a majority of
the electors taking part in the vote, however, not less than
thirty per centum of all persons entitled to vote, shall have
voted against the Bill."

[40]On 31 May 1963 the two new opposition parties, the
Liberals and the Conservatives, challenged four laws dealing
with land use in Denmark. The referendum held on 25 June 1963
resulted in an overwhelming defeat for the Government: with 73%
participating in the referendum the electorate turned down each
of the four proposals by far more than the 30% minimum required
by Section 42, para. 5.

1971, thus gaining eight seats for a total of seventy. But the anti-market Socialist People's Party also gained, moving from a 6.1% share in the popular vote three years earlier to a 9.1% share, thus gaining six seats for a total of seventeen. After a crisis period lasting until October 9, the Social Democratic leader and previous Prime Minister, Jens Otto Krag, was able to organize a minority Social Democratic Government; and with informal support from the Socialist People's Party and the two representatives for Greenland and the Faroes, was able to organize a total of 89 votes against 88 for the opposition "bourgeois group".[41] The coalition was clearly a fragile one, and certaily did not hold together during the vote in Parliament on 16 December 1971 authorizing the Government to undersign the coming Treaty of Accession. The resolution passed with 141 votes for and 32 against. The respective percentages were 81.5% for and 18.5% against. But the five-sixths requirement of Section 20 of the Constitution translates to 83.3%. Thus for the first time in the course of Danish market policy, the five-sixths majority behind the multilateral market policy had disappeared, and the tactic of May had turned into a constitutional necessity. The intransigence of the position of parliamentary anti-marketeers was underscored by the vote on the Enabling Act which was passed by 141 votes to 34 on 8 September 1972, three weeks before the referendum. In the December 1971 vote the anti bloc consisted of all seventeen Socialist People's Party members who voted for the party line, eleven Social Democrats who broke from their party, and four Radical Liberals who voted against their party policy. In the September 1972 vote, these were joined by one additional Social Democrat and the Greenland representative. Thus the anti-market vote increased slightly during the intervening ten months.[42]

---

[41] See *Nordisk Kontakt* 1971: 12, pp. 544-5.

[42] The parliamentary vote on 3 August 1961 to authorize the Government to open negotiations with the EEC was won by 152 votes against 20, the latter all Socialist People's Party members; the vote to renew the second application on 11 May 1967 was exactly

In the event, the constitutionally required referendum authorizing Denmark's membership of the Common Market was held on 2 October 1972, with 63.4% voting yes and 36.6% voting no. The requirement in Section 42, para. 5 of the Constitution that the Bill under consideration by the electors be supported by at least 30% of all persons entitled to vote was easily reached. With total participation at 90.1% of those entitled to vote, the majority voting yes translated to 57% of the total electorate. With the referendum having met all constitutional requirements the ratification process ended and Denmark became a member of the EEC, effective 1 January 1973.[43]

But why did the situation change so much during the third application negotiations that it was necessary to move the final decision from Parliament directly to the electorate? Earlier, it was indicated that there were four contributory reasons, the constitutional, class-partisan interests, the emotional melange of various "nationalisms" and the political structure of the country. The existence of the constitutional provision for a referendum was undoubtedly central in bringing it to the forefront, as was the Social Democratic Party's historic preference for direct democracy in highly controversial situations.

But it was the mixture of the three remaining reasons that produced such a strong anti-market movement that the conventional political process could not handle it. The roots of this are found in the trade unions during the period of the first application, and were complicated by the class-interest basis of the Danish political structure. It will be recalled that at the

---

the same as in 1961, with the same party voting against; the vote to renew the application on 11 November 1970 was won by 119 votes against 13, the latter consisting of the Socialist People's Party and the Left Socialists (the Communists) who had won four seats in 1968, but lost them in 1971; and, when on 18 May 1971, Parliament decided to hold a referendum on EEC membership regardless of whether the five-sixths requirement was reached in Parliament or not, the vote was exactly the same as in the previous November.

[43]*Nordisk Kontakt* 1972: 12, pp. 764-5.

Social Democratic annual party conference in 1961, Hans Rasmussen, the leader of the second largest trade union in Denmark,
not only attacked the Government's decision to enter the EEC but
was also elected vice-chairman of the party at the same time. It
is worth recalling that Rasmussen's attack on the Social Democratic Government's EEC policy was couched in political as well
as economic terms. Indeed, the whole labour movement consistently interpreted the issue of Danish membership of the EEC as an
economic and social clash of interests between workers and farmers, where the farmers would reap profits from the high food
prices in the Community at the expense of the workers, who would
be paying these high prices with either lower real incomes, or
high unemployment, or both. The political arguments marshalled
to support the economic arguments -- which became more complex
with the passing of time as Denmark increased its industrial
sector and did rather well in expanding industrial exports --
became more important and were based on an emotional nationalism
which emphasized the highly "democratic" and "socialist" socio-
political culture of Denmark, and contrasted it to the "capitalist" and "undemocratic" societies of Germany, Italy and France.
The emotional appeal of this argument increased during the third
market negotiation period as the anti-marketeers were able to
point to the contrast between the peaceful parliamentary "egalitarian" politics of the North, and the unstable politics of
"social conflict" and street rioting in Italy, Germany and
France during the late 1960s. And, of course, the appeal to the
"Nordic brotherhood", widely publicized during the abortive
Nordek diversion of 1968-70, found a ready appeal in the labour
movement for the twin reasons that the Nordic labour unions have
very close contacts with each other, and that Denmark's industrial expansion had been accomplished largely as a result of
expanded industrial exports to the other Nordic countries.
    It is the structure of Danish party politics and the struc-
ture of the polity which provides the true explanation why a
relatively small group of activists -- who, despite a decade of
activity and three years of intensive activity, were able to

garner no more than 36.6% of electoral support -- were yet able
to play such an important, indeed dominant role for a time in
Danish politics. First, there is the structure of the labour
movement itself. Although there is a central organization, the
Danish Federation of Trade Unions (*Landsorganisationen i Danmark*,
or *LO*) with between sixty and seventy member unions, there are
three very large and dominant member-unions, the General and
Special Workers Union (*Dansk Arbejdsmand- og Specialarbeider-
forbund*), with over a quarter of a million members, the Retail
Clerks and Office Workers Union (*Handels- og Kontorfunktion-
aerenes Forbund*) with approximately 100,000 members, and the
Smiths' and Machinists Union (*Dansk Smede- og Maskinarbejder-for-
bund*) with about the same number. Although unionization in
Denmark is far-reaching, with membership varying between 95% and
100% in most sectors of the economy, the central organization
(LO) has little effective control over the activities of its
member-unions. And though there are close links between the
Social Democratic Party and the trade union movement, the formal
structural link exists only between the central party organs and
the central labour organization -- which, however, cannot compel
adherence to any Social Democratic Party policy among its members. The class-partisan interests are brought out most clearly
by the left-wing workers' parties, notably the Socialist People's
Party and the small but effective Communist Party, which compete
with the Social Democrats for influence in the trade unions.
Hence, the LO leadership had to tread very carefully in formulat-
ing market policy throughout the EEC debates in order not to lose
influence with its member-unions. Hence also the difficulties of
the Social Democratic Party in keeping the labour movement in
line with its policies on the EEC. These problems increased
during the course of the 1960s as the Socialist People's Party,
which had begun as a splinter group in 1958 with radical Marxist
policies, shed its Marxist image and became more respectable.
Its clearcut rejection of the EEC on emotionally appealing
nationalist, Scandinavianist and cultural grounds, directed
specifically at the industrial worker -- in contrast to the

carefully articulated largely ideology-free economic and political arguments of the Social Democrats, designed to appeal to
all the varied interests in Denmark -- lost the latter much trade
union support on the not unreasonable ground that it was catering
to general national interest and not to particular workers'
interests.

The overall organization of the Danish party structure
played an equally important role in emphasizing the anti-marketeers' arguments. Throughout the 1960s the "ideological" cleavage
revolved around the dichotomy between the three "bourgeois"
parties (the Conservative People's Party, the Liberal Party and
the Radical Liberal Party) and the socialist parties (the Social
Democratic Party and the Socialist People's Party). While the
former have been able to garner between 40% and 50% of the vote,
the latter have together accounted for the remaining 40% to 50%.
Up till 1968, the bourgeois parties were unable to agree on
general policy outlines, while the Radical Party had traditionally been the Social Democrats' coalition partner. In 1968,
however, the Radicals joined with the other two bourgeois parties
and formed the government. This deprived the Social Democrats of
a coalition partner and of a generally moderating "bourgeois"
influence, and forced them to move closer to the more radically
socialist Socialist People's Party. Hence the decision by the
Social Democrats in May 1971 to hold a referendum on the market
question, regardless of the parliamentary outcome of the EEC
accession vote. Hence also the agreement by the bourgeois
parties to support the Social Democrat move, in order not to
alienate any voters and drive them further into the arms of the
anti-marketeers and the Socialist People's Party in the ensuing
September parliamentary elections.

In conclusion, a review of public opinion polls -- which
were taken monthly during the three application periods --
appears to show that it was largely due to the anti-marketeers'
agitation that opposition developed among the public. During the
first two application periods the proportion against fluctuated

between 5% and 9%.[44] In contrast, in October 1970 the proportion
against had risen to 15%, and to 30% by April 1971. Thereafter
it continued to fluctuate between a low of 27% in June, August
and November 1971, and a high of 35% in January and August 1972.
More interesting is the fact that between October 1970 and
September 1972, the percentage of "don't knows" decreased from a
high of 38% in June 1971 to a low of 18% in September 1972, with
most of them going to the opposition column. During the same
period the proportion of the population supporting entry to the
EEC fluctuated between a low of 35% in June 1971 and a high of
49% in September 1972. Clearly, the end-result of the referendum, from the time that it was agreed to in May 1971 to the time
it was held on 2 October 1972, was uncertain.[45]

---

[44]9% in 1961, 5% in February 1967, and 8% in September 1967.

[45]Data taken from a table in Hansen, 1973, op. cit.

CHAPTER 8.   NORWAY: THE HESITANT EUROPEAN

1. Foreign Policy and Economics

Norway, in common with most small states, has been forced to
adapt its policies to external conditions rather than attempt to
influence the external environment to internal demands. In a
democratic state where foreign policy decisions are made on a
parliamentary basis, the success or failure of the adaptation
process depends on elite understanding of the effects on the
sovereignty, independence and welfare of the nation of the forces
to which adaptation has to be made. Generally, the result is
adaptation to external forces, because these are apprehended as
having greater thrust and momentum than internal interests. This
happened in 1948-9 when Norway opted for membership in NATO,
despite a strong emotional predilection for a Nordic Defence
Union. It also happened in 1959 when Norway opted for EFTA, and
again in 1962, 1967 and 1970-1 when Norwegian policy-makers
decided to apply for membership of the European Economic Community, despite similar national/Nordic and cultural tendencies to
the contrary. The consultative referendum result on 25 September
1972, in which the electorate turned down EEC membership, thus
came as a shock.

However, the popular decision of 1972 notwithstanding, Norway's foreign economic policy was not changed thereby. Subsequent economic developments show that September 1972 was merely a convulsion which came about as the result of the temporary transplantation of a carefully balanced complex foreign policy from parliamentary to popular decision. One aspect of foreign policy which had been carefully developed over a long period by the Norwegian political elite was suddenly turned over to the electorate for decision on a simple yes or no basis.

Although there were several immediate causes for the victory of the popular anti-market forces -- in Parliament only the small Centre Party and the Farmers Party, with a combined twenty seats and 10.5% of the electoral vote in the elections of 7-8 September 1969 supported the anti-market stand -- the underlying framework for the referendum result is found in the structure of foreign policy itself. This can best be illustrated with the aid of a 3 x 3 matrix, originally developed by Arne Olav Brundtland:[1]

Norway	s	e	r
A	1	3	2
E	2	1	3
N	3	2	1

In the matrix the top horizontal column shows specific foreign policy objectives: s = security policy, e = economic policy and r = the remainder of non-specific foreign policy. The left vertical column indicates the three specific international political orbits within which the foreign policy objectives may

---

[1]"Norwegian Foreign Policy", *Cooperation and Conflict*, 1968: 3, pp. 169-83.

be satisfied: A = the Atlantic orientation, E = the European
orientation and N = the Nordic orientation. The numerals 1-
3 indicate the relative preference given by the Norwegian political elite to the three international political orientations in
the satisfaction of the three functional foreign policy objectives, s, e and r, during the period under review. Hence it can
be seen that in security matters the Norwegian authorities have
given priority to the Atlantic orientation, with the European
orientation second and the Nordic orientation a trailing third.
In the economic field priority is given to the European orientation, with the Nordic orientation in second place and the Atlantic in third place. In the area of non-specific general foreign
policy, preference is given to the Nordic orientation with the
Atlantic in second place and the European in third.

The foreign policy structure that Norway constructed and
operated during the 1950s and 1960s -- and still does -- was thus
a complex one, which depended on a careful differentiation of
functions and of the orientations or orbits within which these
could be satisfied. While it is relatively easy for an analyst,
or for a diplomatist, to understand and operate within the limits
of such functional and orientational differentiations, this is
more difficult for a politician -- although he understand the
differentiations. For a layman, in contrast, both the compre-
hension of the differentiations as well as their operational
limits are very difficult to understand, and appear to be merely
arcane nonsense. The Norwegian foreign policy elite had apparently forgotten this when they allowed the question of European
Economic Community membership to be placed before the public for
decision.

It may be added that the Norwegian Members of Parliament
themselves, though architects of the foreign policy structure and
overseers of its operation, often reflected in their debates the
citizen-layman inability to differentiate between policy objective and its functional orientation. Hence, for example, the
spillover of the Nordic orientation in the security objective of
NATO membership is demonstrated by the lack of full functional

participation, as shown by the decisions to forbid the permanent stationing of foreign troops in Norway, and the storage and operation of nuclear armaments on Norwegian territory. Similarly, the same Nordic orientation intruded time and again during the consideration of economic objectives in all the market debates. The fact that the Norwegian Parliament decided in 1962 to seek full EEC membership along with Britain and Denmark, and renewed this decision in 1967, 1970 and 1971, does not negate the point just made. The fact is that it took the Norwegian Storting eight months of debate after the British-Danish applications of 9 August 1961 before it decided on 28 April 1962 to apply for full membership in the EEC by a vote of 113-37. In 1967 the Norwegians needed two months after the British application of May 11 to follow the Danes, who had submitted their application on May 12, to decide by a vote of 135-13 on 13 July 1967 to apply for membership. In 1970 the decision to renew the application came on 25 June 1970 with a vote of 132 for and 17 against, some eight months after the Danish decision of 11 November 1970. The main reason why it took so long in each case to decide the application question was that the Swedish-inspired "neutralist" line of a Nordic orientation, with a "looser" relationship to Europe, was exhaustively debated and disposed of before the primarily economic objectives gained decisive weight.

Of course the EEC itself, as well as Britain and Denmark from the mid-1960s but particularly after the Davignon and Werner reports of 1969-70, added a strong political orientation to the whole question of its development and thus gave ample reason for Norwegians to consider the political implications of membership along with the economic ones. Despite this, the parliamentary decisions were made basically on economic grounds while the popular decision in the referendum of 1972 was based as much on the political as on the narrowly economic.

2. Market Policy

It is clear from even a cursory glance at the structure of the

Norwegian economy -- which in fisheries, manufacturing and
shipping has a greater dependency on the external world than do
the economies of any other Nordic country -- and from a reading
of the market debates in parliament during the 1950s and 1960s,
that Norway's economic policy relating to Europe has always been
based on the reduction of trade barriers in order to increase the
access of Norwegian manufacturing and fishery products and
Norwegian shipping to foreign markets. At no time has there been
any desire on the part of Norwegian policy-makers to build an
integrated "common market" with anyone. This objective is in
vivid contrast to the original and continuing purpose of the EEC,
and differs markedly from post-1961 British and even Danish
policy objectives.

Although the Anglo-Nordic group all developed free trade
foreign economic policies in the immediate post-war years and
actively pursued the goal of free or freer trade throughout the
1950s, after the flux of the 1960s only Sweden, Norway and
Finland still pursued free trade in the 1970s as a primary
foreign economic policy goal. Britain deserted that policy in
1961 primarily in the interests of political gains. But it
must also be remembered that Britain's foreign economic and
political policies have usually run parallel, if not contiguous,
courses often supporting one another. Denmark as a small trading
nation tried for a long time to separate the economic and the
political, as was demonstrated for example by its reluctance to
enter into a politically oriented (by definition) customs union
with the other Nordic countries in 1958 and during the entire
WFTA negotiations. This reluctance was transformed into acceptance in 1961-2, when the United Kingdom, one of its two best
customers, decided to join the EEC, the second of its major
customers. The acceptance was transformed into downright enthusiasm by the third round applications ten years later because
Denmark perceived it to be in its best economic interests to
participate in the political control of the economic development
of its major market -- the enlarged Economic Community. That the
tradition of separating the economic and the political had

already been replaced by a policy of combining the two and using one to support the other was illustrated by the Danish proposal to reactivate the Nordic Economic Community in 1958, in the interest not of economic gain (which would have been relatively small for Denmark) but of using the common market of the North for the political purpose of bargaining with the EEC for advantageous economic terms in the expected future enlargement of the latter.

In the case of Norway, the transition from a separation of foreign economic and political policies to combining them was never completed. It should be recalled that during the 1950s Norway was not only a strong supporter of trade liberalization -- along with the rest of the Anglo-Nordic group -- in the OEEC, in GATT and at the WFTA negotiations, but during the ten-year flirtation with a Nordic customs union and common market showed great hestiation in submitting its economy to possible domination by its economically powerful neighbour, Sweden. As it turned out, it was this political fear that finally caused the Nordic Economic Community to founder. A decade later, during the Nordek negotiations, Norway displayed similar apprehensions. This despite the *de facto* economic integration resulting from the Nordic Common Labour Market, the virtual abolition of intra-Nordic trade barriers as the result of EFTA, and the growing political cooperation under the aegis of the Nordic Council. It should, however, be noted that throughout the Nordic *de facto* integration processes, the political and the economic activities were conducted separately and under different rules. In spite of this, a highly integrated cobweb of relations among the Nordic countries had been built up by the end of the 1960s in which it was difficult to differentiate the political from the economic.

But even had the Nordic Common Market in the 1950s, or Nordek in the 1960s, been realized, the problem of relations with the EEC and the United Kingdom would not have been solved for Norway, for the simple reason that the Nordic market would have provided no alternative for the continental and British markets. An alternative between a market with a population of 20 million

196.

and one of 250 million is no alternative at all.

Thus when the United Kingdom, Norway's largest single-country market, and Denmark, part of its Nordic market, made simultaneous applications in 1961 to become full members of Norway's largest market area, the EEC, it was expected on purely economic grounds that Norway would have to follow suit.

That Norway did not immediately do so was an indication that something was wrong. What was wrong was that for Norwegians the political implications of participation in a politically directed economic integration aimed at eventual political unification was even more troubling than the similar objectives in the Nordic Economic Community and Nordek proposals. The underlying cause was a "feeling", between unease and fear, of the possibility that the pursuit of the obvious economic advantages of the EEC would lead to a subversion of Norway's economic and political independence. These feelings were widespread throughout the Norwegian polity. They were strongest at the bottom of the social pyramid and weakest at the top levels of the commercial and shipping elites, and among the foreign policy elite.[2] These feelings were based on nationalism and conditioned by history and geography.

3. Constitutional Amendment

Beginning with the immediate post-war years, the political elite developed close contacts with the other Europeans as a result of OEEC, GATT, NATO and other political and economic cooperative

---

[2]Helge Hveem in 1967 conducted a survey of the elites and opinion makers selected from politicians, civil servants, the mass media, and interest organizations, with a sample of 88 from among the "elites" and 130 from among the "opinion makers" in the sample groups. Of the elite group only 5% had no opinion on the question "On what conditions do you think that Norway should relate itself to the EEC?", 5% indicated that Norway should not relate itself to the EEC, 6% agreed to associate membership and 84% agreed to full membership. See Hveem, *International Relations and World Images*, p. 178. In July 1967 a Gallup Poll showed that 54% of the sample agreed to full membership in the EEC whereas 21% did not think that Norway should become a member, and 25% had no opinion.

activities, and quickly came to the conclusion that the complex-
ities of the modern world required some minimal supranational
structures. As early as 1952, it attempted to amend the 1914
Constitution to permit transfer of authority to supranational
organizations. The Government published a White Paper, *The
Constitution and Norway's Participation in International Organizations*, in which it expressed the view that the concept of
soveriegnty was in a "state of dissolution",[3] and that changes
should be made in the Constitution to permit participation in
international organizations that would require the transfer of
some sovereignty. There was little reaction in the Storting,
because the matter of transfer of sovereignty appeared "academic"
to most politicians, since no policy proposals leading to membership in organizations requiring transfer of sovereignty were
contemplated, even by the Government. The matter was taken up
again in 1956, discussed by the Foreign Affairs Committee of the
Storting and debated briefly in the House in October 1956, but
was defeated unanimously. Clearly the question was not yet an
issue, and there were no immediate prospects for the need for a
transfer of soveriegnty arrangement.

When the matter was again considered by the Foreign Affairs
Committee during the spring of 1960 the situation had changed
considerably: there seemed to be a possibility of an EEC-EFTA
merger of some kind, which would be likely to require the establishment of some minimal supranational organs. As Finn Moe,
Chairman of the Foreign Affairs Committee, put it in a debate in
1960 on the European Free Trade Association, "[I] would regard it
as a great advantage if [the constitutional change] could be
accepted so that we could avoid these constant problems of
Constitutional interpretation ... [it has become] necessary for
us to transfer a certain limited amount of our sovereignty to
supranational organs."[4] After lengthy on-and-off discussions in

---

[3]Stortingsmelding nr. 89, 1951, p. 43.

[4]*Stortingstidende* 1960, p. 2401 as quoted by Trygve Ramberg

the committee and in Parliament, and informal inter- and intra-
party discussions, the Foreign Affairs Committee finally produced
a recommendation to insert a new Paragraph 93 in the Constitution
relating to transfer of authority to international organizations.
The committee's recommendation, however, was not unanimous, and
consisted of one majority and two minority opinions. The majority, consisting of Labour, Conservative and Liberal members,
proposed the following wording and contents for Paragraph 93:

> In order to secure international peace and security, and
> in order to promote international law and order and co-
> operation among nations, the Storting may, by three-
> fourths majority consent that an international organi-
> zation of which Norway is or becomes a member, shall
> have the right, within a functionally limited field, to
> exercise powers which in accordance with this Con-
> stitution are normally vested in the Norwegian author-
> ities, exclusive of the power to alter this Consti-
> tution. For such consent provided above at least two-
> thirds of the members of the Storting -- the same quorum
> as is required for changes in or amendments to the
> Constitution -- shall be present.

> The provisions of the preceding paragraph do not apply
> in cases of membership in an international organization,
> the decisions of which are not binding on Norway except
> as obligations under international law.[5]

The majority's main argument in support of Paragraph 93 was that
it would be necessary in relation to the coming negotiations with
the EEC, but that it would also facilitate Norway's participation
in a number of obligatory forms of international cooperation,
such as nuclear arms control and disarmament.

Of the two minorities one, the Christian People's Party,
agreed to the constitutional amendment but wished both to limit
its application (to exceptional cases) and to make it more
difficult to apply by changing the three-fourths majority to a
five-sixths majority requirement. The second minority, the

---

in Ørvik (ed.), *Fears and Expectations: Norwegian Attitudes
Toward European Integration* (Oslo, 1972), Part II: Sovereignty
and Cooperation, footnote 15, p. 127.

[5]Innstilling S. nr. 100, 1961/2.

Centre Party (formerly the Farmers' Party) was totally against the amendment because it considered it both unnecessary and too broad in application.

After ten amendments and twenty-eight hours of debate covering three days, the final vote was taken on 8 March 1962 with the result that the majority proposal of the Foreign Affairs Committee was passed by a vote of 115-35. It is significant that the only party that voted in a body for the constitutional amendment was the Conservative Party, and the only party which voted against the proposal was the Centre party. The Socialist People's Party also voted against the proposal, but with only two members, which they lost in 1969, they played an insignificant role in the formation of Norway's market policy during the 1960s. All other parties split their votes: of the Labour Party's seventy-four members six voted against, in the Christian People's Party nine out of fifteen voted against, and in the Liberal Party two out of fourteen voted against the proposal. Though there was thus widespread support across the Conservative, Liberal, Labour and Christian People's parties, there was also a significant opposition centred in the Centre Party, with cross-party support in all parties except the Conservatives. Since only the arch-supporters, the Conservatives, who represented the upper classes and the industrial and shipping interests, were able to muster the complete support of their members in the vote on the transfer of sovereignty question, and only their arch-enemies, the Centre Party, the representatives of the farming interests, were able to compel similar complete support of their members, it is clear that Norway was much further removed from internationalism in 1962 than Denmark had been in 1953, when it approved a similar transfer of sovereignty provision in its constitution. Further-more, the intra-party cleavages on the question in the Labour, the Christian People's and the Liberal parties indicated that there was considerable disagreement on both ideological and class bases in the matter of internationalism and the question of its impact on Norway, since the three parties collectively represent approximately two-thirds of the Norwegian electorate, as well as

two-thirds of the social classes, with the Labour Party representing a large percentage of the working class and the Christian
People's and Liberal parties representing large sections of the
middle classes. The intra-party cleavages of 1962 also suggest
that the possibility of substantial shifts from internationalism
to nationalism or *vice versa* within the parties remained a strong
possibility.

The debate itself, though it covered eight or nine diverse
categories of argument[6] including the wording of the proposal,
the three-quarters versus five-sixths majority requirement, the
principles of sovereignty and international cooperation, the
question of need as well as expectations (political, moralistic,
ideological and economic), was nevertheless a very basic confrontation between pragmatic internationalism and idealistic nationalism. Of course, the question of the EEC was in the back of
everyone's mind, since it was, after all, the basic reason why
the question of Paragraph 93 was finally taken up. The fact that
all the other EFTA members had already made application for some
form of EEC membership three months earlier, that the Government
was actively considering an application, and that a debate
determining the fate of the Government's proposal was scheduled
later in the spring session of the Storting, made the debate a
preliminary test of attitudes of its political impact on Norway.
It also created the curious situation whereby the Government
spokesmen tried very hard to get away from the EEC as an issue
and provoked moralistic and idealistic arguments. For example,
Finn Moe, who as chairman of the Foreign Affairs and Constitution

---

[6]Ramberg in his excellent analysis of the 1956, 1960 and
1962 debates on Paragraph 93 divides the arguments into nine
categories: 1. Constitution, 2-A. Principles, and 2-B. Proposals
(the specific wording), 3. Sovereignty and Cooperation, 4. Need,
5. Political Expectations, 6. Peace and Security, 7. Ideological
Expectations, 8. Economic Expectations, 9. Procedure; and discerns
2172 arguments by 78 speakers who made 341 speeches, in which the
arguments were divided 58% pro and 39% contra with 3% both pro and
contra. See Ramberg, op. cit., p. 70, and pp. 78-84.

Committee was the chief spokesman for the proposal, was forced to
conclude his first major speech in the debate with the words,

> I can well understand that many have doubts about the
> European Economic Community, but that we shall determine
> now is ... not our relationship to the Community. It is
> therefore unreasonable to vote against a constitutional
> amendment on the grounds of opposition to the Community,
> when such an amendment is necessary for disarmament and
> peace, whether a Community exists or not. It is those
> who support a change in the Constitution by voting for
> the proposed Paragraph 93 who are in concert with the
> objectives of peace and international law, which have
> been traditions in Norwegian foreign policy since the
> days of the international arbitration agreements. It is
> those who vote against who break with this policy.[7]

Despite the emotional conclusion to his speech, the central
thrust of Finn Moe's arguments in support of the amendment was
placed squarely on pragmatic considerations:

> Today, when the state and national planning plays an
> increasingly larger role in the area of economics, there
> is much greater importance for organized international
> cooperation among states [than in the past]. And I
> believe that one can definitely see that there has been
> a dual revolution in economic-political thinking in
> western Europe during the post-war period. First, both
> the common and the businessman have clearly understood
> that it is the policy conducted by governments, parlia-
> mentary organs and economic-political interest groups
> which determines economic development, social standards,
> the distribution of income, etc....
>
> Secondly, there is a general understanding among
> countries that national economic policy must be re-
> garded in relation to other countries' policies, and
> that the production techniques and the economic system
> of the Western world requires an international plan
> which can coordinate the different countries' policies
> in order to realize their common interests.
>
> In order for this international cooperation to be
> effective it must be of an obligatory character, that is
> to say that those who participate in it must be obliged
> to be bound by the organizations' resolutions and deci-
> sions. And the international organizations must be able
> to make common decisions.[8]

---

[7]*Stortingstidende* 1961/2, p. 2224.

[8]Ibid., pp. 2220-1.

But it was precisely this pragmatic internationalism which led the opposition to unite on a nationalistic basis against the threat of loss of independence to the EEC:

> Had it not been that the proposal in this matter is tied precisely to an eventual membership of the EEC, it is possible that I would have voted for the proposal today. I, of course, agree that Norway should participate in international cooperation, but to the extent that the constitutional amendment is tied to an eventual member ship in the EEC, I cannot vote for it today.

The same member continued:

> I cannot vote for a constitutional amendment which in the future -- eventually leading to joining the Common Market -- will lay the groundwork for a weakening of our sovereignty to the extent that the new Paragraph 93 will.[9]

Although the proponents of the constitutional amendment won the debate with a handsome majority, 115-35 votes, sufficient doubt as to the political impact of the EEC on Norway's political independence had been aroused to force the Government to reassure Parliament. In an intervention on 7 March, Foreign Minister Halvard Lange reiterated the Government's position as presented in White Paper No. 67[10] that though the Government took a favourable view of the closer political and cultural cooperation envisaged in the Bonn Declaration, no such cooperation could be institutionalized except through a new treaty or through changes in the Treaty of Rome. "In both cases the question of Norway's accession must be presented to the Storting for ratification." He added that on the actual form and content of any such proposals would depend whether Paragraph 93 would permit Norwegian accession or whether further changes in the Constitution would be

---

[9]Wirstad (Centre Party), ibid., pp. 2362-3. Wirstad's colleague in the Centre Party Einar Havdhaugen was even more emotional: "... As far as I know, this is the first time in Norway's history that the people are demonstrating against the Storting to protect Norway's Constitution." (ibid., p. 2268) In fact, 5,000 protesters demonstrated outside Parliament during the first day of the debate. *Nordisk Kontakt* 1962: 5, p. 280.

[10]Stortings meld. nr. 67, 1961/2.

necessary. In any case, he pointed out, the Government had not
yet taken any position on the form of a Norwegian application for
negotiations with the EEC: "Before this can be done, the Storting will have taken a position on the ground rules for negotiations of relations with the Community."[11]

4. The 1962 EEC Debate

On 12 April 1962, four weeks after the conclusion of the constitutional amendment debate, the expanded Foreign Affairs and
Constitution Committee presented its report on Norway and the
European Economic Community.[12] As expected, the report contained
three proposals: a Government-majority proposal that Norway
should apply for full membership of the EEC; a Centre-Christian
People's Party proposal that Norway should seek associate membership of the EEC; and a Socialist People's Party proposal that
Norway should seek only a trade agreement with the EEC. The
debate on the proposals took three days before the vote was taken
on 28 April, with the results that the Socialist People's Party
proposal was rejected since it received only the votes of the two
supporters; the associate membership proposal was defeated 112-38;
and the full membership proposal was passed 113-37. As expected,
the line-up of support followed the pattern established a month
and a half earlier with the Conservatives as staunch supporters
of full membership and the Centre almost equally staunch opponents (they lost one member to the full membership support group
and thus did not preserve complete party unity) as well as
unifying around the party proposal for an associate membership.
The other parties split their votes, with the Labour Party losing
eleven to the associate membership group, the Liberal Party
losing two, and the Christian People's Party seven (although two
who voted for full membership also voted for associate member-

---

[11]*Stortingstidende*, 1961/2, pp. 2317-8.

[12]Innst. S. nr. 165, 1961/2.

ship).[13]

The debate itself was highly emotional, and was based largely on nationalistic considerations: two-thirds of the debate dealt with Norwegian problems of social welfare, sovereignty, the economy, religion and culture. Only 5% of it was concerned with foreign policy. The remaining third of the debate related to the internal structure of the EEC and its role as an international factor.[14] Economic considerations of EEC membership constituted only 19% of the Storting debate. This although the main objective of the EEC was economic, and its main impact on Norway was expected to be economic! Daniel Heradstveit concludes that the shift from economic considerations, which had marked the EEC question up to the time of the Storting debates, to mainly political considerations, was conditioned by six factors. First, the economic emphasis of the early phases was mainly due to the fact that the discussion was conducted by experts; secondly, the shift away from the economic followed the shifting of the debate from the expert to the popular level, where "it is difficult to obtain public response to pure economic arguments, which are primarily based on statistics"; thirdly, the economic argument had become saturated; fourthly, as information about the EEC was spread about, it became apparent that the question involved politics as much as economics; fifthly, "be-

---

[13]The votes on 28 April 1962:

Party	Associate Membership		Full Membership	
	For	Against	For	Against
Conservatives	0	29	29	0
Liberals	2	12	12	2
Christian People's	9	6	8	7
Centre	16	0	1	15
Labour	11	63	63	11
Socialist People's	0	2	0	2
TOTAL	38	112	113	37

Source: Compiled from Daniel Heradstveit, "The Norwegian EEC Debate" in Ørvik, op. cit., p. 178.

[14]See Heradstveit, op. cit., p. 186.

cause their position was mainly political in nature, certain groups were anxious to bring the debate into the sphere of politics"; and sixthly, "the question was of great importance for the entire nation, and it was to be handled by politicians." "Consequently," Heradstveit concludes, "the entire political repertory came into play."[15]

The debate in the Storting was the focus of widespread public involvement in the issue. For the three days that they lasted, the newspapers, radio and television followed the parliamentary debates to saturation point and commented freely. At the same time, more direct popular participation took place by means of street demonstrations: 5,000 protesters against EEC membership marched in front of the Parliament Buildings, and 8,000 to 10,000 gathered at a protest rally at the City Hall Square.[16]

The public and political interest did not mean that economic considerations were not present. Indeed, they were often the determinants of the positions of the speakers, particularly among the supporters of full membership. As Nils Ørvik points out,

> In a country whose existence is partly based on shipping and foreign trade, international cooperation is a matter of course. Few politicians would dare to defy this principle. The parties and people who supported the government proposal to apply for membership in the EEC had no difficulties.... They logically and consistently argued for Norwegian membership in the EEC as a means to strengthen the drive for an integrated and closely cooperating Europe.

On the other hand,

> The contra-groups had a much harder time. They could not openly reject international cooperation on principle. This would put them in an impossible position; that of true isolationists.... The way out for the socialist contra speakers was therefore to praise international cooperation as an abstract principle while at the same time condemning the EEC as a wrong approach. Member-

---

[15]Ibid., p. 188.

[16]See Ørvik, op. cit., p. 322; and *Nordisk Kontakt* 1962: 8, p. 467.

ship in the EEC might harm rather than promote coopera-[17]
tion on the international level.

The non-socialist opposition based its arguments more on an
economic base, and related Norwegian agriculture to the question
of national independence and sovereignty. This course was to be
expected since the Centre Party group accounted for the majority
of the non-socialist opposition, with sixteen of the twenty-seven
belonging to the Centre Party which, it will be recalled, repre-
ented the farmers. Of the remaining eleven, nine were members of
the Christian People's Party and two were Liberals. Of these, as
Heradstveit points out, four were farmers, two were principals of
agricultural colleges, two were journalists, and one was an inspec-
tor of schools. "Thus, at least six of the nine were directly
associated with agriculture, as was at least one of the two
Liberals. We may therefore establish that <u>of the non-socialist
opposition's twenty-seven Representatives, twenty-three were closely
connected with agriculture.</u> In other words, we are justified in
saying that the non-socialist opposition was in fact an agrarian
opposition."[18]

Heradstveit further points out that farmers as a group view
European integration with little favour, and refers to Karl
Deutsch's assertion that among all major groups the farmers are
the most difficult to convert to policies of integration.[19]
An investigation undertaken by Norwegian Gallup in September 1961
and 1962 shows that among non-socialist voters the strongest oppo-
sition to Norwegian membership in the EEC was located among Centre
Party supporters.[20]

Given such conflicting economic-political positions as

---

[17]Ørvik, op. cit., p. 322.

[18]Heradstveit, op. cit., pp. 201-2.

[19]Karl Deutsch, *Political Community in the North Atlantic
Area* (Princeton, 1967), p. 175.

[20]Johann Galtung, "Internasjonal samarbeid", in Bjørn Alstad
(ed.), *Norske Meninger* (Oslo, 1969), Vol. I, p. 175.

outlined above, it is not surprising that the debate led to two contrasting assessments of its effectiveness in clarifying the EEC issue. Erik Braadland, the spokesman for the Centre Party, concluded that the conflict between the supporters of full membership and those supporting association had become sharper and more profound, while Prime Minister Einar Gerhardsen concluded that a slow transition towards agreement had been taking place among the three opposing groups in the debate, and that the boundaries of the positions were no longer as sharply differentiated as before.[21]

The Norwegian application for consideration of EEC membership on the basis of Article 237 of the Treaty of Rome was duly made two days after the parliamentary vote, in a brief three-paragraph letter signed by Foreign Minister Halvard Lange. In the letter, the Foreign Minister indicated that the Norwegian Government "would be thankful if negotiations about conditions for accession could be begun in the near future." He added that "Norway's accession to the European Economic Community raises special problems because of the country's geographical location and economic structure. The Norwegian Government hopes therefore that it will be possible, through mutual understanding, to reach satisfactory solutions to these problems during the negotiations."[22] The first hearing took place on 4 July 1962, at ministerial level, when the Norwegian Minister of Foreign Affairs made brief reference to some of the problems which might arise, including the need for protection of Norwegian fisheries and agriculture. The EEC Council of Ministers acceeded to the Norwegian Government's request for the opening of negotiations. Although one meeting at ministerial level followed on 12 November 1962, by the time that negotiations were broken off in January

---

[21]*Stortingstidende* 1961/2, p. 3000 (Braadland); p. 3002 (Gerhardsen).

[22]Letter reprinted in Appendix I of *Rapport om De Europeiske Felleskap*, Vol. VI, 21 April 1971, p. 199.

1963 with Great Britain and Denmark, negotiations proper were not yet under way with Norway (or Ireland, the third applicant for full membership).

5. In Waiting

Between 1963 and 1966 there was little political debate on the EEC. The only significant change was the formation of the first non-socialist coalition government since 1935, resulting from a considerable loss by the Labour Party in the elections of November 1965. Although five of the fifteen new ministers were known supporters of association, rather than full membership, it was assumed the new Government would not initiate any new moves towards the EEC. This proved wrong. In January 1966 the Government announced the establishment of an interdepartmental working committee of officials to re-investigate the problems of Norwegian accession to the EEC. The initiative was supported by all parties except the Socialist People's Party. When in November 1966 it became apparent that the British Government was attempting to reopen negotiations with the EEC, the general Norwegian reaction was positive in support of the British initiative. The Socialist People's Party and the Communist Party reacted negatively as expected, but the reluctance expressed by the Centre Party was considerably muted from its position four years earlier.

As the winter progressed, the question of a renewed application became increasingly real. This time, however, in contrast to the 1961-2 situation, the debate on the question focused more on the actual questions involved as the result of the working committee having presented its first report, which dealt with the structure and operation of the EEC, in February 1967.[23] The second report, dealing with the problems that Norway would face

---

[23]Utenriksdepartementet, *Rapport om Det Europeiske Økonomiske Felleskap* (Marketsutvalget), 24 February 1967.

on accession, followed on 2 June 1967.[24]

During May and June, as a result of the British application of 11 May, most of the political parties considered the question and arrived at clearly stated positions. There was far more unanimity than five years earlier. Within the Labour Party and the Liberal Party no serious splits took place, and both recommended that the Government apply for full EEC membership. The Conservative Party was as staunch and unanimous in its support as in 1961-2. The only problems arose within the Centre Party and the Christian People's Party, which, however, were papered over in order to maintain the coalition Government.

In June, the Government published a White Paper in which it announced its unanimous decision to recommend to the Storting that Norway should again apply for full membership in the EEC. The Government made it clear that it intended to attempt to safeguard Norwegian agriculture during the negotiations -- a reiteration of the position the Labour Government had taken in 1962.[25] A two-day debate took place on 12 and 13 July in which a minority of sixteen, including four Labour members, seven Centre Party members, three Christian Party members and the two Socialist People's Party members attempted to resuscitate the arguments of 1962, and were successful to the extent that they forced consideration of two motions, one attempting to delay the decision of application until the negotiations between the EEC and the United Kingdom had actually begun, and the second proposing an association arrangement rather than full membership. Both were roundly defeated, the first by 130-20, and the second by 133-16. The original motion, presented by the Government and the Foreign and the Constitutional Affairs Committee, proposing that "the Government should seek membership for Norway in the EEC on the basis of Article 237 of the Treaty of Rome," was passed by

---

[24]*Rapport om Norge og de europeiske felleskap* (Del. II av Markedsutvalgets rapport), 2 June 1967.

[25]St. meld. nr. 86. 1966/7.

136-13. Thus in the final vote three Centre Party members who had voted for the association proposal had rejoined the party majority. Only a corporal's guard of opponents was left: four Labourites and two socialists, and seven defectors from the government parties -- three Christian People's Party members and four Centre Party members.

The debate in the House, although following the familiar lines of 1962, was much more restrained, with the supporters of full membership taking up much more of the debate than in 1962 for the simple reason that their size had increased from 75% of members to 89% by 1967. The increase in the supporters' share of the debate was even greater: it had risen from 56% in 1962 to 84% in 1967.[26] The 1967 debate was much less heated than in 1962 because of two main reasons: first, there was "a greater degree of agreement among the public, and ... an increased familiarity with the problem-complex;"[27] and secondly, the economic and interest organizations were far more consistent in their positive response to the EEC question in 1967 than in 1962.[28] Although the Norwegian Farmers Union in 1967 maintained an attitude which was almost as critical as in 1962, it nevertheless left to the Government the decision of the form of application to be submitted to the EEC. The National Federation of Labour (LO) and the Federation of Norwegian Industries supported the Government proposals as strongly in 1967 as in 1962. And it should be pointed out that in 1967, unlike in 1962, none of the main newspapers opposed the Government proposal. But of course, despite the submission of the Norwegian application on 11 May, nothing happened, because General de Gaulle cast his second veto against the British application.

---

[26]See Olav Vefald, "The 1967 EEC Debate", in Ørvik, op. cit., p. 220.

[27]Ibid., p. 209.

[28]See Appendix III to St. meld. nr. 86, 1966/7; and Appendix I to St. meld. nr. 15, 1961/2.

The next two years were largely taken up by Nordek negotiations which excited little enthusiasm among Norwegians, except
among the EEC opponents. When at the end of 1969 the possibility
of Norwegian membership of the EEC arose again, Norway did not
rush to take a position, but followed the EEC's internal negotiations on the points agreed to at The Hague summit in December
1969. After the appearance of the fifth report of the officials'
working committee (established in 1966) on 7 April 1970,[29] which
covered the developments in the EEC during 1969, the Government
produced a short White Paper discussing "the relation of Norway
to the Nordic and European market formations."[30] The White Paper
ended with a reiteration of the 1967 proposal to proceed with an
application for full membership.

6. The Third Application

On 24 and 25 June 1970 the Storting discussed the proposal and
approved it 132-17. The debate in the House this time was a very
tame affair with both the pro- and contra-membership groups
repeating their positions of 1967. In fact, the major difference
was that in 1970 -- largely as a result of the general elections
of September 1969 in which the Socialist People's Party lost its
mandate and a number of new members entered the House -- the
anti-full membership group increased slightly to seventeen, consisting of seven Labour, seven Centre Party and three Christian
People's Party members.

In content the arguments of the proponents were increasingly
based on pragmatic economic considerations, with many stressing
the modification that had taken place within the EEC on the
question of extending its supranational character, while the
anti-full membership group -- now limited more or less to farmers
-- tended to argue the problems of agricultural and general

---

[29]Utenriksdepartementet, *Rapport om de europeiske fellerskap
i året 1969* (Markedsutvalgets rapport V), 7 April 1970.

[30]St. meld. nr. 92, 1969/70.

economic consequences of full membership. In addition, the
opponents also argued that Nordic cooperation should be further
developed as an alternative to the EEC. Little reference was
made to Norwegian cultural and religious life.

On 30 June 1971 Foreign Minister Stray participated in the
formal opening session of negotiations between the EEC and the
four applicant countries. In his opening remarks the Foreign
Minister, after a brief statement that "the Norwegian Government
accepts the Treaty of Rome as a suitable basis for an expanded
European cooperation, with the goals and regulations as set down
in the Treaty and in subsequent regulations and directives",
warned that "the implementation of some of these regulations and
directives in Norway will raise significant problems which we on
the Norwegian side wish to discuss in the coming negotiations."
He then raised the problems of agriculture and fisheries, launched
into a lengthy discussion of the importance of these sectors in
Norwegian regional and population policy, and pointed to the
socio-economic difficulties and the economic restructuring that
an application of the EEC's existing regulations to Norway in
these matters would cause. Therefore, he concluded, Norway would
require special arrangements to safeguard agriculture and fisheries. Only at the end of his presentation did the Minister
briefly indicate that "the Norwegian Government takes a positive
position towards a constructive European cooperation which has as
its goal the strengthening of Europeans both economically and
politically, so that they can play an increasing role in the
struggle to strengthen international peace and security. We
understand that future political cooperation will be discussed in
different contexts."[31]

After the presentation of this most pragmatic-economic
statement, the bilateral negotiations between Norway and the EEC

---

[31]The Foreign Minister's statement on 30 June 1970 at Luxembourg is reprinted as Appendix 5, pp. 205-8 in Utenriksdepartementet, *Rapport om de Europeiske Felleskap* (Markedsutvalgets Rapport
VI), 21 April 1971.

began with a first meeting on 22 September 1970, when the minister repeated much of his formal speech of 30 June and reiterated the problems that agriculture and fisheries would raise. At the meeting, the EEC representatives indicated that they would take into consideration Norway's particular interest in the fisheries question, and it was agreed that negotiations would be conducted on the basis of one ministerial meeting per calendar quarter, and a monthly meeting between officials.

Thereafter negotiations proceeded more or less in parallel with those of the other three membership applicants -- the United Kingdom, Denmark and Ireland -- with solutions being arrived at more or less simultaneously. The only area in which the Norwegian negotiations ran into difficulty was that of fisheries, which meant that whereas the rest of the negotiations were concluded at a meeting on 11-12 December 1971, the fisheries problem had to be put off, being only finally solved at a meeting on 15 January 1972. On 22 January 1972 Norway, along with the United, Kingdom, Denmark and Ireland, signed the Treaty of Accession with the existing members of the EEC.

Eight months later, an advisory referendum took place on 24 and 25 September on the question "Ought Norway to become a member of the European Community?" Of the 79.2% of the electorate who voted in the referendum 53.5% voted "no" and 46.5% voted "yes." Although the referendum was an advisory one, the fact that the Government and the Liberal and Centre Parties and a number of Members of Parliament had specifically bound themselves to abide by the decision of the referendum meant that the four-fifths majority required by Paragraph 93 of the Constitution to ratify Norway's accession to membership in the EEC could not be reached. Hence the Norwegian Parliament did not ratify the Treaty, and Norway did not become a member of the EEC.

7. The Referendum

The referendum of 1972 was not the first in Norway's history. There had previously been four others: two in 1905, on the question of dissolution of the Swedish-Norwegian union and on the choice of king; then one in 1919 on prohibition and another in 1926 on its repeal. Although referenda are not explicitly included in the Norwegian Constitution, the Parliamentary Electoral Rules Commission made it clear in a report in 1952 that the Constitution does not forbid referenda as long as they are advisory and the final disposition remains in the Storting. It is up to the Storting to determine whether it wishes to hold an advisory referendum or not. [32]

In contrast to the Danish situation, where the decision to subject the entire EEC question to a referendum -- whether or not constitutionally required -- was made in May 1971 at the behest of the Social Democratic Party, in Norway the idea of a referendum was present from the very beginnings of the EEC question. The matter was raised for the first time by both the majority and the minority in the 1962 report of the Foreign Affairs and Constitution Committee. [33] In 1967 the Government, in its proposal to reopen negotiations with the EEC, unilaterally declared that it would place the question of a referendum before Parliament when the results of the negotiations were known, and ask Parliament to determine whether or not to hold the referendum. [34] In 1970 the Government reiterated its position of three years earlier. [35] On the basis of the Government's proposal, the Foreign Affairs and Constitution Committee in its report on 20 June 1970 about Norway's relations to the Nordic and European market developments took the position that "an advisory referendum ought to be held. The Storting will make the final determination on the question when the results of the negotiations are

---

[32]See Innst. III, 27 November 1952, B, ch. 4, 1 (pp. 43-47): "To what extent does our Constitution permit the holding of popular votes in matters of state?"

[33]See Innst. nr. 165, 1961/2, p. 330.

[34]See St. meld. nr. 86, 1966/7, p. 100.

[35]St. meld. nr. 92, 1969/70, p. 56.

known."[36] The market debate following this report showed wide-spread support for holding a referendum. During the next two years, both the non-socialist Government and its successor, the minority Labour Government, reaffirmed their intentions of holding a referendum, and the date was finally set in March 1972.[37]

The question that arises naturally out of the conjunction of the history of ten years of overwhelming parliamentary support for full membership in the EEC, and the simultaneous general agreement to hold a referendum on the matter, is: Why did the electorate reverse Parliament's decision? The answer is to be found within a complex of political, social and economic factors. These may be divided into four categories: Norwegian political culture, the partisan-political structure, the elite-mass gap, and Norway's socio-economic structure.

7.1 Political Culture

Of these, Norwegian political culture is basic, underlying the other three categories, and may be divided into two specific factors, Norwegian "democracy" and nationalism.

Although all the Nordic countries are fiercely proud of what they call "Nordic democracy" -- by which is meant an egalitarian, participatory, socio-political system with an emphasis on rights and duties of citizenship within a collective "nation" -- the development of the political cultures in the four Nordic coun-tries has in fact proceeded in two diverging directions. These may best be described by the terms "consensus politics" and the "politics of dissent". Swedes proudly proclaim that their system is one of consensus, and the Finns, though not vocal about it, have been forced, because of the overwhelming might of their eastern neighbour, to develop a Swedish type of consensus poli-tics in all matters that could be of interest to the Soviet

---

[36]Innst. S. nr. 322, 1969/70, p. 599.

[37]See Innst. O. IV, 1971/2.

Union.

The Danes and the Norwegians, on the other hand, have moved
in the direction of dissent. Although this does not mean that
conflicts are rife in their socio-political activities, it does
mean that when differences develop, they are thoroughly and
widely aired. It also means that, should any political or interest group find that its views are at odds with those of other
groups, it does not bow to the majority but attempts to bring its
position forcefully before the widest possible public. In this
process its position hardens, making it difficult for common
ground, let alone a consensus, to be achieved. At the base of
Danish and Norwegian partisan politics is a politics of interests, as fostered by the various economic and ideological interest and pressure groups. The function of the parties is
largely to bridge the interests supporting them. That they are
not always successful in this is demonstrated by the periodic
splintering of parties in both Denmark and Norway. It is further
shown by the enormous impact of the extra-parliamentary interests
on party policy-making. In Norway, even more than in Denmark,
this has led to a growth of "participation" in partisan politics
on the basis of economic, ideological and regional interests
operating on the local Member of Parliament, at the national
interest group level, and at the annual party meeting. In
Norway, moreover, the fact that the population is thinly spread
over a very large geographical area and is directly dependent on
government policy for its wellbeing, leads to a proliferation of
local interests, all seeking satisfaction at the seat of Parliament in Oslo. Thus for Norwegians the Storting is under much
more direct scrutiny by the electorate than is the case in
Denmark, where the population is concentrated in a small and
thickly populated area. The result is that instead of an integration of interests as in Denmark, the tendency in Norway is for
interests to differentiate on a regional basis. Hence there is
an urban-rural split, and an industrial-agricultural cleavage of
interests, in addition to the ideological left-right cleavage and
the standard socio-economic cleavages. The result is a wide-

spread agitation for issues which gives rise to conflicting demands focused on Parliament.

Nationalism in Norway is founded in both history and alienation, and is conditioned by the geographical location of the country. Historically, Norwegians have long been "loners" in a remote part of the world, cut off both by the ocean and by the mountains separating them from Sweden. They have also been dominated by their neighbours, by the Danes for 400 years, and by the Swedes for ninety years until 1905. This has left a residue of distrust of foreigners, at times amounting to xenophobia -- and this includes the Danes and Swedes. Lack of contact with other Europeans, except by the elite and the small seafaring population (approximately 60,000), memories of the German occupation, and the sensation-oriented television contacts with the outside world, have led to a deeply held conviction by most Norwegians that the political-economic-social systems in the outside world are incompatable with the peaceful, discussion-oriented egalitarian liberal system that is Norway. In Norwegians eyes liberty, hard-won only seventy years ago, can be guaranteed only if Norwegians are allowed to be masters in their own house, without external influences. In large parts of Norwegian society there is an ingenuous conviction that because of its moral, democratic, libertarian and egalitarian society, Norway, constitutes the world's most pleasant social, economic and political environment.

During the thirty-year period of overt Nordic cooperation, there has been a grudging acceptance that Swedes and Danes, and even Finns, share many of the values and conditions of existence of the Norwegians. Anti-Swedish and anti-Danish feelings have thus subsided and been replaced by a secondary Nordic nationalism. This was heightened during the Nordek negotiations and during the 1971-2 anti-EEC agitation, when the Nordic alternative to the EEC was held up as being in closer accord with the Norwegian political, social and cultural conditions than "Europe" could ever be.

7.2 Partisan Politics: The Course of Argument

The structure of the party system naturally reflects the political culture within which it operates. It was the participatory nature of Norwegian political culture which brought about the inter-party disagreements in 1971 and emphasized the intra-party interest differences which the parties were unable to resolve in Parliament, and which they left for the electorate to decide in the referendum. Discord on the EEC issue broke out suddenly on the floor of the House during the foreign affairs debate in November 1970. It was both an intra-party and inter-party disagreement. However, the fact that it was also an intra-Government disagreement added to the drama and newsworthiness which instantly re-invigorated the dormant anti-market interests and brought the issue before the public.

The disagreement was brought to the floor of the House by a number of Centre Party members who were concerned at the implications of the acceptance of the Davignon Report by the EEC Council of Ministers, and the contents of the Werner Report presented to the ministers on 27 October 1970. The disagreement gathered added weight when the chairman and parliamentary leader of the Centre Party, Jan Austerheim, took a position in direct opposition to the Government, and argued that the contents of the Davignon and Werner reports changed the ground rules of the EEC beyond anything intended at the time when Paragraph 93 was added to the Constitution. He therefore proposed that the Government should order a judicial inquiry to determine to what extent the proposal of the Werner report to establish an economic and monetary union accorded with the Norwegian Constitution. This show of "uncertainty" on Norway's part was, of course, roundly condemned by other members of the coalition Government and by the Labour opposition. However, the fact remains that at the end of the foreign affairs debate it was decided to send Austerheim's proposal to the Government without a vote being taken on the substance of the proposal.

The split between the Government -- whose policy was to continue negotiations on the established bases -- and the Auster-

heim group in the Centre Party was characterized by the leader of
the opposition, Trygve Bratteli, as "political double dealing".
According to the opposition and the other Government parties, the
split in the Centre Party appeared to be a systematic attempt by
it to create confusion both in the Government and the Storting.
This kind of hesitancy and uncertainty, it was claimed, would
lead to difficulties for Norway's credibility in the EEC negotiations.

The final position taken by Prime Minister, Per Borten,
was a typical coalition ploy: though he agreed that Norway must
show credibility externally, he nevertheless said: "We are also
responsible to show our own people credibility and trust."[38]

During the winter of 1970-1 the disagreement over the EEC
question in the Centre Party grew and led to an increasingly
difficult problem for the coalition Government. The Prime
Minister's credibility decreased as he tried to seek a middle
course between the criticism of his own party and the hitherto
generally accepted policy of his Government and the previous
Government. Nevertheless, both the Prime Minister and the cabinet
made it clear that negotiations must continue because they
involved not only the economic future of Norway but its political
future as well. In his New Year radio and television broadcast,
the Prime Minister took the line that there was no question that
current developments within the EEC extended far beyond the
limits of the Treaty of Rome. The discussions relating to
political and economic union were oriented towards developing
supranational organs with authority to make binding decisions on
its member countries. It was therefore necessary, as the Prime
Minister indicated, for the Norwegian nation to make up its mind
about these goals at the same time as negotiations with the EEC
were continuing.[39] The Foreign Minister, in answer to a question
in Parliament, went even further and underlined strongly that in

---

[38]See *Nordisk Kontakt* 1970: 15, pp. 937-9.

[39]*Nordisk Kontakt* 1971: 1, p. 38.

his view there were compelling security and foreign policy
reasons for an expansion of the European Community. He indicated
further that a failure in this would be a "calamity, not only
economically". He added: "I am particularly concerned about the
political difficulties that will accompany a split in Europe."
Later the same day he confirmed his views in a press conference,
particularly in relation to the compelling security and international political grounds for expansion of the European Community.[40]

The stand taken by the Prime Minister and Foreign Minister
led to a storm of criticism by the anti-market members of the
Centre Party, its newspapers, and the socialist press. The
position taken by the Foreign Minister, a member of the Conservative Party, increasingly focused public attention on the
political aspects of EEC membership in both the House and the
popular press, partly because of his party membership and partly
because it was the first time that a Norwegian cabinet member had
taken such a strong politically oriented pro-EEC position.

The strains that developed on the EEC issue in the cabinet
finally led to a break-up of the coalition. It is noteworthy
that the resignation of the Borten Government, after five and a
half years, took place over an insignificant matter, but one which
involved the EEC question. What happened was that a confidential
report from the Norwegian Ambassador to Brussels, John Halvorsen,
concerning a discussion he had had with J.F. Deniau, a French
member of the EEC Commission, in which Deniau was reported to
have taken the position that Norway could not be a member of the
EEC if it continued to demand permanent special arrangements for
Norwegian agriculture, was leaked to the press and appeared in
the newspaper *Dagbladet* on February 19. Although there was no
indication that the Prime Minister was involved in the leak, the
press nevertheless hinted at the possibility. On February 24 the
Prime Minister stated that neither he himself nor any member of

---

[40]See *Nordisk Kontakt* 1971: 3, pp. 165-6: this took place
on 10 February 1971.

is staff was the source of the leak to *Dagbladet*. Two days
ater, on February 26, half an hour before midnight, the Prime
inister issued a dramatic news release to NTB, the Norwegian
entral press service, in which he admitted that he had shown the
mbassador's report to Arne Haugestad, the leader of the People's
ovement Against Norwegian Membership in the Common Market,
uring a flight from Copenhagen to Oslo. The Prime Minister
nderlined that neither Haugestad nor his two colleagues, who
ere also on the flight, had been the source of the leak to
agbladet -- for which he had their assurance. The Prime Min-
ster concluded his statement by apologising in strong terms for
ommitting the indescretion of showing the contents of a con-
idential document to an outsider.

Under normal conditions a prime minister's right to consult
nyone is accepted, even in Norway, but in the heated atmosphere
f growing public confrontation Prime Minister Borten's admission
hat he had shown a report relating to the confrontation to one
f the opposition leaders who was not even a Member of Parlia-
ent, destroyed the credibility of the coalition arrangement and
orced the Prime Minister to resign on March 2. In explaining
he resignation and his action on the flight, Borten made it clear
hat the report was classified "confidential" and not "secret"
nd therefore did not come under the regulations concerning the
andling of security related documents. He explained that the
ther two Centre Party members of the cabinet did not view the
indiscretion" as a cause for resignation, but all twelve min-
sters from the other three coalition parties took the view that
t was.[41]

Following the Borten Government's resignation, attempts were
ade to form a new four-party non-socialist coalition but they
oundered when it was seen that the differences on the EEC
uestion were simply too deep to permit a majority government.
ence, the Labour Party formed a minority government with Trygve

---

[41]See *Nordisk Kontakt* 1971: 4, pp. 232-5.

Bratteli as Prime Minister. The new Government immediately took a strong pro-EEC position, to which it adhered through the heated and increasingly public debate in the ensuing year. Indeed, the Bratteli Government went so far during the extraordinary party conference in the spring of 1972 as to declare that the advisory referendum would be considered as binding on the Government. At the end of August 1972 the Prime Minister declared that the Government would resign if the majority voted against the Government position in the referendum. And, of course, the Government did resign immediately after the referendum.[42]

The debate on the EEC question was carried on throughout 1971 and right up to the referendum in 1972. In the Storting it was raised frequently during 1971 and almost weekly during 1972. Major debates took place on the occasion of White Papers or other documents being presented. In 1971 the Government presented a White Paper on 21 May on its position on the EEC question;[43] on 14 January 1972 the new Foreign Minister, Andreas Cappelen, gave a report of the results of negotiations at Brussels which led to a lengthy debate in the House on 20 and 21 January; on 10 March 1972 the Government released its White Paper on the negotiations together with the Treaties that Norway had signed, which led to a series of interpellations and caused debates between the opponents and the proponents of membership;[44] and on 6-8 June the final marathon debate on EEC membership was held, introduced by the Foreign Affairs Committee which presented a report, on 26 May 1972, that was unanimous only in one recommendation, namely that there should be no final vote on the substance of membership during the parliamentary debate.

The Foreign Affairs Committee split on the question of form

---

[42]And was replaced by a Christian People's Party cabinet which included almost the whole party and was based on a 9.4% electoral minority position.

[43]St. meld. nr. 90, 1970/1.

[44]St. meld. nr. 50, 1971/2, with appendices; and Saerskilt Vedlegg 1 and 2 til St. prp. m. 126, 1972/3.

of membership -- ten out of twelve, including the Labour, Conservative and Liberal Party representatives, agreed with the Government policy that full membership of an expanded EEC was not only the best economic solution but was historically correct and necessary. In the majority's view, the political difficulties connected with Norwegian membership would be solved in the transition. The real question was how Norway would solve the problems that it would meet in any case, regardless of the form of relationship with the EEC. "Membership of an expanded European Community will place us in a better position to solve these problems," they argued.[45] The minority of two, consisting of Per Borten, the former Prime Minister and representative of the Centre Party, and Lars Korvald, the future Prime Minister and representative of the Christian People's Party, took the position that though a relationship with the EEC was necessary, it ought to be an economic one. Therefore a free trade arrangement would meet the economic and trade problems, while retaining freedom of action in general political and economic questions. "As a result of such a solution our country will not be bound by the common policies and common regulations which are continually being implemented in ever more fields within the Community." The significance of freedom of independent action was underscored:

> Even if we, regardless of our form of relation with the EEC, will be influenced by its decisions, we will nevertheless, through a free trade area solution, remain freer in the choice of instruments and in our use of resources to pursue the development of our society that we desire.[46]

The entire debate from 1971 onwards was focused on the two forms of relations with the EEC, full membership versus a free trade arrangement, and the arguments used to support them were formulated along the lines expressed by the majority and minority statements in the 26 May 1972 report of the Foreign Affairs Committee. The arguments of both the proponents and opponents of

---

[45]*Nordisk Kontakt* 1972: 10, p. 666.

[46]Idem., pp. 666-7.

EEC membership became increasingly political. Whereas the former presupposed an interdependent world where national choice, especially for a small society-polity-economy such as Norway, was limited, the latter believed that the limitations of international interdependence could be overcome -- or at least expanded -- by refusing to be bound to any external authority in decisions as to what was best for Norway. The argument of the proponents, that direct ongoing participation in decisions affecting an interdependent world actually increased one's freedom of action, was rejected by the opponents out of hand, on the grounds that it would lead instead to increasing control from abroad.

The positions of the parties hardened as 1971 turned into 1972. The Liberal Party at its April 1971 annual conference showed a relatively small but vocal minority against membership, but papered over the differences by agreeing to support the continuation of membership negotiations and to leave the determination of a final position until the next year. A year later, at the extraordinary party conference held on 3-4 March 1972, the party split, with 128 votes against membership and 95 in favour.[47] Similarly the Christian People's Party, at its annual meeting held on 20-22 May 1971, agreed to leave the final disposition to the following year. When it met again at an extraordinary conference on 7-8 April 1972, a majority voted against membership.[48] Thus two parties which at the beginning of negotiations in 1970 had taken a relatively strong stand (though with minority dissent) in favour of EEC membership had reversed their positions by the spring of 1972 and now had majorities opposed to membership.

Two parties took a strong united stand. Already at its annual meeting in 1971 the Centre Party indicated that it was moving away from the position taken by its former coalition

---

[47]See *Nordisk Kontakt* 1971: 8, p. 517; and *Nordisk Kontakt* 1972: 5, p. 313.

[48]See *Nordisk Kontakt* 1971: 10, p. 644; and *Nordisk Kontakt* 1972: 7, p. 451.

cabinet members, and within a few months came out wholly against full membership and in favour of a free trade arrangement -- even the former Prime Minister, Per Borten, and the former cabinet ministers acceded to the new policy. The Conservative Party took a similarly strong stand at its March 1972 annual conference and voted 252 in favour of supporting a yes vote at the September referendum, against 5 blank ballots.[49] The ruling Labour Party, at its annual meetings, strongly supported the Government line but, with significant, if small, minorities dissenting. The result was that the dissenters decided to form an anti-EEC pressure group within the party. The two Norwegian political parties which had not achieved parliamentary representation at the elections of 1969, the Socialist People's Party and the Communist Party, took very strong anti-EEC positions.

By the time that the marathon market debate of June 1972 took place, the Norwegian political parties presented a confusing set of coalitions, which, however, were clearly aligned either in favour of, or against, membership in the EEC. In favour were the Government, supported by the vast majority of its party members both in the House and in the national party organization, and the Conservative Party, both in Parliament and nationally. On the opposition side were the Centre Party with all its members in Parliament, supported by the national party organization, the extra-parliamentary Socialist People's Party and the Communist Party. Majorities of the national organizations of the Christian People's Party and the Liberal Party supported the opposition, while minorities in both, nationally, supported the Government position. In Parliament the two parties were similarly split, with approximately half supporting the Government and the other half supporting the opposition. To this "coalition" must be added the vocal minority in the Labour Party -- both within and outside Parliament -- which had split with official policy.

The situation was extremely confusing to the average sup-

---

[49]See *Nordisk Kontakt* 1971: 7, p. 449; and *Nordisk Kontakt* 1972: 6, p. 384.

porter of all the parties represented in Parliament, except the
Centre and Conservative parties. Thus, for example, the Labour
supporter was faced with the unheard-of situation in which his
party was officially in league with its sworn enemies, the
Conservatives, whereas a small group was in a strange coalition
with rabid socialists, communists and their class enemies, the
farmers and middle classes, as represented by the Centre and
Liberal parties. Although the socialists were able to make
considerable political capital out of the Labour-Conservative
"coalition", the latter was unable to exploit the "unholy alliance" of Labourites, farmers and middle class liberals. However,
despite the strange coalitions and the copious public outpourings
of both the proponents and opponents in Parliament, by the time
of the marathon market debate in early summer, a head count of
those who had declared themselves against the EEC added up to
only thirty-eight members, with the rest either actively or
passively in the pro-market column.

7.3 The Elite-Mass Gap

This situation came about as a result of an elite-mass gap or, as
one commentator put it, the "generals and soldiers were out of
step".[50] By and large, it was a centre-periphery conflict, with
cross-cutting divisions in five socio-economic sectors, including
social status, educational level, age and income. In addition,
there was a geographical distribution to the conflict. The basis
of the conflict was, of course, the difference in the positions
taken on the EEC question by the centre (positive), as opposed to
the periphery (negative).

A survey taken in February 1972 showed that, whereas the
total sample showed a 26% pro-EEC stand, the lowest social level
showed only a 15% "pro" stand; the next level, 21%; the next,
29%; and the top level 53%.[51] An analysis of a number of opinion

[50]Nils Petter Gleditsch, "Generaler og fotfolk i utakt",
Internasjonal Politikk, 1972: 4B, pp. 795-809.

[51]Ibid., p. Table 4 on p. 799.

surveys taken in 1971-2, and the in-depth surveys taken by the Statistical Central Office immediately after the referendum of 1972, show a positive correlation between education, age and income and attitudes to the EEC question: the higher the level of education, the closer in age to the middle years, and the higher the income, the stronger the support for membership.[52] Similarly there was a clear centre-periphery cleavage between the supporters of membership and the opponents, as shown by the statistics of the referendum: the larger the community, the larger the "pro" vote.[53] In addition, there was also a clear difference among occupational groups, with farmers and fishermen opposing membership by 85%, industrial workers by 60%, civil servants by 45% and the self-employed by 40%.[54]

The centre-periphery cleavage had three sources: the difference in elite-mass expectations, historic foreign policy differentiations, and the grass roots organization and activity of the anti-EEC mass movement. Whereas the elite, with their closer contacts with Europe both in their occupations and economically, and a better political appreciation of international cooperation, considered EEC membership necessary in the context of an interdependent world, and expected it to bring both political and economic benefits to Norway, the periphery had the opposite expectations: a fear that external political control -- already demonstrated by what they considered an unacceptable agricultural and fisheries settlement in the Treaty of Accession[55] -- would not only progressively remove their livelihood but would determine the conditions under which they could earn that liveli-

---

[52]Ibid., see Table 3 on p. 799.

[53]See Central Bureau of Statistics, *The Advisory Referendum on Norway's Accession to the EEC* (Oslo, 1972), Vol. I, Table 6, p. 44.

[54]See Gleditsch, op. cit., Table 2 on p. 798.

[55]See the Treaty, Protocols 20 (Norwegian agriculture) and 21 (fisheries arrangements for Norway).

hood. For the opponents, EEC membership must clearly lead to an abrogation of self-determination and a transfer of political authority from the Norwegian people to a foreign supergovernment at Brussels, which operated, not on Norwegian rules of political conduct, but by alien ones.

The foreign policy differentiations took three forms. The first two were the differentiation between foreign and domestic policy, and the consequent differentiation in elite-mass involvement in the former as opposed to the latter. This, of course, is not unusual or limited to Norway. In almost every country the electorate leaves the conduct of foreign policy to elites most of the time, as is demonstrated by the fact that very little parliamentary time is devoted to foreign policy matters. What was unusual was that in 1971-2 the foreign policy issue of the Common Market became a domestic issue in Norway, but with a continuing differentiation between the elite and the masses: the former continued to regard it as a foreign policy matter and approached it as such, whereas the latter regarded it as a domestic question, approached it from a completely different angle and handled it differently. The cleavage between the elite and the masses was further exacerbated by the third form of differentiation, the traditional separation of political, economic and security objectives in foreign policy. Whereas the elite continued to differentiate between the three -- although in somewhat reduced form, as shown by the EEC supporters' arguments in Parliament -- the masses saw no differentiation at all between the political and the economic.[56] Hence the situation in Norway during the third application negotiations and referendum differed markedly from that in Denmark. Whereas in the latter the Government and the proponents of the EEC membership argued -- as they had done since 1962 -- on a political-economic nexus as well as a foreign and domestic policy relationship, in Norway the Government and proponents of EEC membership separated both the foreign and the

---

[56]The security aspect was left largely untouched by both the elite and the masses.

domestic, and the political and the economic. The result was that in Denmark the issue of EEC membership was joined on grounds chosen by the proponents, whereas in Norway there was one issue for the proponents and another for the opponents.

The third source of the centre-periphery cleavage is found in the grassroots organization and the activity of the anti-EEC mass movement. The People's Movement Against Norway's Membership in the Common Market (*Folkebevegelsen Mot Norsk Medlemskap i Fellesmarkedet*) was organized as a cover organization for all opponents of Norwegian membership within a few months of the beginning of negotiations in 1970. Structurally, it had grown out of the 1962 opposition groups which were mainly based on farmers' organizations. The new organization that was set up in 1970 differed markedly from its predecessors in that it was an idea-based organization which was open to anyone on an individual basis who opposed EEC membership. Hence it was possible for all kinds of strange bedfellows to work together without regard for differences of opinion, ideology or interests on other matters, and the organization became a truly grassroots one composed of individuals from every part of Norway. Its strength lay in its singleness of purpose, its independence from all other organizations, and in its internal structure: its central council was composed of representatives of councils representing every county of Norway, which councils in turn represented nearly every municipality in the country. It was the most thoroughgoing grassroots structure that has ever existed in Norway. As a result of its independence, the organization was able to garner a large amount of financial support from other interest and pressure groups, as well as individuals, and because of its single-mindedness, was able to attract a number of prominent academics and other intellectuals. These two factors meant that the organization was able to produce reams of well thought-out and logically constructed arguments supporting its cause, and that it was able to send articulate "agitators" to speak to small groups of supporters all over the country. The grassroots structure of the organization meant that it was able to operate on a personal

230.

basis, with the convinced members in a local area proselytising
their friends, acquaintances and co-workers, using as data and
inspiration material supplied by the "agitators" and the intel-
lectual resource group.

The high point of the anti-EEC movement's activity came
during the winter and spring of 1972, when on 19 April 1972,
after less than five months of preparation, it was able to issue
a 285-page "white paper" opposing the Government's final White
Paper of 10 March 1972.[57] It presented a series of detailed
arguments opposing the Government's position, and formed the
basic source-book for arguments against EEC membership during the
last few months of the campaign before the referendum.

In contrast to the anti-EEC mass movement, the pro-EEC
movement (*Ja til EF*) was not even organized until the beginning
of 1972, because supporters argued that a popular appeal for
support or opposition to EEC membership would make little sense
until the results of the negotiations were known. Despite
feverish activity to organize a popular grassroots counter-appeal,
the organization never got off the ground. In fact, during the
week when the anti-EEC movement held its press conference in
which it released its anti-Government "white paper", the pro-EEC
movement was just moving into offices to house its headquarters.

---

[57]*Folkebevegelsens melding om Norges forhold til De Europeiske Felleskap* (EF), Oslo, 19 April 1972.

CHAPTER 9.   THE POLITICS OF THE ECONOMICS OF NEUTRALITY

1.   Sweden: The Politics of Independence

In contrast to those of Denmark and Norway, Sweden's and Finland's economic policies are politically, and not just functionally, dependent variables of general foreign policy, and of
security policy in particular. All foreign policy decisions are
taken on the basis of security considerations, so that they will
fit within the parameters of security politics. The process in
Sweden may often be more real than apparent, because in public
discourse the meaning of security has become totally subsumed to
the concept of neutrality, which has taken on connotations far
beyond the strict legal meaning of the term neutrality, to the
extent of having become "in a word" a description of Swedish
foreign policy. Because since 1814 Sweden has managed to stay
out of wars, credit for this is given to the policy of neutrality,
while the attributes of that policy are often imprecisely understood. The fact that the policy has enjoyed widespread public
support for a century and a half and has become, during the
decades following the Second World War, a national "sacred cow",
means that it has become identified as a basic national value and
an expression of "Swedishness", which may be questioned only by
placing one's loyalty to Sweden at peril.

1.1 The Demands of the Credibility of Neutrality

Despite this, Sweden's political and administrative elites have
clearly understood the basic character of neutrality and that it
has two sources, one external and the other internal. Moreover,
there is agreement that the external source is the main determining one. Swedish policy-makers accept the fact that Sweden
has been able to remain a non-belligerent in past wars mainly
because its territory has neither been of strategic importance in
the wars of others, nor a threat to any belligerent. The first
condition is a passive one over which Swedish decision-makers
have no control, but the second is active: Sweden must make
clear in advance to all potential belligerents that it will not
permit the use of its territory for the advantage or disadvantage
of any belligerent. It may not require active intervention
during the course of hostilities for the original declaration to
be upheld. What is most important is that internal policy makes
clear throughout that no deviation from the original declaration
of neutrality is contemplated.

What has been described so far is in fact legal neutrality,
and Sweden has been consistent in remaining legally neutral.
But, this kind of neutrality will keep a state out of war only if
the potential belligerents agree, throughout the course of
hostilities, that it is in their mutual interests to respect the
neutrality of the declarant. This, however, is only possible if
it is clear beyond doubt to all belligerents that the enemy will
in no case be tempted to invade the neutral state in order to
gain either a strategic or a tactical advantage in the war. And
this is only possible if the geographic situation of the neutral
state offers no such advantage.

At any given time there are few states which fulfill the
geographic conditions for legal neutrality. Sweden has never
been one of these. In fact, the evidence provided by the wars of
the twentieth century shows that in the European context only
Switzerland has consistently fulfilled these conditions. During
both the First and the Second World Wars the legal declaration of
neutrality was cavalierly treated by one of the belligerents,

Germany, and all European neutrals -- with the exception of
Switzerland and Sweden -- had their neutrality violated either
territorially or functionally. During the Second World War,
Switzerland and Sweden were again the only European neutrals to
escape encroachment on their policies by the belligerents, but
for two entirely different reasons. Whereas Switzerland was able
to maintain neutrality on a strictly legal basis because it was
supported by the geopolitical requirements outlined above, Sweden
maintained its neutrality mainly because of a widely publicized
internal decision to support the declaration with adequate
military force. In contrast to Switzerland's passive legal
neutrality, Sweden's neutrality was an active armed one.

After the war Sweden converted its wartime armed neutrality
policy to peacetime uses. Swedish foreign policy is generally
formally characterized as being based on "a policy of freedom
from alliances during peacetime aiming to preserve Swedish
neutrality during wartime". Freedom from alliances in peacetime
is considered a prerequisite for the ability to maintain neutrality in case of a war between the two superpowers in the bipolar
system. The reason for this requirement is simply that a state
that seeks neutrality during hostilities must in peacetime pursue
a policy that gives credibility to its claim to neutrality in
wartime, and which creates an external belief in that state's
will and ability to preserve neutrality during hostilities.

1.2 The Constraints of Neutrality and Policy-Making

The pursuit of such a self-imposed policy demands stringent consistency in order to ensure external credibility. Moreover it
requires rigid adherence to the principle that all policies should
be coordinated and subsumed to the demand for credibility of
neutrality. In the Swedish case this has given rise to three
main sets of constraints in policy-making. First, it has produced a demand for consistent independence in all policy so as to
emphasize Sweden's lack of political dependence on any other
state or bloc of states. This demand has taken the practical
term of an interrelated set of objective and subjective demands.

The objective demand is to retain the credibility of Sweden's
historic geopolitical security position, and the subjective one
is the demand to maximize independence of action. The two are
closely interrelated, with the objective demand both providing
the basis for the subjective one and creating it, and the subjective demand reinforcing the credibility of the objective one.
In a speech made by Prime Minister Tage Erlander to the Second
Chamber of the Ridsdag on 24 November 1959, the interrelation-
ships are made clear:

> If, without binding ourselves by undertakings made under
> an alliance, we nevertheless fervently and constantly
> take the part of one side in the political groups exist-
> ing in our divided world, we should lose every chance we
> have of working for peaceful co-existence and the recon-
> ciliation of the peoples of the world. We should thus
> forfeit the chance to undertake an important and positive
> task which is otherwise a natural one for a country like
> ours.[1]

In his speech Prime Minister Erlander also emphasized the
importance of the Swedish "official" policy line being credible
externally, and argued for the necessity of self-restraint in the
utterances of Swedish political leaders in order to enhance the
credibility of the official policy.[2]

The second set of restraints imposed on Swedish policy-
making by the demand that the neutrality policy should be credible
is a military-financial one. The credibility of Sweden's claim
to neutrality in case of hostilities between the great powers
requires the maintenance of armed forces strong enough and equipped with matériel of sufficient technological sophisitication to
make a potential attack on Sweden by any single great power so
costly that the potential attacker will be deterred from attack-
ing for trivial or secondary reasons. Although this is not the
ideal aim, it is the minimal solution for Sweden's credibility of
neutrality demands. The ideal solution cannot be envisaged

---

[1]Royal Ministry for Foreign Affairs, *Documents on Swedish
Foreign Policy 1959* (Stockholm, 1960), pp. 46-7.

[2]Ibid., p. 47.

by Sweden as practicable either financially or from the point of view of personnel, since its population of 8 million and its Gross National Product of U.S. $32 billion both represent but a fraction of the resources of the great powers. But even the minimal solution places a heavy burden on the Swedish economy. For example, from 1968 to 1971 Sweden's defence expenditures ranged between 3.7 and 3.9 per cent of its GNP, a percentage that was consistently higher than for any West European country except Great Britain and Portugal, although France, Greece and Turkey exceeded the Swedish percentage in some of those years. However, Sweden's per capita defence expenditure in 1971 was absolutely the highest in Europe at U.S. $145, exceeding the closest competitors -- Norway, West Germany, France and Britain -- by over 40%.[3] Although the cost is high, it must still be borne by the Swedish taxpayer in order to maintain a level of military power in peacetime which makes the Swedish official policy of neutrality consistently believable in the eyes of the external world.

It is the demand to make the deterrent power credible that has forced Sweden to develop an independent military industry to produce matériel for its armed forces which will be on a par with those of the great powers. The growing costs involved in this activity forced Sweden during the 1960s to reduce the diversity of its military hardware and to redeploy forces to save costs while maintaining the quality of the deterrent force. The growing costs of research and development have increased the pressure on Sweden to maintain its position as one of the main armaments exporters. This latter activity could be regarded as being at odds with Sweden's policies of neutrality and pursuit of peaceful solutions to conflicts. However, Swedish governments reduce the conflict between policies and economic necessity by consistent refusal to sell arms to any state involved, or likely to be involved, in hostilities.

---

[3]See IISS, *The Military Balance*, annual.

The third set of restraints imposed on Swedish policy-makers by the demand for a credible policy of neutrality is an economic one. Again to maintain external belief in its ability to remain outside great power conflicts, Sweden must pursue economic policies in peacetime which will permit its society and economy to operate in wartime as an independent entity: without reference to the external world, it must be able to maintain the functioning of its economic and social organization and a minimum standard of physical wellbeing for the population; and provide the economic strength necessary to maintain its defensive capability. To avoid being drawn into a great power conflict, it must organize its economy in such a way as to be able to withstand an economic blockade for some "reasonable" period of time.

To achieve these objectives, Sweden has been pursuing policies of "total defence" during the past two decades, in which the economy and its organization occupies the central position. The principles underlying the economic defence were defined in 1971 as follows:

> The formation of economic defence is determined essentially by our security policy and by the structure of our economy today and in the future. Planning and measures of preparedness in peacetime are directed towards making it possible for our economy to have at hand in case of war, blockade or other crisis, the necessary goods and services.[4]

In its pursuit of a policy of neutrality, Sweden is restricted in its economic policy options during peacetime. Not only do the demands of realistic economic defence and of Sweden's claim to maintain credible neutrality during hostilities make it impossible for Sweden to form political alliances with other states or blocs of states in peacetime, but they do not even allow Sweden to join in peacetime international economic organizations which could call in question its ability to maintain an economy not crucially dependent on these organizations. The Government made its position clear on this point as follows:

---

[4]Nils Andrén, *Den Totala Säkerhetspolitiken* (Stockholm, 1972), p. 105.

The country cannot participate in such forms of cooperation involving foreign political, economic, monetary and
other questions, which, according to Swedish assessment,
could jeopardize the possibilities of pursuing a consistent policy of neutrality. This means that Sweden cannot
undertake binding responsibilities in international cooperation within any group of states with the objective
of forming common positions. [Such cooperation] must be
limited by boundaries to prevent the possibility of
accepting a transfer of the right of decision-making from
national to international organs.[5]

1.3 The Constraints of Neutrality and the Economy

The necessity for clearly visible limits to foreign economic
policy is underscored by the strong internationalizing tendencies
in the operation of the Swedish economy. Sweden's economic development during the period 1950-70, along with the growth of
industrial output and consumption that took place, led to progressively increased integration of the Swedish economy as a
whole -- and the militarily sensitive technologically advanced
engineering and electrical sectors in particular -- with that of
Western Europe. In other words, de facto integration is taking
place -- and has been doing so for some time -- between Sweden
and the European core. From a security point of view, the
"normal" development and growth of the Swedish economy has
contradictory implications. On the one hand, the de facto intre-
grative process tends to destabilize the Swedish security position built on the policy of neutrality, since it obviously binds
the Swedish economy to the coordinating and developing common
economies of the EEC, whose members during the shift of the
1960s to the 1970s became formally committed to economic central-
ization and political union. In addition, all the EEC members
except Ireland are members of the NATO military alliance. On the
other hand, the credibility of the policy of neutrality demands a
strong economy which, in the industrialized world, can only be
achieved by small industrial societies by an international

---

[5]Handelsdepartementet, Inför Sveriges EEC förhandlingar
(Stockholm, 1971), p. 19.

division of labour which, however, brings with it *de facto* integration of economies. In the Swedish case there is a further demand in that the military credibility pursued by Sweden in the interests of making the neutrality policy credible requires that the economy should be able to produce military hardware and control systems equal to those of the great powers. This can only be done with a strong and sophisticated economy, which, in the case of a small country like Sweden, unfortunately requires international division of labour. Over time, the cycle of strength, development and sophistication through international division of labour leads progressively towards ever greater functional integration of similar strong, developed and sophisticated economies. The price for the economic and technological basis of Sweden's military credibility supporting the credibility of the neutrality policy is economic integration with other similar economies, in fact with the expanded EEC.

Up to the beginning of the 1970s Sweden had been able to contain the contradictory pressures of the functional economic demands by insisting on subsuming all questions, whether political, security or economic, to the demands of the credibility of the neutrality policy. This was made possible during the 1950s and most of the 1960s for three reasons: first, because the degree of internationalization of the Swedish economy had not reached a critical point; secondly, because the functional integration that had taken place between the Swedish economy and the economies of Western Europe was split among a number of economies controlled by separate political authorities; and thirdly, because the EEC, though aiming towards political unification, had done little more than coordinate the economic policies of the member-states. With the beginning of the 1970s, however, the situation changed rapidly and radically. Militarily and politically sensitive sectors of the Swedish economy -- the engineering and electronic sectors -- had become overwhelmingly integrated with the economies of the EEC countries; and, the EEC had expanded to include the United Kingdom -- a significant economic partner of Sweden -- and had decided to implement the original objective of political unification by 1980.

Hence Sweden must be even more careful in making clear that all policies are made on the basis of maintaining the neutrality policy inviolable and untainted by external factors. For this reason Sweden chose in 1971 to make it clear that it would not formally accede to any economic or political integration with the EEC. The fact that Sweden could not, however, disrupt the ongoing functional integration demanded that it come to some kind of agreement with the EEC -- in the event, a free trade area -- and that it coordinate its economic policies with those of the EEC insofar as the self-imposed limits should permit. For the neutrality policy to remain credible under conditions of increasing functional economic integration with the EEC, Sweden must consistently make it clear to the outside world that its economic policy decisions are always made independently by Swedish authorities and are never based on any prior external commitments. This has been the policy line to which Swedish governments have firmly adhered throughout the decade of negotiations with the EEC.

1.4 The Course of Market Policy: 1961-1962: From Division to Consensus

In all open societies and highly developed economies, different interests are articulated and become politicized. This happened in Sweden. As soon as the United Kingdom announced in July 1961 that it had decided to apply for Common Market membership, a debate arose concerning the effect of the British *volte face* on Sweden and concerning the optimal course of action to follow. Although the debate lasted until General de Gaulle's veto on 14 January 1963, the battle lines were drawn early, during the four-month period preceding the Swedish decision to apply for associate Community membership in December 1961. In contrast to what happened in Denmark and Norway, in Sweden only a single formal "market debate" took place in Parliament, during October 1961.

In theory there were four options open to Sweden: to apply for full membership, to apply for association according to

Article 238 of the Treaty of Rome, to ask for negotiations on a
trade agreement, or to do nothing at all. The last option was
uniformly rejected by all interest groups and political parties,
for the simple reason that it was evident that the structure of
the Swedish economy was heavily trade oriented. Hence the
question was not whether to react but how to react to the impending appearance of a big trade bloc composed of almost all of
Sweden's trading partners, including the old Six, the United
Kingdom, Norway and Denmark, which were expected to join the
Community should the British negotiations prove successful.
Therefore, the debate revolved around the first three options.
Although the Government immediately ruled out application for
full membership, the main weight of the debate was nonetheless
focused on the question of how to become a full member without
the political obligations of full membership. The trade agreement option was generally relegated to a residual position --
something that could always be taken up if the preferred alternatives did not materialize. In broad terms, three considerations entered into the debate: the sovereignty argument, the
culture argument and the economic interest argument. The anti-
EEC forces tended to emphasize the necessity of continuing the
neutrality/non-alignment policy in order to maintain continued
Swedish independence -- which, it was argued, would not be
possible within a politically directed EEC composed of NATO
members. In short, the EEC could not be considered as a strictly
economic organization such as EFTA. Indeed, the very foundations
of the EEC were predicated on the concept of an eventual political union; a framework of supranational organs to be operated
on an elaborate majoritarian basis was already outlined in the
Treaty of Rome, which also expressly prohibited any kind of
secession from membership. Clearly, full membership in the EEC
would mean a transfer of sovereignty out of the country, and an
abrogation of Sweden's cherished independence. The cultural
arguments of the anti-EEC group were much more emotional, and on
the whole echoed the similar Danish and Norwegian sentiments.
The two main components were, first, the fear that Sweden's high

standard of economic development and highly developed welfare
state might be adversely affected by the relatively "backward"
stages of economic and social organization in the non-Nordic
components of the enlarged EEC. Indeed, the Treaty of Rome
demands a considerable degree of harmonization of industrial,
financial, employment and social policies, and the standard to be
applied would clearly not be the Swedish/Nordic one, but the
continental one. Secondly, there was the frankly chauvinistic
pride in "Nordic democracy" which created not only distrust but
downright antagonism towards the authoritarian, Roman Catholic and
unstable political systems and cultures of continental Europe.

In addition, the anti-EEC forces also found considerable
support among economic interests antagonistic to the EEC. The
farmers, for example, were afraid of competition with the lower-
cost agriculture of the continent. The fear was a highly rational one, since agricultural policy in Sweden since 1947 has
maintained a high price system in order to fulfill both social
and foreign policy objectives: to attain income parity between
farmers and industrial workers, and to sustain a viable agricultural sector as a basis for a modicum of self-sufficiency in food
production in the interests of a credible neutrality policy in
case of war or blockade. The farmers of Sweden, accustomed to a
protective wall against foreign agricultural produce maintained
by a system of import levies and internal fiscal supports, had
real cause for apprehension in the light of the various proposals
for rationalizing agricultural production in the EEC. Similarly,
small businessmen, in Sweden as elsewhere, feared the competition
from the commercial giants of the EEC and the United Kingdom,
which they felt Common Market membership would swiftly bring
about.

In contrast, the pro-EEC forces tended to emphasize the
economic interests of Sweden above political interests. The
Federation of Swedish Industries (FSI) -- the industrial cover
organization which coordinates industrial policy and relations
with labour unions and with the government for the whole of
Sweden's private industry -- argued in stark and simple economic

terms: because the export sector generates such a large part of
the national income and employs such a large proportion of the
Swedish labour force, it was imperative that Sweden associate in
some way with the EEC, preferably as a full member, in order to
avert the inevitable disaster of economic stagnation, including a
falling standard of living, which non-adherence to the Treaty of
Rome would eventually bring about. Similarly, the Federation of
Swedish Wholesale Merchants and Importers (FSWMI) took a strongly
pro-EEC position based on the same "doom-and-gloom" projections
of the consequences of non-adherence.

The fact that the industrial and commercial establishments
of Sweden were the only supporters of full membership, and that
their arguments were strictly economic (tradition prevents the
FSI and the FSWMI from engaging in extensive debate in foreign
policy) doomed the full-membership drive. The economic arguments, nevertheless, had a considerable effect on the Government
and on the position that it took in its initial letter of application in December 1961. The reason was not because pressure
group tactics shifted public opinion or convinced politicans, but
because it is generally recognized in Sweden, and well understood
at the level of partisan political activity, that Sweden is a
trading nation dependent for its high standard of living on easy
access to West European markets. Hence the pro-EEC drive did
little more than underscore this fact of life. Also, politics in
Sweden operates on the basis of consensus rather than brokerage.
Moreover, decision-making tends to be centralized within the
framework of Parliament, where the different political parties
present their views after processing the inputs of their supporting interest groups through a "filter of responsibility". It
could be said that Swedish politicians and political parties tend
to take Burke's representative theory of representation seriously. The result is that the opposition parties do not oppose for
the sake of opposition, nor do they pursue pet programmes or
ideologies; instead, they tend to argue variations of the national consensus. From this the government tends to draw a further
consensus, which then becomes national policy. National policy-

making in Sweden tends to operate very much like policy-making within a British Conservative cabinet, or a Canadian federal Liberal or Conservative cabinet. Such a process of consensus politics took place during the fall of 1961.

Within a few days of the British and Danish announcements of their intentions of requesting EEC membership, Foreign Minister Undén in an interview with the press on 5 August 1961 expressed scepticism over the possibility of combining membership with Sweden's policy of neutrality. His main reason for this was that the development of the EEC was proceeding in a political direction intended to produce a political federation in time. Sweden, in contrast, was interested only in a purely economic arrangement because such political objectives were contrary to its interests. Consequently, if EEC membership had to be excluded, either because of the position taken by the Six or because Sweden could not accept it, "in contrast an economic association agreement would constitute a completely different question." Sweden clearly had an interest in an economic arrangement.[6] To this Bergquist adds that even if the Government had not formally taken a position, Undén's interview set the direction for the debate to follow.[7] The interview was followed on 17 August by a meeting of the Parliamentary Committee on Foreign Affairs, which discussed the question of negotiations with the EEC in general terms. On the same day the Prime Minister issued a statement in which he stressed the willingness of his Government "to negotiate on closer economic cooperation in Western Europe". He said that there was general agreement that "the outcome of the negotiations must not be allowed to change the conditions that made it possible for Sweden to pursue its policy of neutrality. The economic coordination with the EEC that we sought thus presupposed special provisions to make this coordination compatible with our policy of neutrality and to satisfy

---

[6]Press interview reported in Mats Bergquist, *Sverige och EEC* (Stockholm, 1970), p. 46.

[7]Ibid., p. 46.

other vital Swedish interests."[8] The leader of the Centre Party,
Gunnar Hedlund, took a public position on 19 August in support of
association with the EEC and against membership.[9] On 22 August,
Prime Minister Erlander delivered a long speech to the Congress
of the Swedish Steel and Metal Workers Union which was largely
anti-EEC in content, and which made it clear that the Swedish
Government had decided not to seek full EEC membership since this
would be incompatible with Sweden's policy of neutrality. There
was no indication in the speech whatever that the Government had
an application for association in mind; indeed, apart from
criticizing the EEC and declaring Sweden's decision not to seek
membership, the Prime Minister made no reference to any other
possible form of agreement with the EEC.[10] Bergquist, however,
points out that two days earlier the president of the Swedish
Federation of Labour Union had made a speech similar in tone to
the Prime Minister's, in which he had specifically supported association with the EEC.[11] Parenthetically, it should be noted that
the ties between the Government and the Swedish Federation of
Labour Unions (*LO-Landsorganisationerna*) are very close, and that
the LO leadership takes its political direction exclusively from
the Social Democratic Party leadership -- in fact from the
cabinet. The Government, nevertheless, made no reference to
association as a preferred form of adherence to the Treaty of
Rome until the "market debate" in Parliament on 25 October 1961.

In the meantime, on 25 August the Liberal Party argued that
the Government ought to consult further with the various economic
and labour organizations before taking a further position; and
that Sweden should first make an attempt to discover whether it
would be possible to become a member of the EEC with certain
escape clauses to satisfy Sweden's policy of neutrality; and, if

---

[8]*Documents on Swedish Foreign Policy 1961*, p. 111.

[9]Bergquist, op. cit., p. 47.

[10]*Documents on Swedish Foreign Policy 1961*, pp. 111-25.

[11]Bergquist, op. cit., p. 47.

this did not prove possible, then to seek an association arrangement.[12] On 28 August the leader of the Conservative Party, Gunnar Heckscher, took the same position as the Liberal Party.[13] Three days later, in a statement issued on 31 August, the Centre Party agreed with the Government's position and recommended association [sic] with the EEC. In addition, it proposed that contact should be made with "other militarily neutral countries which find themselves in the same position as Sweden".[14] Finally, the central committee of the Communist Party issued a statement on 10 September in which it took a strong position against EEC membership which it regarded as a political, capitalistic bloc. Moreover, it noted with satisfaction that the Government and the farmers opposed such membership, but the party warned that even "a so-called association with the EEC may take forms which would involve the giving up of Swedish neutrality and independence."[15]

Thereupon the Government took contact with the governments of Austria and Switzerland which culminated in a ministerial meeting among the three in Vienna on 19 October 1961. The results were stated in a press release:

> On the basis of previous studies, the Ministers were able to establish that, as regards the form of the future relationship with the EEC, they see in the same light the problems posed by the neutrality status of their countries. They, however, found themselves also confirmed in their view, that neutrality does not constitute an obstacle to their participation, through association in appropriate form, in the economic integration of Europe, and to their taking the measures necessary for the functioning of an integrated European Market.[16]

On 4 October the Government held a meeting at the prime

---

[12]Ibid., p. 48.

[13]Ibid., p. 48.

[14]Ibid., p. 48.

[15]Ibid., p. 48.

[16]*Documents on Swedish Foreign Policy 1961*, p. 127.

ministerial country residence of Harpsund with representatives of
the industrial and agricultural organizations: industry reiterated its fear of the consequences of non-membership; agriculture emphasized the necessity of maintaining the principle of
income parity, and the importance both of maintaining a balanced
agricultural production sector, with sufficient production to
provide for the self-sufficiency necessary to support the
neutrality policy, and of providing continuing government support
for small farming; and the forestry industry emphasized its
dependence on exports and therefore the importance of Swedish
entry into the EEC.[17]

On 25 October 1961 the market debate took place in Parliament. The Government announced that "it is ... the Government's
intention to submit Sweden's application for association to the
Community within the near future."[18] Despite a lengthy and wide-
ranging debate, the positions taken by the parties did not
change: the Social Democratic and Centre parties argued for
association, the Conservative and Liberal parties for membership
with escape clauses for Swedish neutrality, and the Communist
Party for remaining wholly outside the Community.[19] However, the
debate made it clear that the national consensus on the importance of Sweden's policy of neutrality had been renewed during the
period since Britain and Denmark had submitted their membership
applications on 31 July, and that a further consensus had developed among the four democratic parties -- in which the two
Communists in the Upper House and the five Communists in the
Lower House did not join -- whereby it was agreed that Sweden
should seek some form of adherence to the Treaty of Rome, without
jeopardizing its policy of neutrality. The acceptable form
appeared to be association. Of course, the emerging consensus

---

[17]Reported in Bergquist, op. cit., pp. 48-9.

[18]*Documents on Swedish Foreign Policy 1961*, p. 136.

[19]See *Documents on Swedish Foreign Policy 1961*, pp. 128-37;
and *Nordisk Kontakt* 1961: 12, pp. 703-9.

did not indicate unity: the differences in orientation of the
pro-membership and the anti-membership partisan blocs remained.
Thus, for example, the Government and the Centre Party continued
to emphasize the overriding importance of Sweden's independence
in the interests of its policy of neutrality, whereas the Conservative and Liberal parties emphasized the importance for
Sweden's economy of participating in at least some of the decision-making organs within the Community, without however giving
up the policy of neutrality.[20] The application for associate
membership, delivered together with the Austrian and Swiss
applications on 15 December 1961, reflected this consensus. In a
statement on the same day the Prime Minister said:

> We wish to create through direct negotiations with the
> Community a large European market comprising 300 million
> people. Our country's interest in participating in econ-
> omic cooperation now developing in Europe, and our will
> to do so, has the support of practically unanimous Swe-
> dish public opinion.... At the same time Sweden has stead-
> fastly resolved to abide by her neutrality.... Thus, what
> we want to achieve for Sweden is an economic association
> with the European Economic Community which is compatible
> with our neutrality. Whether or not we succeed naturally
> depends on the outcome of the negotiations now proposed
> by the Government.[21]

Bergquist, in an analysis written in 1969, adds:

> In fact, the policy thus formulated was an elegant solu-
> tion. For at the time we are dealing with here, it is

---

[20]See in particular *Nordisk Kontakt* 1961: 12, pp. 705-6. It
is interesting to note the general attitude in Sweden, throughout
the decade leading to the trade agreement in 1973, which tended to
emphasize the consensus, and to play down the differences. The
headline in *Nordisk Kontakt* on the market debate in Parliament is
typical of this: "Unity in the long market debate on alliance-
free cooperation with the EEC." Bergquist's study of the 1961-2
national debate tends, in contrast, to emphasize the cleavages.
It should be pointed out that few Swedish academics, politicians
and colleagues of Bergquist's in the Swedish Foreign Ministry,
where he is an official, agree with his approach, because Swedes
simply do not think in terms of cleavages, and that cleavage
studies are foreign to their own analyses of the country's
society and polity. The fact is that as soon as cleavages
develop, they are deliberately minimized through the operation of
the politics of consensus.

[21]*Documents on Swedish Foreign Policy 1961*, pp. 139-40.

not entirely clear what association would actually mean,
since so far there existed only one such agreement --
disregarding those with the former dependencies -- namely
that with Greece. There may have been an intentional
policy on the part of the Government to give an interpretation to the association concept that the Community
had not envisaged but nevertheless would find suitable,
once it was convinced by the Swedish Government, or
rather by the three neutral countries, Austria, Sweden
and Switzerland.[22]

The consensus developed further during the winter and spring
of 1962. It became evident that the Government had moved some
distance to accommodate the economic arguments of the industrial
and commercial establishments when the Minister of Commerce on 23
January 1962 reviewed the debate.[23] The Minister first dealt
with the political problem. He said:

> I should ... like to stress ... that membership of the
> Economic Community, in the form envisaged by the Treaty
> of Rome, has not at any time whatsoever, been in the
> Government's mind as a conceivable solution for our part
> to the market problem. Our line of foreign policy fol-
> lowed its pre-determined course -- and it is not possible
> for us to make any compromises about it -- and in the
> current international situation it is surely almost
> superfluous to emphasize that, instead, our vigilance in
> this respect must be increased. The Treaty of Rome ...
> is a political treaty. Were Sweden to accede to this
> Treaty, the interpretation would inevitably be that we
> had made a clear departure from the foreign policy we had
> pursued until now. The alternative therefore was in the
> first place to seek to bring about an association accord-
> ing to Article 238 of the Treaty of Rome and it was in
> accordance with this Article that we transmitted on 15
> December an application for negotiations to achieve asso-
> ciation between this country and the Community.[24]

He then turned to the economic argument and made it clear
that "we must do everything we can so as not to be left outside
the European larger market," and noted that the Government,
in close collaboration with the business and labour organizations,

---

[22]Mats Bergquist, "Sweden and the European Economic Community", *Cooperation and Conflict*, Vol. 4, 1969, p. 7.

[23]*Documents on Swedish Foreign Policy 1962*, pp. 121-30.

[24]Speech to First Chamber of Riksdag. Ibid., pp. 123-4.

was analyzing the possible ramifications of the Treaty of Rome on the Swedish economy.[25]

That the Government had moved further from its initial strictly political position towards accommodating the economic arguments is clearly demonstrated by the speech of the Minister of Commerce to the EEC Council of Ministers six months later, on 28 July 1962. Parenthetically it might be added that the speech could have been made by any of the other three democratic parties' front-benchers. Save for the differences of emphasis that these would have added, the speech was a masterly elucidation of the final consensus:

> At the outset I would like to make it clear that the Swedish Government does not for its part propose to ex- clude from the negotiations any subject matter covered by the various chapters of the Treaty of Rome. With regard to the economic aspect we share the view of the Community that integration not only implies the abolition of cus- toms tariffs and quotas in trade between the countries concerned but also entails a number of economic and social measures designed to ensure a good result. Like the original and prospective Member States, we have of course specific points of economic interest to defend and in this context the possibilities of derogations and suspension may have to be discussed. But we are ready to negotation with the Community in an instructive and posi- tive spirit.[26]

He then went through parts 2, 3 and 4 of the Treaty of Rome. Thereafter he approached the political problems that association with the Common Market would create for Sweden: "Here I would like to emphasize strongly from the outset that we have been meticulous in not letting economic interests as such influence our position. We take our policy of neutrality much too ser- iously to risk compromising it by cloaking economic desiderata in neutrality terms."[27] He then posited three reservations:

> The first of the neutrality points relates to trade poli- cy towards third countries.... As a neutral country, we would have to keep a certain liberty of action and to

---

[25]Ibid., p. 126.

[26]*Documents on Swedish Foreign Policy 1962*, p. 151.

[27]Ibid., p. 152.

reserve the competence to negotiate and sign agreements with third countries in our own name. On the other hand we are prepared, within institutional arrangements for consultation, to coordinate our tariff and trade policy closely with that of the Community. Experience leads us to expect that there should in practice be no significant divergences between Sweden's policy and that of the Community.

. . . .

The second neutrality point relates to the safeguarding of certain supplies vital in wartime. The Rome Treaty itself contains special provisions regarding war materials. There are, however, in addition to war materials, certain supplies of for instance pharmaceuticals and vital foodstuffs which must be safeguarded partly through the maintenance of domestic agricultural production.

. . . .

The third point has to do with a neutral country's needs to be able to take or abstain from measures according to the requirements of neutrality. It may, for instance in cases of war and grave international crisis, have to introduce controls on trade or refrain from taking part in sequestration of property directed against the belligerent. That derogation from any common action in an integrated market, which this need might imply, would be of varying importance according to the circumstances. But it is not excluded that it might go as far as a suspension of parts of, or the whole of, the agreement of association or withdrawal from the agreement. We have noted that Article 224 of the Treaty of Rome gives certain rights of derogation to the Member States of the Community. A corresponding provision in agreement of association will have to be drafted in such a way as clearly to cover our neutrality requirement.[28]

This is the point at which the Swedish application for associate membership of the EEC remained until 1967, since no further discussions took place with the EEC before the first round of negotiations was terminated by General de Gaulle's press conference on 14 January 1963. During the ensuing four-year period, until the spring of 1967, Sweden's Common Market policy remained more or less dormant. The time was taken up with sporadic discussion of various schemes to overcome the trade bloc division of Europe, and with the Kennedy Round negotiations

---

[28]Ibid., pp. 152-3.

within GATT.

1.5 From Second Application to Accession to Trade Pact: Increasing the Consensus

When the United Kingdom submitted its second application for membership in the summer of 1967, a debate once more took place in Sweden as to how it should make a new approach to the Community. The main question was whether Sweden should stick to its 1961 application, which had never been withdrawn, or submit a new one, and if so, in what form. The Conservative and Liberal parties again proposed their preferred position, that Sweden should apply for full membership with escape clauses. The Communists stuck to their position of independence and non-membership. The different interest groups reiterated their old positions. The Conservatives and Liberals, however, had a new, and apparently telling argument, namely, that the political thrust of the EEC had been dissipated even further since 1961-2 through General de Gaulle's policies. Hence, they argued, a solution along the lines they proposed would be even more probable now than four years earlier. In the event, the Government apparently accepted this argument, for it decided to seek "negotiations with the Community with the aim to ensure that Sweden will participate in the enlarging of the European Economic Community in a manner consistent with the Swedish policy of neutrality."[29] Thus, the Government had changed its mind and had left the form of membership open to negotiation. Of course, nothing came of this application, and the EEC had not proceeded to examine the Swedish application by the time that General de Gaulle held his semi-annual press conference on 27 November 1967 and slammed the door once more.

The decision of The Hague summit meeting of the EEC on 1-2 December 1969 to proceed with the opening of negotiations with Britain for expansion of the Community created little excitement in Sweden. As late as 29 April 1970, during the parliamentary foreign and trade policy debate it was clear that Swedish poli-

---

[29]Utrikesfrågor 1967, p. 139.

ticians did not think it likely that the EEC question would be
solved for some years.[30] Hence, it was not until 10 November
1970, the date when Sweden had been invited to make its first
statement to the Council of Ministers of the EEC at Brussels,
that the question appeared on the Swedish political agenda. In a
nine page Government statement presented by Minister of Commerce
Kjell-Olof Feldt the 1967 position was reiterated with greater
precision given to the reservations. As usual, the political
considerations of participation in the EEC were strongly emphasized:

> International ties cannot be accepted which make the
> possibility to choose neutrality in time of war illusory.
> The policy must be supported by a strong military defense
> and the economic life so organized that the nation can
> endure a large-scale blocade during a fairly long
> period.[31]

The statement went on to add two reservations relating to
the Davignon Report, which had been accepted by the EEC's foreign
ministers on 27 October 1970, and the Werner Report which had
been presented, but not yet acted on by the EEC Council of
Ministers,

> We cannot participate in such forms of cooperation in
> foreign policy, economic, monetary and other matters
> which, in our judgement would jeopardize our possibil-
> ities to pursue a firm policy of neutrality. This means
> that we cannot participate within a certain group of
> States in a cooperation in matters of foreign policy which
> is binding and which aims at the working out of common
> policies. Limits are also set to our possibilities to
> accept a transfer of the right of decision-making from
> national to international institutions within the frame-
> work of an economic and monetary union.[32]

Despite these strongly worded reservations the Government,
nevertheless, left the form of participation in the EEC open,

---

[30]*Nordisk Kontakt* 1970: 7, pp. 420-1.

[31]Cited in "On Sweden and the European Economic Community"
(Swedish Government Memorandum, 18 March 1971 [extract]), *Cooperation and Conflict*, Vol. 7, 1972, p. 344.

[32]Ibid., p. 344. See also three-page resumé of Government
statement in *Nordisk Kontakt* 1970: 14, pp. 871-3.

though the Minister did emphasize the importance of a customs union between Sweden and the EEC.

On the same day in Stockholm the opposition party leaders in reacting to the Government statement in Brussels reiterated their by now familiar positions. Communist Party leader Hermansson repudiated both the membership and customs union concepts and saw the statement as surprisingly friendly towards the EEC. He repeated his party's position that Sweden ought to be satisfied with a trade agreement with the EEC. The Democratic opposition parties' leaders took largely consensus positions with the Government but added their particular partisan avowals. Centre Party leader Gunnar Hedlund and Liberal leader Gunnar Helén approved the Government statement by and large but underscored that much would depend on the skill with which the Government handled the coming discussions with the EEC Commission and the negotiations which would follow. Conservative Party leader Yngve Holmberg expressed disappointment that Sweden had not sought full membership in order to ascertain during the negotiations whether it would be possible to combine membership with the policy of neutrality. Leading members of the industrial and commercial establishment echoed this view.[33]

The question of the application was not raised in Parliament until the first day of the general political debate on 19 January 1971. It was not so much a debate as an attempt to show moderation and increase the consensus, as all party leaders -- except for the Communist Party leader, who stood fast in his anti-EEC attitude -- attempted to come to grips with the conflicting political demand of neutrality and the economic demand of close participation with the EEC. For example, the Centre Party leader found that Swedish membership in the EEC was not excluded but explained that he had become more pessimistic as a result of the Davignon Report. However, he emphasized that a position with respect to the form of membership could not be taken until the points at issue had been clarified. The leader of the Liberal

---

[33]*Nordisk Kontakt* 1970: 14, pp. 869-71.

Party criticized the "national self-sufficiency" which a number
of EEC opponents exhibited. According to him, a close association with the EEC was of great importance to all Swedes:
"Although it is not possible to form an opinion as to the final
form of membership as yet, nevertheless, we will have to pay
dearly if even a customs union at the very least does not materialize." The Conservative Party leader, Gösta Bohman, criticized
the lack of knowledge, and the predetermined positions and
political superstitutions which marked large parts of the Swedish
EEC debate. According to him, "we ought firstly to seek full
membership with safeguards for neutrality. We must create as
good conditions as possible within Swedish opinion and at Brussels
for such a form of membership which will best safeguard Swedish
and European interests."[34] The Prime Minister, Olof Palme,
argued that it was also in other countries' interests that
Sweden's policy of neutrality would be firmly followed. He said,
"We cannot participate in foreign policy cooperation which would
commit us to a particular group of States.... The Government will
gather a broad opinion around the base lines of Swedish foreign
and trade policies and attempt to reach a constructive agreement
with the EEC."[35]

Four months after the initial statement to the EEC Council
of Ministers on 10 November 1970, the Swedish Government issued a
follow-up memorandum on 18 March 1971 which definitely excluded
the possibility of any formal membership. The new declaration of
Sweden's position was based on a thorough analysis of the meaning
of the Davignon Report and of the implications of the Werner
Report, accepted by resolution of the Council of Ministers of the
EEC on 8-9 February 1971. After a lengthy introduction outlining
the history of Swedish EEC discussions and negotiations, and
interpreting the significance of the Commission's attitude toward
the Werner Report, the memorandum analyzed the implications of

---

[34]Ibid., p. 174.

[35]Ibid., p. 174.

the Davignon Report:

> The conclusion which we must draw is that Swedish member-
> ship of the EEC would result in cooperation in the field
> of foreign policy along the lines of the Davignon Report.
> Consequently, the question of Swedish membership of the
> communities depends on whether cooperation in the field
> of foreign policy in accordance with the Davignon plan is
> compatible with the policy of neutrality. The coopera-
> tion aims at a harmonization of the foreign policy....
> The aim is to 'show the whole world that Europe has a
> political mission'. The arrangement is conceived only as
> a first step towards a closer cooperation in future.
>
> ....
>
> The aim of the Swedish policy of neutrality is to keep us
> out of a possible future war. It also serves to maintain
> stability and calm in Northern Europe and thereby consti-
> tutes a contribution towards peace in the whole of
> Europe. This view is shared by all countries in the East
> and the West. A basic principle of our policy of neu-
> trality is that our position should be taken freely and
> according to our own independent judgment. In an acute
> situation of tension it is particularly important that we
> do not give the rest of the world the impression that our
> conduct is dependent upon consultations with a certain
> group of States.
>
> The countries which have taken the initiative and co-
> operation in the field of foreign policy on the basis of
> the Davignon plan are all members of NATO. The countries
> which have applied for membership are all -- with the
> exception of Ireland -- also members of this military
> alliance.
>
> ....
>
> To conclude:
>
> ....
>
> Swedish participation in the foreign policy cooperation
> drawn up on the basis of the so-called 'Davignon Report'
> is not compatible with a firm Swedish policy of neutral-
> ity. Members of the EEC are expected to take part in
> this cooperation and accept the political goals behind it.
>
> Swedish participation in an economic and monetary union,
> which implies an abandonment of the national right of
> decision-making in important fields, is not compatible
> with a Swedish policy of neutrality.[36]

---

[36]"On Sweden and the European Economic Community" (Swedish
Government Memorandum, 18 March 1971 [extract]), *Cooperation and
Conflict*, Vol. 7, 1972, pp. 344-6.

Nevertheless, the memorandum concluded,

We have, *inter alia*, declared that we are prepared to participate in a customs union comprising both industrial and agricultural goods.... The form of cooperation between Sweden and the Communities will have to be a special agreement in which the rights and obligations of the parties are clearly defined. This will be the object of negotiations.[37]

With this declaration Sweden's policy toward the EEC was fixed. Nothing remained but to negotiate the customs agreement; and the negotiations were duly instituted by a letter dated 6 September 1971 to the member governments of the EEC and its Commission. The letter outlined the development of a toll-free market between Sweden and the EEC as the foundation for a treaty between the two. Sweden declared its readiness to remove both customs duties and quantitative restrictions for industrial products in its trade with the EEC, to coordinate its customs duties and other trade regulations with the EEC, and to negotiate an agreement that the two parties should start to coordinate trade policies against third countries. Furthermore, Sweden declared its preparedness not to exclude any sectors from customs duty reduction.[38]

The negotiations with the EEC duly took place in parallel with the other neutral countries, Austria, Finland and Switzerland, and the treaty between Sweden and the EEC was signed at Brussels on 22 July 1972. The treaty which entered into force on 1 January 1973 provided for customs duty reductions by 20% per year from 1 April 1973 to 1 July 1977, at which point a virtually complete customs union between the EEC and Sweden would exist. Sweden was also given the right according to Article 21 of the Treaty (as was the EEC) to take unilateral steps, regardless of other sections of the Treaty, to safeguard its security during war or "serious international tension."[39]

---

[37] Ibid., pp. 346-7.

[38] *Nordisk Kontakt* 1971: 12, pp. 793-4.

[39] See Treaty, p. 14, Article 21.

Although hindsight shows that the decision taken in the
Swedish Memorandum of 18 March 1971 was the only possible one
given the absolute and historical consensus on the inviolability
of Sweden's policy of neutrality the period between March 1971
and November 1972, when the ratification debate took place in
Parliament, nevertheless, saw an apparent break-up of the consensus on policy towards the EEC that had developed among the
democratic parties during the previous decade. This was surprising since as early as 10 November 1970, when Sweden presented
its initial statement to the EEC Council of Ministers, the EEC
reaction was negative. For example, the chairman of that meeting, the German Foreign Minister Walter Scheel, openly stated
that the general opinion in Brussels towards possible Swedish
membership of the EEC was negative.[40] It should also be pointed
out that at no point had any leading Swedish politician even
suggested that Sweden should give up its policy of neutrality.
Nevertheless, as late as 4 September 1971, at the meeting of the
foreign policy committee which considered the letter delivered on
6 September to the EEC member-governments and the Commission, the
Conservative and Liberal parties' leaders protested, that the
Government should ask for association according to paragraph 238
of the Treaty of Rome.[41] Only the Centre Party supported the
Government's position. The reason for this obvious rearguard
action of the Conservatives and Liberals appears to lie not so
much in their convictions as in the fact that both parties are
heavily supported by the industrial and commercial establishments. These, throughout the three applications, strongly
polemicized their economic arguments for full membership, or at
least associate membership. During the third application period,
the pressure tactics of these groups reached fever pitch, culminating in a two-day meeting in January 1972, organized by the
Export Association and the Federation of Swedish Industries, at

---

[40]*Nordisk Kontakt* 1970: 14, p. 869.

[41]*Nordisk Kontakt* 1971: 12, p. 793.

which 175 industrial and commercial leaders sharply criticized
the Government's handling of the EEC question. By this time it
was too late.

2. Finland: the Politics of Sovereignty

While Swedes think in terms of maximizing independent policy
options, Finns think in terms of necessity of state and reason of
state -- in other words, the preservation of the state's very
existence. In the Finnish view, the existence of the state as a
discrete entity depends on Soviet security perceptions and on
Soviet goodwill. Neutrality is regarded as a political necessity, the only possible response to Soviet demands for security
and the only possible safeguard to sovereignty. Since Finnish
neutrality functions as an adaptive response to a single external
demand, it is more stable than the Swedish form of neutrality,
but it is also coloured by its dependence on Soviet security
perceptions. Consequently, Finland has constantly to reassure
the Soviet Union that its foreign activities do not undermine
Soviet security.

The "Note Crisis" of 1961 illustrates this dependence. In
a speech to the National Press Club in Washington on 17 October
1961, President Kekkonen sought to explain what he referred to as
the "Finnish paradox" by saying: "The better we succeed in
maintaining the confidence of the Soviet Union in Finland as a
peaceful neighbour, the better are our opportunities for close
cooperation with the countries of the Western world."[42] Two
weeks later, while on vacation in Hawaii, he was informed that
the Soviet Union wished to open "consultations in accordance with
the Finnish-Soviet Treaty on Friendship, Cooperation and Mutual
Assistance, on measures for the defence of the borders of the two
countries against the threat of armed aggression on the part of
West Germany and states allied with it."[43] Kekkonen met this

---

[42]Urho Kekkonen, *Neutrality: The Finnish Position* (London,
1970), p. 89.

[43]*Ulkopolittisia Lausuntoja ja Asiankirjoja 1961* (hereafter

crisis, which resulted from the then current Berlin situation, with a typical initiative: he flew to Novosibirsk in Siberia to meet Khrushchev whom he persuaded that the holding of military consultations between Finland and the Soviet Union would arouse concern and fear of war in the other Scandinavian countries, and that consequently the Soviet Union's logical course was to withdraw its proposal and thus lessen tension. Kekkonen also pointed out that the Soviet Union would thus give evidence that it was sincere in its desire for coexistence, in dangerous as well as in uneventful times. The Note incident resulted in a net gain to Finland. Paasikivi's interpretation of the provision for consultation in the Treaty -- that both parties had to recognize the threat of aggression before consultations could take place -- was now confirmed by the course of events: the Soviet claim that a threat existed had failed to bring about consultations. "But the Novosibirsk statement went further. It suggested that it was up to Finland to take the initiative for consultations. This amounted to the reinterpretation of ... the Finnish-Soviet Treaty that further strengthened Finland's neutrality."[44]

Similarly, in the case of EFTA, in its attempts to safeguard its economic interests in the face of European economic demands, Finland managed both to integrate its trade activities with EFTA and to expand its political independence, but only by scrupulous and careful attention to Soviet economic interests and Soviet confidence in Finnish friendship. Two years of intricate negotiations between the Soviet and Finnish governments were concluded by Kekkonen's personal interventions with Premier Khrushchev in September and November 1960, when Finland signed a treaty with the Soviet Union on tariffs, to come into effect if or when Finland should reach agreement with EFTA. In the treaty, Finland

---

ULA), pp. 209-13.

[44]Max Jakobson, *Finnish Neutrality* (London, 1968), p. 79. See also speech by Kekkonen, "The Results of the 'Note' Crisis", in Kekkonen, op. cit., pp. 102-8. It should be noted that President Kekkonen disavows Ambassador Jakobson's contention that it is up to Finland to initiate consultations and reaffirms the bilateral character of the provision. See *ULA 1969*, pp. 59-60.

agreed to reduce duties on Soviet manufactured goods by the same
amount and at the same rate as it was to reduce duties on EFTA
goods. This concession, however, was not made with reference to
the Most Favoured Nation principle because the Soviet Union was
not a member of GATT and did not wish to recognize it. Instead,
the concession was based on "neighbourly relations" existing
between the two countries. As a result, the agreement was made
palatable to all concerned: the Soviet Government could claim
that the MFN clause with Finland remained intact, the Finnish
Government could claim that the concession to the Soviet Union
had been made on grounds that were unique and therefore not
applicable to any other state outside EFTA, and EFTA members
could argue that the integrity of the free trade area had not
been breached.[45]

Partly to assuage Soviet dislike of the "instrument of
imperialist policy" -- as the Soviets regarded EFTA -- and partly
to safeguard certain quantitative import restrictions for the
maintenance of imports from the Soviet Union necessary to continue bilateral trade with the Soviet Union, Finland did not
become a member of EFTA. Instead, a separate free trade area
comprising Finland and the seven member-states of EFTA -- FINEFTA
-- was created by a treaty signed on 27 March 1961. This meant
in practice that Finland acquired all the advantages of EFTA membership, while sacrificing none of its security interests. In
the process Finnish sovereignty was strengthened.

During the first and second rounds of applications for EEC
membership, Finland bided its time and did not react at all,
either internally or externally. By 1970, however, it had become
clear that the EEC was indeed going to be expanded and that
Finland would be faced with two foreign trade problems. First,
two of Finland's principal trading partners, Britain and Denmark,
had decided to enter the enlarged EEC; and, secondly, two of
Finland's leading competitors in the Common Market, Sweden and

---

[45]Jakobson, op. cit., p. 65. See also *ULA* 1960, pp. 112-6.

Norway, were either about to enter (Norway) or to negotiate an
arrangement to penetrate the tariff walls of the enlarged Community (Sweden). Clearly, Finland had to come to terms with the
EEC, or its competitiveness in the West European markets would
suffer a major setback. As President Kekkonen put it in his
opening speech to Parliament on 6 April 1970:

> Our struggle to mind our economic interests is not
> limited ... to the Nordic countries. It presupposes the
> maintenance and improvement of our competitive powers
> everywhere and in all directions. Actually, this struggle
> runs parallel with the realization of our neutrality
> policy. It constitutes an important precondition for the
> success of our neutrality policy. A great part of
> Finland's foreign trade is with the European Free Trade
> Area, with the European Economic Community and with the
> socialist countries. Our position as an associate member
> of EFTA and our long-term trade agreements with the
> socialist countries have effectively contributed to the
> positive development of our foreign trade. The question
> of the European Economic Community has opened a possible
> change in the European market constellation. In this
> situation we must safeguard the preconditions of our com-
> petitive ability in this direction as well.[46]

As expected, the President began his preparations for
negotiations with the EEC by making an unofficial visit to the
Soviet Union on 24-26 February 1970, followed by an official
visit five months later on 17-20 July 1970, followed by another
unofficial visit on 23-25 February 1971, and yet another unofficial visit on 17-18 November 1971. The immediate upshot of
this series of visits was the agreement between the President and
the Soviet Government to renew the Finnish-Soviet Treaty of
Friendship, Cooperation and Mutual Assistance -- consequent upon
a Soviet initiative during the July visit -- a full five years
before it was due to expire in 1975.[47] A few days after his
visit to the Soviet Union, the President paid an official visit
to the United States where he explained the prolongation of the
Treaty in a speech in Washington on 23 July 1970:

---

[46]*ULA 1970*, pp. 16-17.

[47]The treaty was formally renewed on 20 November 1970.

The Treaty had another five years to run. But no one can be certain about the development of the European situation in the coming years. We have reason to hope that we are moving towards greater security in Europe. But in this period of transition, the position of different countries may become subject to uncertainty or speculation. We wish to remove any possible doubt about the consistency of our policy.

This is all the more important in view of Finland's vital interest in maintaining her trading position in all markets. Whatever arrangements that may have to be made to this end must of course be in accord with our policy of neutrality.[48]

Clearly the Soviet Union had so far not been convinced of the wisdom of supporting Finland's desire to come to terms with the EEC. Indeed, in a television interview shortly after his February 1971 visit to the Soviet Union, the President indicated that although the European economic integration question had been discussed with the Soviets, he did not wish to go into this in detail but merely pointed out that the Soviets "as is known, regard international economic blocs with extreme mistrust".[49] Nevertheless, the President had apparently convinced the Soviets sufficiently of the necessity and validity of his making an approach to the EEC for Finland to be able to put in its application within a few days of the President's November 1971 visit to the Soviet Union. Since by constitutional authority, and historical precedent since the Second World War, foreign affairs are conducted by the President and since, by precedent also, the sphere of Soviet-Finnish relations has been exclusively in the hands of the President, very little is known about informal discussions that take place between him and his interlocutors in Moscow.[50]

---

[48]*ULA 1970*, pp. 219-20, English original.

[49]*Nordisk Kontakt* 1971: 4, pp. 209-10.

[50]Soviet-Finnish relations are based on a very high degree of personal interaction between President Kekkonen (and Paasikivi before him) and the Soviet leaders: for example, the February 1971 visit to the Soviet Union was President Kekkonen's seventeenth.

Nonetheless, Finland's negotiations with the EEC began in November 1971 -- after a series of exploratory talks beginning in the Spring of 1970 -- and moved smoothly to a conclusion in July 1972 when a free trade agreement between the EEC and Finland was initialled. According to Article 3 of the Agreement, "Customs duties and imports shall be progressively abolished", beginning with a reduction to 80% of the basic duty on 1 April 1973 and reduced to nil over a four-year period ending on 1 July 1977. However, the transition period for the abolition of tariffs in the forestry and pulp and paper sector is a long eleven years, in addition to a temporary increase in British and Danish duties against Finnish goods.[51] The reason for this was the state of the forestry industry in the Common Market, which faces modernization problems and does not wish to be exposed to Finnish competition, whether directly or through re-export via Denmark, Britain and Ireland.

Over agriculture, Finland made no concessions to the EEC because of the counterbalancing difficulties in the forestry products sector that developed during the negotiations. In fact, agriculture was excluded, but the Agreement does leave the door open for future negotiations on this matter.

Because of the importance of the forestry products sector in the Finnish economy, a special arrangement was conceded by the EEC by granting Finland two decalage timetables, one of twelve and the other of eight years, covering mainly the labour-intensive branches, to counterbalance the negative effects of the EEC conditions in the pulp and paper sector.[52]

Another noteworthy exception in the Finnish agreement, compared with the Norwegian and Swedish free trade agreements,

---

[51]See *Agreement between the European Economic Community and the Republic of Finland*, Protocol No. 1, Concerning the Treatment Applicable to Certain Products.

[52]See *Agreement*, Annex D, List 1: Products Originating in the Community for which the Customs Duties Imposed upon their Importation into Finland will be Progressively Abolished over a Period of 12 Years; and List 2: Products ... a Period of 8 Years.

is the retention of qualitative restrictions on fuels -- a continuation of the FINEFTA arrangement.[53] The petroleum products exception is of political as well as economic importance to Finland, since it depends almost exclusively on the Soviet Union for petroleum and other fuels. The EEC Agreement thus allows the continuation of the Soviet-Finnish bilateral trade arrangements without interference. Furthermore, the political demands of Finnish-Soviet trade are safeguarded by Article 12 which provides for equal treatment on tariff questions with third countries:

> A Contracting Party which is considering the reduction of effective level of its duties or charges having equivalent effect applicable to third countries benefitting from most-favoured-nation treatment, or which is considering the suspension of the application, shall, as far as may be practicable, notify the Joint Committee not less than 30 days before such reduction or suspension comes into effect. It shall take note of any representations by the other Contracting Party regarding any distortions which might result therefrom.[54]

Hence Finland has no need to negotiate with the EEC in order to satisfy the demands of Soviet-Finnish bilateral trade; simple notification suffices.

In addition to the Free Trade Agreement with the EEC, Finland and the Soviet Union concluded a treaty very early in the course of Finland's EEC negotiations (on 23 December 1971), on economic, technological and industrial cooperation. Furthermore, Finland opened negotiations with Comecon on agreement in principle for cooperation, which was initialled during the spring of 1973.

That the former agreement was in the economic interests of Finland is clear from President Kekkonen's reply, in a TV and radio interview on 18 February 1974, to the question "Did your talks concern concrete new economic cooperation projects between Finland and the Soviet Union?":

> Quite a lot ... For example, I had a list of the objects that Finnish industry is ready to offer to the Soviet

---

[53]See Article 14 of the *Agreement*.

[54]Article 12 of the *Agreement*.

Union, and in fact we went over [very many] major projects.
The attitude to the Finnish offers was very favourable.
It is perhaps pointless to discuss them in this phase, as
negotiations have already begun on certain projects and as
completely new matters were taken up. I can perhaps men-
tion one matter that will obviously soon be in a decision-
making phase. A new chemical pulp mill, an acetate pulp
mill producing 140,000 tons, will be built in Svetogorsk.
This is extremely gratifying for us. The construction
work in Svetogorsk will end in 1975, and this quite sizeable project will begin then.[55]

That the Comecon agreement was a strictly political ploy on
the part of the Finns to satisfy the demands of Finnish neutrality and not to satisfy economic demands is made clear in the
protestations of a senior official in the Ministry for Foreign
Affairs who in a public speech in Copenhagen on 3 May 1973 said,

You may be interested in our Comecon (SEV) agreement,
which makes us the first market economy to conclude such
an agreement. I need hardly explain to this audience
what Comecon is and what it is not. I would simply point
out that it is not an economic community in the sense that
the EEC is; it is one with which it is not possible to
negotiate a tariff agreement. It is illogical, therefore,
to think of our agreement with Comecon as a counterbalance
to the agreement we negotiated with the EEC. The Comecon
agreement is a framework within which cooperation, in the
first place exchange of information, can be organized.
Our starting point was that a better knowledge of the
norms, methods and other facts of that group might
further bilateral trade between Finland and the Comecon
members.

He added:

In general, vistas of this kind are opening up to the
countries of Western and Eastern Europe which have recently started to engage in livelier and fruitful economic
dialogue. The Conference on Security and Cooperation in
Europe will be very important for efforts to develop East-
West trade. Such trends will give added impetus to trade
negotiated on a bilateral basis and a commercial policy
along traditional lines, as well as to securing the expansion of trade in the long term. Trends of this nature
are also essential in a situation where regional groupings
in Europe, both in the East and in the West, concomitantly
increase in their internal cooperation.[56]

---

[55]Ministry for Foreign Affairs, *Finnish Features*, 1, 1974.

[56]Pentti Uusivirta, Head of Commercial Policy Department,
Ministry for Foreign Affairs, at the Conference "Scandinavia,

But surprisingly for Finland, where foreign questions seldom become political issues, the matter of the free trade agreement with the EEC became embroiled in domestic politics. This was the result of two factors, the Communist Party's opposition to any arrangement with the EEC and the peculiarity of the Finnish political structure, including the partisan configuration and constitutional requirements. The Communist Party's opposition to any arrangement with the EEC continued stiff and unyielding till the bitter end: it was the only party that voted against ratification of the Agreement on 16 November 1973. The party's unyielding opposition was all the more strange since the Soviet Union had raised no public objections -- either in diplomatic notes or in articles in *Pravda* or *Izvestia*. Unfortunately, it could not be simply disregarded, because the party is the second largest "socialist" party in Finland and consistently polls one-fifth of the electoral votes. Furthermore, it and the Social Democratic Party (Finland's largest party, with a quarter of the electoral vote) share the support of the labour movement in Finland.

But the neo-Stalinist opposition to the "capitalist" EEC could easily have been overcome by the other parties uniting in support, had the internal political-economic-constitutional structure not created three years of confusing conflicts. The origins of these lay in the 1970 central collective agreement to solve wage settlements on an economy-wide basis, and the formation of the five-party coalition government, including the Communist Party, to solve this and other pressing problems of the economic recession of 1969-70. However, in March 1969 the Communist Party withdrew from the coalition since it did not wish to be tainted with the unpopular measures considered necessary to enforce labour peace and orderly growth. But even the four-party rump coalition (the Social Democrats, the Centre Party, the Liberal People's Party and the Swedish People's Party) was unable

---

Britain and the European Community" on 3 May 1973 in Copenhagen. *Finnish Features*, 9, 1973.

to overcome the internal conflicts over the same issue, and
resigned on 29 October 1971. The President called an election
for 2-3 January 1972 and appointed a civil servant caretaker
government, which was only replaced on 23 February by a Social
Democrat minority government -- one and a half months after the
elections in which only minor changes in the parliamentary
configuration took place.[57] On 4 September 1972 this ministry,
after a seven-week crisis involving economic questions, resigned.
Thereupon a four-party coalition government, consisting of the
Social Democrats, the Swedish People's Party, the Centre Party
and the Liberal People's Party, took office.

What mainly brought about the downfall of the series of
governments were economic questions. In the summer of 1972 these
were centred on the enabling acts, and included the enactment of
a market disturbance law, the granting of price control powers of
a permanent nature to the government, the creation of a permanent
contra-cyclical system of a tax-like nature, and statutory
control of capital flows. During the late summer of 1972 the
Social Democrats, at their annual party congress, decided to tie
the ratification of the EEC Free Trade Agreement to the passage
of the enabling acts. The reason for this was that under the
Finnish Constitution the government cannot, by a simple majority
of votes in Parliament, obtain authority to impose price controls, a contra-cyclical taxation system or a system for direct-

---

[57]

	ELECTIONS			
	15-16 March 1970		2-3 January 1972	
Party	Seats	% Votes	Seats	% Votes
Social Democrats	52	23.4	55	25.8
Conservatives	37	18.0	34	17.6
Centre	36	17.1	35	16.4
Communists	36	16.6	37	17.0
Rural	18	10.5	18	9.2
Swedish People's	12	5.7	10	5.3
Liberals	8	6.0	7	5.2
Christian	1	1.2	4	2.5
Workers & Small Farmers	0	1.4	0	1.0
	200	100.0	200	100.0

ing capital flows: they all require a five-sixths majority. As
the right-wing parties -- all in opposition -- commanded well
over one-sixth of the seats in Parliament, and in the recent past
had opposed the granting of such powers to the government, and as
the right-wing parties insisted on the EEC Free Trade Agreement,
the Social Democrats linked the two matters together to obtain
leverage for the passage of the economic package. Despite the
pressure game, it took well over a year before satisfactory
arrangements were worked out among the parties and the enabling
acts were revised and finally agreed to. The EEC Agreement --
which had become critical because of the time limits involved in
the initial round of reduction of tariffs -- was signed in
Brussels on 5 October and ratified by Parliament on 16 November
1973.

3. The Political and Psychological Requirements of Swedish and Finnish Neutrality

As we have seen in chapter 2 and the present chapter, the Swedish
and Finnish policies of neutrality are only minimally related to
the concept of legal neutrality. The legal objective of neutrality is to enable a state to remain a non-participant during a
war.[58] The claim of the right to non-participation in a war
imposes the duty on the neutral to maintain an impartial attitude
towards the belligerents. The condition of impartiality, however, requires behaviour in peacetime that will make the declaration of neutrality in the event of war credible in the eyes of
the belligerents. The demand for credibility is paramount; this
was shown in the refusal of Switzerland to become a member of the
United Nations for fear of compromising its position of impartiality, even though its neutrality has been guaranteed for a
century by an international convention signed by all the major

---

[58]"Neutrality represents an impartial attitude or policy or a
third state which, as a non-participant in a war, envokes special
rights and duties in relation to the belligerents." William L.
Tung, *International Law in an Organizing World* (New York, 1968),
p. 460.

powers. In the case of Sweden and Finland, neither of which has
any international undertakings supporting its policy of neutrality, the credibility demand provides the main support for the
claim to impartiality in the event of war.

Hence the Swedish and Finnish policies of neutrality have
two interdependent objectives: first, to create and maintain
conditions which make neutrality possible in the event of war
and, secondly, to maintain and increase independence of political
decision prior to the outbreak of war. The former is the credibility argument and the latter the sovereignty argument.

It is not possible to design foreign policies in the ab-
stract; specific countries must be the objectives of specific
foreign policies. Swedish and Finnish neutrality policies are
directed towards the superpowers and the possible outbreak of war
between them. Hence the two interdependent objectives of the
policy of neutrality must ensure the growing credibility of the
two countries' neutrality policies *vis-à-vis* both superpowers.
Sweden and Finland must ensure that their international behaviour
in peacetime serves this end.

The necessary emphasis on superpower acceptance of the
policy of neutrality may, however, become a constraint leading
to third parties and/or one of the superpowers considering the
neutral's policies not impartial but tending to support the
superpower whose demands for the demonstration of credibility are
being accommodated, either because that superpower makes greater
demands than the other, or because the neutral considers it more
important to pre-empt the demands of one superpower than those of
the other. Thus Finland has been regarded by many third parties
as being Soviet-dominated, and Sweden as being pro-Soviet or at
least "left-leaning", particularily during the long period of
Swedish criticism of the American involvement in Vietnam. And it
is true that both Finland and Sweden are more concerned with
showing the Soviet Union that they are not anti-Soviet than they
are in demonstrating to the United States that they are not anti-
American. Finland may with some justification be accused of
being pro-Soviet, rather than merely impartial, in the conduct of

its foreign policy; certainly the intention of the Paasikivi-Kekkonen line is to reassure the Soviets that Finland will not only do nothing that would lead to a weakening of Soviet security, but will actively attempt to increase it to the extent of its ability. Although the necessity for the Paasikivi-Kekkonen line is rooted in the two countries' Second World War experiences, the geographic position of Finland and the power differential between the two, and is therefore an understandable and necessary policy for Finland, and although the United States and the major powers accept its necessity, the fact that there is no policy towards the United States counterbalancing the Paasikivi-Kekkonen line (because the United States has made no demands for such a policy) often leads third parties -- and Western public opinion -- to regard Finland as pro-Soviet. Sweden's attempt to demonstrate concern for Soviet security needs produces a similar impression, although its geographic, historical, strategic and military power conditions are different from those of Finland.

It is to lessen the constraints imposed by the Soviet demands, and the assumption by American and third party opinion that these are the determining forces in their foreign policies, that the two countries have expanded their involvement with third parties to demonstrate their independence. This démarche has become possible largely because of the increase in the number of independent states, the increasing economic demands made by the newly-emerged states on the industrialized world and the increasing participation of these states in world politics. Because they have no colonial past, are industrialized, have well-established democratic cultures and are neutral *vis-à-vis* the two superpowers, Sweden and Finland have been able to engage in independent political and economic relations with the Third World without fear of compromising the credibility of their neutrality policies. Increased relations with states outside the superpower blocs makes the independence of the two countries' foreign policy activities more visible, and reduces their concentration on superpower-oriented policy activities. Moreover, all the Nordic countries -- not only Sweden and Finland -- believe

that an increase in multilateral webs of relationships based on
non-security concerns will reduce international tensions and
shift attention from security problems to the economic-based
problems of welfare and wellbeing.

The European economic integration movement and the increasing interdependence of contiguous highly developed industrialized
economies has provided an opportunity for the two Nordic countries to add a European and economic dimension to their foreign
policies, thus reducing relatively the superpower oriented
concentration on security policy. This, however, has not been as
easy as the expansion of activity into the Third World because of
the extensive overlapping of membership of the EEC and NATO, the
supranational political character of the decision-making system
in the EEC, and the proclaimed intention of the EEC to form an
eventual political union. These factors clearly prevented the
two neutral countries from actively pursuing full membership in
the EEC because of the limitations that this would place on their
freedom to make independent policy decisions. The impartiality
of a neutral is inevitably suspect when it formally transfers any
of its sovereign authority to make decisions affecting any part
of its foreign or internal activities to a supranational authority; when it undertakes formally to place any part of its economy
under the direction of collective policy; or when it undertakes
to make any kind of decision which will formally bind its economy
with economies under foreign political direction. However, the
dilemma created by the political impossibility of full membership
and the economic demand for participation had to be solved to
ensure the continuing growth of the two economies. The solution,
in the form of free trade agreements between Sweden and the EEC,
and between Finland and the EEC, in the non-agricultural sectors,
with escape clauses, is testimony to the acceptance by the EEC
membership of the neutrality policies of the two countries.
Moreover, the fact that two other neutrals, Austria and Switzerland, and another highly developed industrialized country,
Norway, also had to be accommodated on a free trade basis assisted in demonstrating to the Soviet Union that the Swedish and

Finnish accords with the EEC were part of a basic West European
intra-regional economic arrangement among like highly industrialized economies, and not politically anti-Soviet in intention or
character. The fact that an economic rapprochement began between
Western Europe and the Soviet Union during the late 1960s assisted in determining the form of the Swedish and Finnish solutions.

In practical terms, however, the Swedish and Finnish economic accords with the EEC have increased daily political contact
with the EEC and its members. Because of increasing concern
everywhere with economic wellbeing and an increasingly obvious
interdependence among not only the highly industrialized economies but between the less developed and the industrialized, and
between the larger and the smaller even across ideological and
security bloc boundaries, a general shifting of emphasis in
international politics is taking place from the traditional
security-oriented "high" politics toward an economically oriented
"low" politics. If this shift continues, the economic relations
of the two neutral Nordic countries with the EEC will increase in
importance at the expense of the security-oriented relations with
the superpowers. However, as long as a possibility of war exists
between the two superpowers, the two neutrals must carefully
heed the constraints implicit in making their claim to impartiality credible. Because the EEC is ideologically anti-
communist, culturally Western, and eight-ninths part of the
American superpower bloc, Finland and Sweden must be very careful
constantly to show the Soviet Union that, despite their increasing economic relations with the EEC, they are not so dependent on
it that they cannot maintain a position of impartiality in the
event of a war between the superpower blocs.

Hence the carefulness of both Sweden and Finland in not
aligning their foreign policies, including their foreign economic
policies, with any group, not even with the non-aligned. The
objective is to show the superpowers and all third parties that
they conduct independent foreign policies and that their behaviour is not dependent on any prior commitments to any foreign
powers, but is always based on the requirements of the policy of

neutrality -- the maintenance of sovereign independence and an
impartial attitude towards the superpowers.

There is one exception to this, the intra-Nordic non-security-oriented activities. Here Sweden and Finland try to accen-
tuate their belonging to the Nordic group, which claims a peculiar cultural and political position apart from the rest of the
world. It was this claim to which President Kekkonen appealed in 1961
when he made clear to the Soviet leaders that Finland would
remain a Nordic type of democracy even if "the rest of Europe
should turn communist."[59]

Instead of becoming part of the non-aligned group, the
Nordics tend to support Third World aspirations on a case basis,
both as a group and individually, in the interests, first, of
building third party appreciation of their independence from the
superpowers; secondly, of increasing the importance of "low"
politics in international relations; and thirdly, of strengthening the non-security-oriented web of relations among nations.
Nordic membership in the non-aligned group -- composed as it is
of diverse, intensely nationalist, and economically underdeveloped countries with unstable political structures and undemocratic political cultures -- would tend to undermine rather than
support these objectives. For the only thing that the Nordics
have in common with the non-aligned countries is the desire to
remain outside superpower bloc politics. Moreover, the Nordics
as a group have been much more successful than the non-aligned in
this quest. Sweden and Finland have not only maintained their
independence from superpower domination but have increased the
acceptance of their policies of neutrality in the eyes of the
superpowers. Denmark and Norway, although aligned with NATO,
have carefully reduced their obligations to it to a "semi-neutrality" and have emphasized their Nordic position by coordinating their Third World policies with Sweden and Finland. In
addition, Denmark, although a full member of the EEC, neverthe-

---

[59]Cited by K. Korhonen, "Finland and the Soviet Union", *Essays
in Finnish Foreign Policy* (Helsinki, 1969), p. 32.

less regards itself as politically and socially an integral part
of the Nordic group and a member of the EEC for economic reasons
only.

The Nordics, furthermore, are able to maintain the neutral-
ist-oriented Nordic solidarity -- Finnish and Swedish neutrality,
Danish and Norwegian "semi-neutrality" -- because of the internal
stability of their political and economic structures, the homo-
geneity of their populations and cultures, and the politics of
Nordic consensus. Hence Sweden and Finland not only have no need
to look beyond the Nordic area for countries with which to make
common cause, but are prevented from doing this by the necessity
for maintaining Nordic solidarity. This solidarity provides
vital support for the neutrality policies of the two countries:
both superpowers are fully aware of the four countries' common
determination to keep the Nordic area out of superpower rivalry
as much as possible. Moreover, all four are actively, conjointly
and cooperatively engaged in the promotion of any activity that
will reduce world tensions and hence the likelihood of war. This
is the ultimate objective of the Swedish and Finnish policies of
neutrality.

10. A SUMMING-UP

In the three decades since the Second World War, it has been
clear that all the four Nordic countries have given primary value
to the sovereign independence of the political, social and
economic systems represented by the concept nation-state.
Although this emphasis finds different expressions in the four,
it may be analyzed under three operational headings: security,
political independence and economic interdependence.

Because of geographic, cultural and historical factors, the
problem of security -- i.e. the continued survival of the existence of a sovereign state entity -- has formed the fundamental
framework within which national policy has been pursued in the
Nordic countries since the Second World War. All four, culturally Western and ideologically democratic, found themselves
because of their geographic location on the strategic and cultural frontier between the superpowers and their nascent blocs as
these were formed in the immediate post-war years. Throughout the
three decades since the beginning of the cold war, although the
confrontation between the superpower blocs has changed from a
strategy of ideological and cultural annihilation to one of
political and economic competition, the Nordic countries have
never been permitted to forget their exposed ideological, cul-

tural, political and economic positions. Moreover, although it
may be fashionable in an era of economic cooperation and political détente, to downgrade or even disregard military strategy,
the Nordic countries -- because of their geographic location in
the continuing confrontation of military-strategic deployment of
forces in the North Atlantic and the North Cap areas, their
proximity to the political/military strategic confrontations over
Berlin and the Soviet Union's decisive actions in Eastern Europe
to maintain its hegemony -- have been forced constantly to re-
evaluate their policy options according to the demands of the
continuing superpower military-strategic confrontation. The fact
that two of the four -- Norway and Denmark -- have been structurally part of one of the superpower blocs throughout the
period, and physically adjacent to the hostile superpower while
removed by 4,000 miles from the friendly superpower, has not only
heightened the awareness of the continuing strategic confrontation; it has also demanded a careful and continuing evaluation of
superpower interests and policy positions, and constant formulation of foreign and domestic policy to adapt to the superpowers
so as to decrease -- or at least not increase -- the interest of
the hostile superpower while increasing the interest of the
friendly superpower.

Although the argument applies particularly to Norway and
Denmark (not equally and with varying intensity at different
times) it also applies to the two neutral countries Sweden and
Finland, again with unequal force in the case of each and at
different times. The reason for this is, of course, geographic:
because of their location, the Nordic countries form a region
with two focal points -- the North Cap and the Baltic Straits.
This means that both Sweden and Finland must be as careful in
paying attention to superpower interests and démarches as must
Norway and Denmark. Indeed, the former must be even more careful
in some respects in the implementation of their policies than the
two NATO members. Because Finland and Sweden have no external
guarantors for the inviolability of their territories, because
both depend on the credibility of the operation of their policies

of neutrality and because both perceive the main threat to
security as coming from the Soviet Union -- just as the two NATO
members do -- they must make doubly certain that their foreign
policy actions are not perceived in a hostile light by the Soviet
Union.   In the Swedish case this process has become institutionalized as the ritual of invoking the "sacred cow" of neutrality
in all foreign policy statements, and as the framework within
which long-term foreign and economic policies are formulated.   In
the case of Finland, because of the geographic factor of the long
and indefensible common border with the Soviet Union, the experiences of the Second World War and the clearly Western
character of Finnish culture, political culture and political
sympathies, this operates as a very carefully elaborated process
of implementation of a policy of friendship for the Soviet Union,
designed constantly to demonstrate that Finnish foreign and
domestic activities will in no way decrease the security of the
Soviet Union, but might, on the contrary, increase it.

Indeed, the concept of the Nordic Balance may be regarded as
the conceptual framework used by the Nordic countries to evaluate
the possible effects of one country's actions on the others --
and the feedback effects thereof on them -- within the context of
the bipolar system.   At the very least the concept underlines the
importance of the four Nordic countries as a regional subsystem
within the international bipolar system.   It also emphasizes the
fact that the four Nordic countries do not form an entity but
rather subsystems within the Nordic region.

Although the problem of political independence as a functional expression of sovereign independence of the state entity
has been met in different ways by the four Nordic countries,
because of differing demands of security, the functional base for
all has been the same: the Nordic tradition of neutrality and
non-involvement.   In the event, although only Sweden has been
able to take advantage of this and proclaim itself politically
independent of other states, the three others reflect varying
degrees of that same Nordic desire for non-involvement.   For
example, Finland, whose neutrality policy has always been suspect

in the eyes of both West and East, has made a virtue of the need
to be independent politically to buttress its neutrality. It has
been eminently successful insofar as the external indicators of
political independence are concerned: in a quarter of a century
it has been able to move from the position of an economic vassal
of one of the superpowers, forced to deliver almost half its
industrial production as war reparations, to a state with an
economy whose foreign sector is overwhelmingly directed towards
the market economies of the West; from a position where it was
excluded from participation in international organizations to one
in it which is a full member of the United Nations, the OECD,
GATT, the Nordic Council, and almost all other non-regional
multilateral organizations. Furthermore, as of November 1973
Finland has had a free trade pact with the EEC. Moreover, as the
host country to the first phase of the SALT I negotiations and
the convenor of the Conference on Security and Cooperation in
Europe, it has enhanced its prestige as an independent international agent acceptable to both superpowers and their respective cohorts. For all this the Finns have had to pay a price
which reduces the claim to political independence: Finnish
political independence is predicated on the Treaty of Mutual
Cooperation and Friendship with the Soviet Union -- the superpower more distrusted by the Finns -- and an energetic self-
censorship combined with an unceasing effort to assuage Soviet
psychological fears of Finland's sincerity and the security
provided by Finland as an independent buffer. Nonetheless, when
all is said and done, Finnish political independence in the mid-
1970s is not only a far cry from the position in the mid-1960s or
the mid-1950s, but is probably as secure as that of any European
state given the politics of bipolarity.

Like Sweden and Finland, the two NATO members have also
pursued the Nordic objective of political independence within the
constraints of their security demands. Both have rejected the
permanent stationing of foreign troops and of nuclear weapons on
their territories in peacetime, and both have been highly vocal
in their criticisms of such "undemocratic" NATO members as

Greece, Turkey, Portugal and Spain, both within and outside NATO councils.

Sweden rejected EEC membership for the political reasons that a formal political undertaking to bind the Swedish economy to that of a group of NATO members would call its independence in question and would violate its security policy. For Finland the question of EEC membership never even arose because such action would have been incompatible with its neutrality and policy of independence, as understood by both the Soviets and the Finns. As for Norway, its rejection of EEC membership is directly attributable to Norwegian popular fears of loss of sovereignty. In Denmark similar fears were widely expressed and were only overcome by the demands of economic necessity, as aided and abetted by such facile political arguments that participation in the councils of the EEC would increase Denmark's influence in the making of decisions affecting Denmark's economy, that Denmark would be in good "democratic" company with Great Britain, home of the Mother of Parliaments, and that it would increase its political role in the Nordic area by acting as a bridge between the EEC and the Nordics. It can justifiably be said that Denmark did not become a member of the EEC for idealistic or political reasons but because pragmatic economic considerations left no alternative.

Perhaps the most convincing evidence that the four Nordic countries hold sovereign independence -- the right to be masters in their own house -- as the primary political value is to be found in their relations among themselves. Although Denmark, Norway and Sweden-Finland were united under a single crown in the Kalmar Union, that Norway was part of Denmark for centuries, that Finland was part of Sweden for 600 years, and that Norway and Sweden were united in a personal union under the Crown until 1905, that the ideology of "Scandinavianism" has become over the past century part of the Nordic cultural mythology, and that various and diverse organizations and activities ranging from monetary coordination to the harmonization of laws have been actively promoted for almost a century, the four Nordic countries

are no closer to political integration today than they were after
the break-up of the Swedish-Norwegian union in 1905. The Nordic
Council's active and energetic cooperative efforts in the harmonization of social, traffic, communications, educational and even
economic legislation notwithstanding, the Nordic parliaments and
their supporting political systems simply refuse to give up the
exclusive right of each national parliament to make binding
decisions for the nation. In the Nordic countries and in the
Nordic Council it is clearly understood that sovereignty resides
-- and will continue to reside -- in the Danish Folketing, the
Finnish Eduskunta, the Norwegian Storting and the Swedish Riksdag.

The problem of economic interdependence is the most complex
of the three operational factors of sovereign independence. This
is for two reasons: first, because complex highly industrialized
economies are naturally interdependent rather than independent;
and secondly, because the economy provides the wherewithal to
implement security and political independence policies, as well
as more mundane welfarist objectives. In other words, there is a
dual set of interdependences: on the one hand among economies and
on the other hand between an economy and its dependent political
and security systems. But it is equally true that political and
security systems affect economic systems. Hence, to reduce the
impact of economic interdependence on the political and security
systems, and thereby to increase sovereign independence, the
economy must be carefully politically directed to conform with
security and political objectives. Simply put, economic welfare
objectives cannot be allowed to direct the process of economic
growth and development, but must be subservient to the interests
of the "high politics" of security and political interests of the
nation. Among other things, this means that the state should not
make any formal commitments to any other state or bloc of states
which might reduce its sovereign control over its own economy.
And this, in short, is the reason why the Nordic countries have
consistently pursued the ideal of free trade, rather than economic bloc-building -- right up to the moment when it becomes clear
that the economic advantages of formal dependence on a bloc

outweigh the political advantages of formal economic independence. However, the argument is only partially valid, since only Denmark and Norway have fully tested it -- though with differing results because of domestic political engagements.[1] The Swedish test was purely internal and consisted of a decade of calculations -- primarily at the elite level -- of the economic opportunity costs of not joining set against the security costs of joining. For Finland, even the possibility of making these calculations was not available because of the overwhelming demands of Soviet security interests.

The Swedish calculations were the more difficult and "honest" ones, because the Swedes had to calculate fully the interdependence of the security, political and economic factors, whereas the Norwegian and Danish calculations could leave out -- except at a secondary level -- the calculation of security costs, since both were already members of the NATO alliance, and a further integration of their economies with other NATO members would not affect their security positions. Indeed, insofar as non-economic calculations entered into the Norwegian and Danish decisions to enter the EEC, these involved the twin problems of political independence and of the psychological trauma of making a political decision to place their economies under the joint political authority of continental political systems generally regarded by the Nordics as "un-democratic" and not in tune with the "democratic" social objectives of the Nordic political and economic systems. The only saving grace, as the Nordics saw it, was the fact that the United Kingdom, widely regarded by them as a Nordic-type "democracy", with similar social objectives, would also become a member of the EEC.

In any case, the idea that economic independence is today any longer possible for such highly industrialized states as the

---

[1]The validity of the argument is not affected by the fact that, as the result of a popular referendum, Norway did not follow through and become a member of the EEC. Popular referenda, as witness Switzerland, often bring into play irresponsible emotional forces in direct contradiction to calmly calculated elite policies.

Nordic ones is a chimera. As our analysis of the direction of
trade shows, all the Nordic countries during the two decades
between 1950 and 1970 were becoming more and more dependent on
the similar industrialized economies of Western Europe. Economic independence simply is not possible. However, what is
possible is the decision of a state to retain the political
authority to make the "day-to-day" decisions of directing its own
economy within the constraints of international interdependence.
But to make such a decision, the state needs a reason more potent
than a mere desire to retain formal control over its economy, and
even than the desire to use this means to maintain its political
independence. In fact, as the Nordic countries demonstrate, it
requires the demand of security.

Clearly, as is shown by the review of the three decades of
developments in the security, economic and political fields,
the Nordic countries have been very reluctant to integrate, either
with each other or with Western Eruope, because for all of them
sovereign independence has been the operative objective. Despite
this, considerable *de facto* integration of Nordic economic
systems with the economic system of the EEC has taken place.
Formal integration, however, has been limited to Denmark.

Therefore, the question is: Does the analysis of the three
decades under review indicate that the Nordic countries are
integrating -- with each other and/or with Western Europe? The
answer depends entirely on the definition of the concept of
integration. If integration is defined as a process of community
building through the sharing to a greater or lesser degree of some
values, interests and beliefs, then the Nordic countries are
integrating both with each other and with Western Europe -- and
indeed with the whole world of Western industrialized powers --
because there has been an increasing sharing of values, interests
and beliefs, but in particular of values and interests.[2] Es-

---

[2]Compare Ernst B. Haas, *Beyond the Nation-State* (Stanford
University Press, 1964), p. 29: "I conceive of integration as
referring exclusively to a process that links a given concrete international system with a dimly discernible future concrete
system."

pecially within the Nordic region, common linguistic, cultural,
religious, industrial and organizational features and interests,
and increasing transactions resulting from rapid technological
developments, have produced a very high degree of sharing of most
economic, social and political values -- a very high degree of
economic, social and political integration. This, however, has
not produced any discernible movement, either between 1905 and
the Second World War, or since the Second World War, towards
formal, *de jure* reorganization of the structure of politically or
constitutionally authoritative national community decision making
on a regional non-national community basis. In other words, if
integration is defined as "a process whereby two or more actors
form a new actor"[3] or as "the process whereby political actors in
several distinct national settings are persuaded to shift their
loyalties, expectations and political activities toward a new
centre, whose institutions possess or demand jurisdiction over
the pre-existing national states",[4] or even as "the development
of devices and processes for arriving at collective decisions by
means other than autonomous actions by national governments",[5]
then political integration has not taken place within the Nordic
area. Indeed, as the result of the *de facto* increase in shared
values, interests and beliefs, the Nordic countries -- including
both their elites and their masses -- have become increasingly
aware of their separate identities, and have concluded that these
can only be safeguarded in an increasingly "integrating", interdependent social, economic and political world by the continuing exercise of sovereign independence by their national
parliaments. Hence, for example, the conduct of regional politics in the social, economic and political spheres, by means of

---

[3]Johan Galtung, "A Structural Theory of Integration", *Journal of Peace Research* V: No. 4 (December 1968), p. 377.

[4]Ernst B. Haas, *The Uniting of Europe* (Stanford University Press, 1968 ed.), p. 16.

[5]Leon Lindberg, *The Political Dynamics of European Economic Integration,* Stanford University Press, 1963, p. 5.

the consensualism of the lowest common denominator.

On the question of political integration with Western Europe, the answer is similar. The only difference is that in each case of "integrating" with Europe, the arguments of sovereign independence have been clearly stated, whether in support of a decision not to "integrate" or of a decision to "integrate". And, when a decision to "integrate" has been taken, it has been on the basis of practical necessity, rather than as a matter of community-building, or the idealistic desire to form a new "actor". In each case a minimum of authority, consonant with the perceptions of practical necessity, has been transferred from the national parliament. This was the case when Norway and Denmark joined NATO, and this was the case when Norway decided to enter the EEC -- but did not -- and when Denmark became a full member of the EEC.

It may be concluded then that the three decades since the Second World War have seen a considerable increase in intra-Nordic interactions conducive to community-building, and a similar increase in interaction between the Nordic countries and Western Europe, again conducive to community-building. However, the period has not seen any transfer of authority from the national parliaments to a regional authority in the Nordic area, nor has it seen any willing transfer of authority from a national parliament to any international or supranational authority. What has happened is a minimal transfer -- to NATO in the case of Norway and Denmark, and to the EEC in the case of Denmark -- consonant with the retention of optimal sovereign independence, and given the increasing interdependence of security and economic interests. The desire to conserve the nation in the form of a sovereign independent nation-state has produced not only reluctant Europeans, but reluctant Nordics of the Nordic countries.

APPENDIXES

Appendix I

TABLE I

EXPORTS AS A PERCENTAGE OF GDP

	1950 %	1955 %	1960 %	1965 %	1970 %
Denmark	21.2	25.0	25.5	23.0	22.0
Finland	13.8	20.2	22.5	20.0	23.6
Norway	15.9	20.7	21.4	20.5	23.6
Sweden	20.5	20.9	20.2	19.3	23.1

SOURCES: Compiled from, *UN Yearbook of International Trade Statistics*, 1953, 1956, 1960, 1968, 1971 (Exports) and *UN Yearbook of National Account Statistics*, 1957, 1969, 1970, 1971 (GDP).

TABLE 2a

All Nordic Countries: Exports: *Value by region; percentage share by region; percentage changes by region 1950 to 1970*

	1950		1955		1960		1965		1970		PERCENTAGE CHANGE					
	Millions U.S.$	%	Millions U.S.$	%	Millions U.S.$	%	Millions U.S.$	%	Millions U.S.$	%	1950/55	1955/60	1960/65	1965/70	1950/60	1960/70
World	2550.2	100	4192.3	100	5899.9	100	9115.7	101[2]	14829.4	100	164	141	155	163	231	251
EEC	692.8	27	1185.8	28	1726.4	29	2617.9	29	3817.1	26	171	146	152	146	250	221
EFTA	1023.2	40	1700.9	41	2372.3	40	3879.5	43	6778.7	46	166	139	164	175	232	286
Nordic [1]	380.0	15	607.6	14	1003.4	17	2027.1	22	3453.4	23	160	165	202	170	264	344
U.K. [1]	585.1	23	1004.9	24	1111.6	19	1578.8	17	2311.4	17	172	111	142	146	190	208
U.S. & Canada	160.2	6	269.6	6	445.3	8	689.2	8	1078.0	16	168	165	155	156	208	242
East Europe	196.1	8	329.5	8	408.7	7	548.0	6	874.0	6	168	124	134	159	208	214
Rest of world	477.9	19	706.5	17	947.2	16	1381.1	15	2281.6	15	148	134	145	165	211	240

TABLE 2b

All Nordic Countries: Imports: *Value by region; percentage share by region; percentage changes by region 1950 to 1970*

	1950 Millions U.S. $	%	1955 Millions U.S. $	%	1960 Millions U.S. $	%	1965 Millions U.S. $	%	1970 Millions U.S. $	%	PERCENTAGE CHANGE 1950/55	1955/60	1960/65	1965/70	1950/60	1960/70
World	3098.7	101[2]	5022.8	100	7192.2	100	11041.1	101[2]	17728.0	100	162	143	154	161	232	246
EEC	792.3	26	1738.7	35	2702.0	38	3794.9	34	5460.9	31	219	155	140	144	341	202
EFTA	1183.9	38	1663.9	33	2306.7	32	3836.9	35	7119.8	40	141	139	166	186	195	309
Nordic[1]	402.2	13	628.2	13	873.7	12	1952.1	18	3937.7	22	156	139	223	202	217	451
U.K.[1]	637.8	21	915.5	18	1057.8	15	1504.6	14	2408.1	14	144	116	142	160	166	228
U.S. & Canada	302.4	10	484.6	10	821.3	11	1049.7	10	1611.9	9	160	169	128	154	272	196
East Europe	211.2	7	375.8	7	468.3	7	614.0	6	985.8	6	178	125	131	161	222	211
Rest of World	608.9	20	759.8	15	893.9	12	1745.6	16	2549.6	14	125	118	195	146	147	285

[1] Percentages for 1950, 1955, 1960, 1965, 1970 are of World Imports and Exports respectively.

[2] Percentages total more than 100 as a result of rounding to nearest full percentage point.

SOURCES: Compiled from UN Yearbook of International Trade Statistics 1953, 1956, 1960, 1968, 1971.

TABLE 3a

DENMARK: EXPORTS: *Value by region; percentage distribution by region; percentage change by region 1950 to 1970*

	1950		1955		1960		1965		1970		PERCENTAGE CHANGE					
	Millions U.S. $	%	Millions U.S. $	%	Millions U.S. $	%	Millions U.S. $	%	Millions U.S. $	%	1950/55	1955/60	1960/65	1965/70	1950/60	1960/70
World	665.9	99[3]	1041.5	101[2]	1463.3	100	2273.2	101[2]	3285.2	100	156	141	155	145	220	225
EEC	175.6	26	299.1	29	411.1	28	621.7	27	680.9	21	170	137	151	110	234	166
EFTA	386.1	58	517.0	50	649.4	44	1059.0	47	1632.7	50	134	126	163	154	168	251
Nordic[1]	86.5	13	145.9	14	224.1	15	464.7	20	864.0	26	169	154	207	186	259	386
U.K.[1]	279.3	42	347.8	33	393.0	27	507.1	22	621.6	19	125	113	129	123	141	158
U.S.& Canada	13.4	2	67.2	6	145.8	10	176.9	8	290.0	9	502	217	121	164	1088	199
East Europe	16.2	2	36.9	4	59.9	4	84.3	4	113.7	3	228	162	141	135	370	190
Rest of World	74.6	11	121.3	12	197.1	14	331.3	15	567.9	17	163	163	168	171	264	288

TABLE 3b

DENMARK: IMPORTS: Value by region; percentage distribution by region; percentage change by region 1950 to 1970

	1950 Millions U.S.$	1950 %	1955 Millions U.S.$	1955 %	1960 Millions U.S.$	1960 %	1965 Millions U.S.$	1965 %	1970 Millions U.S.$	1970 %	1950/55	1955/60	1960/65	1965/70	1950/60	1960/70
World	853.8	100	1173.0	101[2]	1794.9	99[3]	2811.2	101[2]	3800.1	99[3]	137	153	157	156	210	244
EEC	228.2	27	443.9	38	707.7	39	1000.0	36	1275.1	33	195	159	141	146	310	206
EFTA	419.1	49	490.4	42	686.2	38	1020.2	36	1808.0	41	117	139	149	177	164	263
Nordic[1]	126.9	15	168.3	14	272.7	14	549.9	20	1001.6	23	133	162	202	182	215	367
U.K.[1]	269.0	32	293.2	25	341.8	25	374.0	13	609.0	14	109	117	109	163	127	178
U.S. & Canada	79.3	9	94.4	9	178.2	10	249.7	9	350.3	8	119	189	140	140	225	197
East Europe	39.9	5	44.5	4	79.2	4	105.2	4	147.4	3	112	178	133	140	199	186
Rest of World[1]	87.3	10	99.8	10	143.6	8	455.1	16	622.1	14	114	144	317	137	165	433

[1] Percentages for 1950, 1955, 1960, 1965, 1970 are of World Imports and Exports respectively.
[2] Column totals more than 100% as a result of rounding individual percentages to nearest percentage point.
[3] Column totals less than 100% as a result of rounding individual percentages to nearest percentage point.

SOURCES: Compiled from UN Yearbook of International Trade Statistics 1953, 1956, 1960, 1968, 1971.

TABLE 4a

NORWAY: EXPORTS: *Value by region; percentage distribution by region; percentage change by region 1950 to 1970*

	1950		1955		1960		1965		1970		PERCENTAGE CHANGE					
	Millions U.S. $	%	Millions U.S. $	%	Millions U.S. $	%	Millions U.S. $	%	Millions U.S. $	%	1950/55	1955/60	1960/65	1965/70	1950/60	1960/70
World	390.2	101²	634.5	101²	880.8	100	1442.6	101²	2457.0	100	165	139	164	170	226	279
EEC	105.0	27	153.0	24	226.2	26	361.1	25	730.3	30	146	148	160	202	215	323
EFTA	143.5	37	258.5	41	400.1	45	645.8	45	1134.9	46	180	135	161	176	279	284
Nordic[1]	63.7	16	107.0	17	180.1	20	357.9	25	634.6	26	168	164	199	177	283	352
U.K.[1]	70.7	18	137.2	22	199.1	23	256.8	18	440.2	18	194	145	129	171	287	221
U.S. & Canada	39.7	10	60.6	10	64.3	7	137.6	10	153.5	6	153	106	214	112	162	239
East Europe	21.9	6	37.7	6	40.6	5	51.3	4	60.6	3	172	108	126	118	185	149
Rest of World	80.1	21	124.7	20	149.6	17	246.8	17	377.7	15	134	120	165	153	187	252

TABLE 4b

NORWAY: IMPORTS: *Value by region; percentage distribution by region; percentage change by region 1950 to 1970*

	1950 Millions U.S. $	%	1955 Millions U.S. $	%	1960 Millions U.S. $	%	1965 Millions U.S. $	%	1970 Millions U.S. $	%	PERCENTAGE CHANGE 1950/55	1955/60	1960/65	1965/70	1950/60	1960/70
World	678.5	100	1089.4	101[2]	1461.3	99[3]	2205.7	101[2]	3702.0	100	161	134	151	168	215	253
EEC	123.3	18	301.5	28	480.7	33	643.9	29	919.8	25	245	159	134	143	390	191
EFTA	290.1	43	469.1	43	559.4	38	924.6	42	1645.7	45	162	119	165	178	193	294
Nordic[1]	129.6	19	232.4	19	306.1	21	600.7	27	1062.8	29	179	78	334	177	139	590
U.K.[1]	150.2	22	218.2	20	219.3	15	266.4	12	455.9	12	309	91	134	171	282	229
U.S. & Canada	94.8	14	137.4	13	193.9	13	237.4	11	444.3	12	145	141	122	187	205	229
East Europe	32.6	5	39.4	4	46.9	3	62.1	3	82.2	2	121	119	132	132	144	175
Rest of World	137.7	20	142.0	13	180.4	12	337.7	15	610.0	16	103	127	187	181	131	338

[1] Percentages for 1950, 1955, 1960, 1965, 1970 are of World Imports and Exports respectively.

[2] Column totals more than 100% as a result of rounding individual percentages to nearest percentage point.

[3] Column totals less than 100% as a result of rounding individual percentages to nearest percentage point.

SOURCES: Compiled from *UN Yearbook of International Trade Statistics* 1953, 1956, 1960, 1968, 1971.

TABLE 5a

SWEDEN: EXPORTS: *Value by region; percentage distribution by region; percentage change by region 1950 to 1970*

	1950		1955		1960		1965		1970		PERCENTAGE CHANGE					
	Millions U.S.$	%	Millions U.S.$	%	Millions U.S.$	%	Millions U.S.$	%	Millions U.S.$	%	1950/55	1955/60	1960/65	1965/70	1950/60	1960/70
World	1102.5	101[2]	1728.2	101[2]	2566.9	101[2]	3973.1	100	6780.8	100	157	149	155	171	233	264
EEC	321.9	29	555.8	32	811.8	32	1234.9	31	1869.8	28	173	146	152	151	252	230
EFTA	369.4	34	687.1	40	989.5	39	1691.5	43	3014.5	44	186	144	171	178	268	305
Nordic[1]	186.0	17	308.5	18	509.4	20	1023.5	26	1826.2	27	166	165	201	178	274	359
U.K.[1]	156.9	14	337.1	20	410.3	16	527.5	13	847.3	12	215	122	129	161	262	207
U.S. & Canada	73.6	7	96.4	6	185.3	7	286.4	7	503.9	7	131	192	155	176	252	272
East Europe	78.3	7	64.0	4	119.2	5	132.2	3	338.3	5	82	186	111	105	152	284
Rest of World	259.3	24	324.9	19	461.1	18	628.1	16	1054.3	16	125	142	136	168	178	229

TABLE 5b

SWEDEN: IMPORTS: *Value by region; percentage distribution by region; percentage change by region 1950 to 1970*

	1950 Millions U.S.$	%	1955 Millions U.S.$	%	1960 Millions U.S.$	%	1965 Millions U.S.$	%	1970 Millions U.S.$	%	PERCENTAGE CHANGE 1950/55	1955/60	1960/65	1965/70	1950/60	1960/70
WORLD	1178.8	100	1991.0	99[3]	2876.1	100	4378.5	101[2]	7004.1	101[2]	169	145	152	160	244	244
EEC	341.6	29	824.5	41	1154.0	40	1643.3	38	2375.6	34	241	140	142	145	338	206
EFTA	350.1	30	482.5	24	742.9	26	1424.1	33	2637.4	38	138	154	192	185	212	355
Nordic[1]	89.4	8	148.4	8	273.5	10	609.9	14	1308.7	19	166	184	223	215	306	479
U.K.[1]	234.6	20	272.6	14	375.9	13	642.7	15	996.8	14	116	138	171	155	160	265
U.S.& Canada	105.1	9	205.6	10	377.3	13	453.1	10	668.4	10	196	184	121	148	359	177
East Europe	73.9	6	87.0	4	126.8	4	157.5	4	330.9	5	118	146	124	210	172	261
Rest of World	308.1	26	391.4	20	475.1	20	700.5	16	991.8	14	127	121	147	142	154	209

[1] *Percentages for 1950, 1955, 1960, 1965, 1970 are of World Imports and Exports respectively.*

[2] *Column totals more than 100% as a result of rounding individual percentages to nearest percentage point.*

[3] *Column totals less than 100% as a result of rounding individual percentages to nearest percentage point.*

SOURCES: Compiled from UN Yearbook of International Trade Statistics 1953, 1956, 1960, 1966, 1971.

TABLE 6a

FINLAND: EXPORTS: Value by region; percentage distribution by region; percentage change by region 1950 to 1970

	1950 Millions U.S.$	%	1955 Millions U.S.$	%	1960 Millions U.S.$	%	1965 Millions U.S.$	%	1970 Millions U.S.$	%	PERCENTAGE CHANGE 1950/55	1955/60	1960/65	1965/70	1950/60	1960/70
World	391.6	100	788.1	100	988.9	100	1426.8	100	2306.4	100	201	126	144	162	253	233
EEC	90.3.0	23	177.9	23	277.3	28	400.2	28	536.1	23	197	156	144	134	307	193
EFTA	124.2	32	238.3	30	333.3	34	483.2	34	996.6	43	192	140	145	206	268	299
Nordic[1]	43.8	11	46.2	6	89.8	9	181.0	13	527.9	23	106	194	202	292	205	588
U.K.[1]	78.2	20	182.8	23	235.8	24	287.4	20	402.3	17	234	129	122	140	302	171
U.S.& Canada	33.5	9	45.4	6	49.9	5	88.3	6	130.6	6	136	110	177	148	149	262
East Europe	79.7	20	190.9	24	189.0	19	280.2	20	361.4	16	240	99	148	129	237	191
Rest of World	63.9	16	135.6	17	139.4	14	174.9	12	281.7	12	212	103	126	161	218	202

TABLE 6b

FINLAND: IMPORTS: *Value by region; percentage distribution by region; percentage change by region 1950 to 1970*

	1950		1955		1960		1965		1970		PERCENTAGE CHANGE					
	Millions U.S. $	%	Millions U.S. $	%	Millions U.S. $	%	Millions U.S. $	%	Millions U.S. $	%	1950/55	1955/60	1960/65	1965/70	1950/60	1960/70
World	387.6	101[2]	769.4	101[2]	1059.9	100	1645.7	101[2]	2637.3	100	199	138	155	160	274	249
EEC	99.2	26	168.8	22	359.6	34	507.7	31	708.7	27	140	213	141	140	363	197
EFTA	124.6	32	221.9	29	318.2	30	564.3	34	1028.7	39	178	143	177	182	255	323
Nordic[1]	56.3	15	79.1	10	147.4	14	287.9	18	564.6	21	141	186	145	196	262	383
U.K.[1]	63.5	16	131.5	17	141.0	13	221.5	14	346.4	13	207	107	157	156	222	246
U.S. & Canada	23.2	6	47.2	6	71.9	7	109.5	7	148.9	6	203	152	152	136	310	207
East Europe	64.8	17	204.9	27	215.4	20	289.2	18	425.3	16	316	105	134	147	332	197
Rest of World	75.8	20	126.6	17	94.8	9	175.0	11	325.7	12	167	75	185	186	125	344

[1] Percentages for 1950, 1955, 1960, 1970 are of World Imports and Exports respectively.

[2] Column totals more than 100% as a result of rounding individual percentages to nearest percentage point.

SOURCES: Compiled from UN *Yearbook of International Trade Statistics* 1953, 1956, 1960, 1968, 1971.

APPENDIX II

Resolution adopted at the Ministerial meeting of the Seven in
     Stockholm; 19th - 20th November, 1959.

The existence of two groups, the European Free Trade Association and the European Economic Community, inspired by different
but not incompatible principles, implies the risk that further
progress along these lines be hampered if such a danger could
not be avoided by an agreement to which all countries interested
in European economic cooperation could subscribe.

Such an agreement, based on the principle of reciprocity,
should not cause any damage to the measures taken by the European Free Trade Association and the European Economic Community.
Moreover, it should allow member States of either organisation
to eliminate in common the obstacles to trade between them, and
more generally, to seek to solve the problems they share.
Among those, there is the problem of aiding the less developed
countries in Europe and in other continents, which is one of the
foremost tasks of the more advanced countries.

Common action in these fields would strengthen the already
existing bonds between the European countries as well as the
solidarity arising from their common destiny, even if their
views on the way in which European integration should be
achieved are not always identical.

For these reasons, the seven Governments who will sign the
Convention establishing the European Free Trade Association,
declare their determination to do all in their power to avoid
a new division in Europe. They regard their Association as a
step towards an agreement between all Member countries of OEEC.

To this end the seven Governments are ready to initiate
negotiations with the members of the EEC as soon as they are
prepared to do so. Meanwhile views should be exchanged through
diplomatic channels or in any other way, on the basis upon which
such negotiations may profitably be opened.

SELECT BIBLIOGRAPHY

1. GENERAL

A. Official publications:

European Free Trade Association:

EFTA Secretariat, *The Stockholm Convention Examined.* Geneva, 1963.

Agreement creating an association between the member states of the EFTA and the Republic of Finland. Geneva, May 1964.

Agricultural agreements between the EFTA Countries. Geneva, January 1966.

Jantzen, Torben (Trade Policy Dept., EFTA), *The operation of a free trade area.* Geneva, 1965.

Green, S.A., and K.W.B. Gabriel (EFTA), *The Rules of Origin.* Geneva, 1965.

Annual review of agricultural trade. Geneva, annual.

Annual Reports. Geneva, annual.

International Labour Organization:

Yearbook of Labour Statistics. Geneva, annual.

Nordic Council:

Nordisk Kontakt (Parliamentary review), approximately 12-15 issues a year during the parliamentary session.

Nordisk Undredningsserie (NU) [Nordic Report Series]. Over 200 publications in Danish, Norwegian and Swedish, since 1960, appearing at a rate of 20 - 23 per year during the 1970s. Stockholm.

Nytt från Nordiska Rådet. A compilation of excerpts from the Nordic press concerning Nordic matters. Appeared between 1960 and 1968. Since discontinued.

Yearbook of Nordic Statistics. Stockholm annual.

Organization for Economic Co-operation and Development:

OECD Economic Surveys, Denmark. Paris, annual.

OECD Economic Surveys, Finland. Paris, annual.

OECD Economic Surveys, Norway. Paris, annual.

OECD Economic Surveys, Sweden. Paris, annual.

The growth of output 1960-1980. Retrospect, Prospect and Problems of Policy. Paris, December 1970.

United Nations:

Yearbook of International Trade Statistics. New York, annual.

Yearbook of National Accounts. New York, annual.

B Periodicals:

Danish Association for Foreign Affairs, *Fremtiden*, monthly.

Finnish Political Science Association, *Politiikka*, quarterly.

Nordic Committee for the Study of International Politics, *Cooperation and Conflict*, quarterly.

Norwegian Institute of International affairs, *Internasjonal Politikk*, quarterly.

Norwegian Institute of International Affairs, *Nupi-Notat*. Irregular series of mimeographed reports and articles. Oslo.

Paasikivi Society, *Ulkopolitiikka-Utrikespolitik*, quarterly.

Political Science Associations in Denmark, Finland, Norway and Sweden, *Scandinavian Political Studies*, annual.

Swedish Institute of International Affairs, *Världspolitikens Dagsfrågor*, monthly.

C. Books and articles:

Alcock, W.J., "The Evolution of Scandinavian Foreign and Defence Policies, 1919-1969": Unpublished thesis. Kings College, University of London, 1971-2.

Anderson, Stanley, U., *The Nordic Council, A study of Scandinavian Regionalism*. Seattle, University of Washington Press, 1967.

Atlantic Treaty Association, *The Soviets and Northern Europe*. Paris, 1971.

Bjøl, Erling, *Internationell Politik* [International Politics]. Stockholm, 1968.

Bjøl, Erling, *Öst-Västkonflikten* [The East-West Conflict]. Stockholm, 1971.

Herlitz, Nils, *Nordisk folk-styrelse* [Nordic Self-rule]. Stockholm, Föreningarna Nordens Förbund, 1972.

Kleppe, Per, *EFTA-Nordek-EEC*. Stockholm, 1972.

Lagerkvist, M. and O. Kleberg, *Ekonomi och politik i Europa* [The Economics and politics of Europe]. Stockholm, 1972.

Miljan, Toivo, "The Nordic Countries: Europe's Reluctant Partners" in Peter Stingelin, *The European Community and the Outsiders*. Toronto, 1973.

"Nato and European Security". *Orbis*, Vol XIII (Spring 1969): Nr. 1. Special Issue.

The Scandinavian Market, 1971. Copenhagen, 1971.

Saeter, Martin, *Det Politiske Europa* [Political Europe]. Oslo, 1971.

Wendt, Frantz, *The Nordic Council and Cooperation in Scandinavia*. Copenhagen, 1959.

2. DENMARK

A. Government Publications

Ministry of Foreign Affairs. The Economic secretariat. *Danmark og de Europaeiske Markedsplaner* [Denmark and the European Market Plans]
Nr. 1 - Markedsplaner og erhvervsudvikling inderfor industrivaereområdet
       [Market plans and economic development in the industrial sector]
Nr. 2 - Afsaetningsforholdene for landbrugseksporten
       [Alternatives for agricultural exports]
Nr. 3 - Problemer verdrørende arbejdsmarkedet og socialpolitikken
       [Problems concerning the labour market and social policy]
Nr. 4 - Konkurrenceforhold og monopolkontrol
       [Competition and monopoly controls]
Nr. 5 - Adgang til erhvervsudøvelse
       [Towards economic development].
       Copenhagen, 1958.

Ministry of Foreign Affairs, Committee on Denmark's relations with the European Communities. *Danmark og de Europaeiske Faellesskaber* [Danmark and the European Communities],
Vol I, 1968.
Vol II, 1968.
Supplement 1, 1969.
Supplement 2, 1970.
Supplement 3, 1971.
Supplement 4, 1972.

Det Økonomiske Råd: Formandskabet [Economic Council: Presidium], *Markedsperspektiver og Strukturporblemer* [Market perspectives and structural problems]. Copenhagen, October 1971.

Ministry of Foreign Affairs. *Redegørelse for resultatet af Forhandlingerne om Danmarks medlemskab i Faellesskaber* [Report of the results of negotiations on Denmark's membership in the Communities]. December 1971.

Ministry of Foreign Affaris, *Economic Survey of Denmark.* Copenhagen, annual.

B. Books, pamphlets and articles

Brixtofte, Peter (ed), *Facts om Faellesmarkedet* [Facts about the Common Market]. Holte, Ef-Forlaget, 1971.

Dansk Arbejdsgiverforening. [Federation of Danish Employers], *Arbejdsgiverne og EF* [The Employers and the EEC]. Copenhagen, 1972.

Dansk Smede- og Maskin-arbeiderforbund [Danish Smiths' and Machinists' Union], *Skal Danmark ind i faellessmarkedet?* Should Denmark enter the Common Market?]. Copenhagen, 1972.

Fischer, Jean, et al., *En piece om Faellesmakedet: EEC - et barn av borgerskabet* [A story about the Common Market: EEC - a child of the bourgeoisie]. Copenhagen, 1971.

Gade, Sven Ove, og Koch, Ejlea, *For og imod EF* [For and against the Common Market]. Det Danske Forlag, 1971.

Haagerup, Niels J., *Dansk Sikkerhedspolitik og det Nye Europe* [Danish security policy and the New Europe]. Copenhagen, 1972.

Haagerup Niels J., "Norden i det internationale system: Danske forestillinger og forventninger" [The North in the international system: Danish views and expectations], in Karl E. Birnbaum (ed) *Nordiska Framtids-perspektiv* [Nordic future perspectives]. Stockholm, 1970.

Haagerup, Niels J., "Norden, Nato og Europa: et dansk synspunkt" [The North, NATO and Europe: a Danish viewpoint] in *Norden, NATO og Europa* [The North, NATO and Europe]. Aarhus, 1969.

Haagerup, Niels J., *Europa og NATO, Faellesmarkedet og sikkerhedspolitikken* [Europe and NATO, The Common Market and security policy]. Copenhagen, 1971.

Haagerup, Niels J., "Réactions Scandinaves à la Politique Atlantique du Président de Gaulle, *Politique Etrangère*, 1966:3, pp 237-72.

Haagerup, Niels J., "Denmark's Security Policy", *Survival*, May 1971, pp 172-8.

Haagerup, Niels J., "Dänemark und Norwegen vor der Enscheidung über den EWG-Beitritt", *Uropa-Archiv*, 1972:17, pp 601-8.

Haekkerup, Per, "Europe: Basic Problems and Perspectives", *International Affairs*, Vol 41, No. 1 (1968), pp 1-10.

Haekkerup, Per, *Danmarks Udenrigspolitik* [Denmark's foreign policy]. Copenhagen, 1965.

Haekkerup, Per, "Denmark's Foreign Policy", *The American-Scandinavian Review*, Liv, Dec. 1966.

Hansen, Peter, "Denmark and European Integration", *Cooperation and Conflict*, Vol 4 (1969), pp 13-46.

Hansen, Peter, "Die Formulierung der dänischen Europapolitik", *Österreichische Zeitschrift für Aussenpolitik*, 1973:1, pp. 3-31.

Hansen, Peter, Nikolaj Petersen and K.W. Redder, *Foreign Policy Attitudes in the Danish Population. Working Paper No. 4*, Questionnaire with Marginals. Aarhus 1973.

Heurlin, Bertel (ed), *Danmarks udenrigspolitik efter 1945*, Kilder til belysning af Danmarks udenrigspolitiske mål [Denmark's foreign policy goals]. Copenhagen 1970.

Landbrugsraadet [The Agricultural Council], *Faellesmarkedet i en nøddeskal* [The Common Market in balance]. July, 1971.

Landsorganisationen i Danmark [Federation of Labour Unions], *Danmark og ECC* [Denmark and the EEC]. 1971.

Landsorganisationen I Danmark, *Rapport*. Landsorganisationens foretningsutvalgets besøg i Bruxells 29 november - 2 december 1971 [Report. The visit of the business committee of the LO to Brussels 2 November - 2 December 1971].

Lykketoft, Mogens (ed)., *Magtspil og sikkerhed* [Power play and security]. Copenhagen, 1968.

Nielsson, Gunnar Prebar, "Denmark and European Integration: A small Country at the Crossroads", University of California, 1966: Unpublished Ph.D. dissertation. On file at University Microfilms, Ann Arbor.

Olsen, Ole, *Dansk Økonomi og EF* [The Danish economy and the Common Market]. Dragør, Forlaget Prometheus, 1972.

Ørvik, Nils, and Niels J. Haagerup, *The Scandinavian Members of NATO. Adelphi Papers*, No. 23 (1965).

3. FINLAND

A. Government Publications

Bank of Finland, *Monthly Bulletin*. Helsinki, monthly.

Bank of Finland, *Financial Markets in Finland*. A series of Articles which appeared in the Bank of Finland Monthly Bulletin in 1970-72. Helsinki, 1972.

Bank of Finland, Institute for Economic Research, *Economic Indicators for Finland*. Helsinki, quarterly.

Commission for Foreign Investment in collaboration with the Bank of Finland, *Establishing a Business in Finland*, n.d.

Ministry of Finance, Economic Department, *Economic Survey of Finland*. Helsinki, annual.

Ministry of Finance, Economic Department, *National Budget for 1968 for Finland (summary)*. Helsinki, 1968 and annually.

Ministry for Foreign Affairs, *Documents concerning conference on European Security and Cooperation*. Helsinki, 1973.

Taloudellinen Suunnitteelukeskus [Economic Planning Centre], *Suomen kansantalouden kehitysmahdollisuudet vuoteen 1980*. Also published in English, *Growth Prospects for the Finnish Economy up to 1980*. Helsinki, 1973.

Ulkoasianministeriö [Ministry for Foreign Affairs], *Ulkopoliittisia Lausuntoja ja Asiakirjoja* [Statements and Documents on Foreign Policy]. Helsinki, annual.

Ulkoasianministeriö, *Yhdistyneiden Kansakuntien Yleiskokouksen toimintaan* [The United Nations General Assembly Report]. Helsinki, annual.

Ministry for Foreign Affairs, *Finnish Features*. Press releases, statements and speeches. Helsinki, irregular.

B. Books, periodicals and periodicals articles

Anckar, Dag, *Om riksdagsmännens utrikespolitiska debattaktivitet* [Concerning the foreign policy debating activities of Members of Parliament]. Åbo, 1968.

Anckar, Dag. "Finnish Foreign Policy Debate: The Saimaa Canal Case", *Cooperation and Conflict*, 1970:4.

306

Anckar, Dag, *Partiopinioner och utrikespolitik* [Party opinions, and foreign pqlicy], *Acta Academiae Aboensis*, Ser A., Vol 41. Åbo Akademi, Abo, 1971.

Apunen, Osmo, *Neutral European Countries and European Security*. INFO-UI:n julk-sarja 27/1971.

Blomberg, J. and P. Joenniemi, *Kaksiteräinen miekka. 70 - luvûn puolustus politiikkaa* [The two-edged sword. Defense policy in the seventies]. Helsinki, 1971.

von Bonsdorff, Göran, *Faktorer av betydelse för Finlands relationer till Sovjetunionen* [Important factors in Finland's relations with the Soviet Union]. *Ulkopoliittinen instituutti Sovjetologisia tutkimuksia*, 1968:4. Helsinki, 1968.

von Bonsdorff, Göran, *Finlands politik after kriget* [Finnish policy after the war]. *Världspolitikens dagsfrågor*, 1950:9. Helsinki, 1950.

von Bonsdorff, Göran, *Suomen ja Neuvostoliiton suhteet toisen maailmansodan jälkeen* [Finnish-Soviet relations after the Second World War]. *Neuvostoliittoinstituutin vuosikirja*, No. 22 (1971). Helsinki, 1971.

Brodin, Katarina, *Finland 1956-1966*. Utrikespolitiska Institutet, Stockholm, 1966.

Brodin, Katarina, *Finlands utrikespolitiska doktrin*: En innehållsanalys av Paasikivis och Kekkonens uttalanden åren 1944-1969 [Finland's foreign policy doctrine: A content analysis of Paasikivis and Kekkonens speeches 1944-1969]. Stockholm, 1969.

Brodin, Katarina, *Finlands Utrikespolitiska Doktrin* [Finland's foreign policy doctrine]. Swedish Studies in International Relations 2. Stockholm, 1971.

Finnish Political Science Association, *Finnish Foreign Policy*. Studies in foreign policy. Helsinki, 1963.

Finnish Political Science Association, *Essays on Finnish Foreign Policy*. Vammala, 1969.

Gripenberg, G.A., *Neutralitetstanken i Finlands politik* [The concept of neutrality in Finnish policy]. Orebro, 1960.

Hagalehto, Ilkka (ed), *Suomen ulkopolitiikan kehityslinjat 1809-1966* [Trends in Finnish foreign policy 1809-1966]. Porvoo, 1968.

Hakovirta, Harto, "The Finnish Security Problem", *Cooperation and Conflict*, 1969:4.

Hakovirta, Harto, *Suomen turvallisuus-politiikkaa* [Finnish neutrality policy]. Helsinki, 1971.

Halsti, Wolf H., *Suomen puolustus-kysymys* [Finland's defence in question]. Helsinki, 1954.

Halsti, Wolf H., *Me, Venäjä ja muut* [We, the Russians and others]. Helsinki, 1969.

Heikkila, Raimo, *Finland, the Land of Cooperatives*. Institute of Cooperation, University of Helsinki, 1963.

307

Hyvärinen, Risto, "Finland's foreign policy" in *Finland in Focus, 1966*. Helsinki, 1966; and in *Introduction to Finland*. Porvoo, 1963.

Jakobson, Max, *Finnish Neutrality*. Finnish foreign policy since WW II. London, 1968.

Jansson, J-M, (ed), *Studier i finländsk politik* [Studies in Finnish politics]. Stockholm, 1968.

Julkunen, Martti (ed), *Suomi ja muuttuva Eurooppa* [Finland and a changing Europe]. Rauma, 1970.

Junnila, Tuure, *Noottikriisi tuoreeltaan tulkittuna* [An interpretation of the Note crisis while it is still fresh]. Porvoo, 1962.

Kallas, Hillar and Sylvie Nickels (eds), *Finland: Creation and Construction*. Helsinki, 1968.

Kansallis-Osake-Pankki, *Kansallis-Osake-Pankin Kuukausikatsaus* [Kansallis-Osake Bank's monthly review]. Helsinki, monthly.

Kare, Kauko, *Tähän on tultu* [We have come this far]. Helsinki, 1967.

Kare, Kauko, *Tähän on tultu 2:* Paasikivenlinjalta Kekkosen kolmanteen [We have come this far 2: From the Paasikivi line to the Kekkonen approach]. Helsinki, 1969.

Kekkonen, Urho, *För fosterlandet*. Tal och artiklar 1938-1955 [For the fatherland. Speeches and articles 1939-1955]. Helsingfors, 1955.

Kekkonen, Urho, *Puheita ja kirjoituksia I*. Puheita vuosilta 1936-1956 [Speeches and articles I. Speeches 1936-1956]. Helsinki, 1967.

Kekkonen, Urho, *Puheita ja kirjoituksia II*. Puheita presidenttikaudelta 1956-1967 [Speeches and articles II. Presidential speeches 1956-1967]. Helsinki, 1968.

Kekkonen, Urho, *Brobygga*. Tal 1943-1968 [Bridge-building. Speeches 1943-1968]. Stockholm, 1970.

Kekkonen, Urho, *Neutrality: The Finnish position*. Speeches. London, 1970.

Killenen, Kullervo, *Kansallinen etu ja kansainvälinen kehitys* [National interest and international development]. Helsinki, 1967.

Loikkanen, Jouko, *K-linja* [K-line]. Helsinki, 1967.

Luoto, Reima (ed). *Suomen turvallisuuspolitiikan perusteet* [The foundations of Finnish security policy]. Tampere, 1972.

Määttänen, Sakari, *Tapaus Jakobson* [The Jakobson episode]. Helsinki, 1973.

Nousiainen, Jaakko, *Suomen poliittinen järjestelma* [The political structure of Finland]. Helsinki, 1959.

Ørvik, Nils, *Sicherheit auf Finnisch*. Stuttgart, 1972.

Paasikivi, J.K., *I Puheita vuosilta 1944-1956* (I speeches from 1944-1956]. Helsinki, 1962.

Pajunen, Aimo, "Finlands Säkerhetspolitik" [Finlands security policy], *Strategisk bulletin*, 1967:4.

La politique extérieure de la Finlande. Notes et études documentaires, 26 novembre 1971. La Documentation française. Paris, 1971.

Puntila, L.A., Suomen polittiinen historia [Finnish political history]. Helsinki, 1971.

Puntila, L.A., Finlands Politiska Historia 1809-1966 [Finland's political history 1809-1966]. Helsinki, 1972.

Repo, Eino (ed), Urho Kekkonen: Människan och statsman [Urho Kekkonen: the man and the statesman]. Helsingfors, 1960.

Salonen, Ahti, M., Linjat [The line]. Helsinki, 1972.

Törnudd, Klaus, Suomi ja Yhdistyneet kansakunnat [Finland and the United Nations]. Helsinki, 1967.

Törnudd, Klaus, The Electoral System of Finland, London, 1968.

Wahlbäck, Krister, Från Mannerheim till Kekkonen. Huvudlinjer i finländsk politik 1917-1967 [From Mannerheim to Kekkonen. The main lines of Finnish politics 1917-1967]. Stockholm, 1967.

Warner, Oliver, Marshal Mannerheim and the Finns. Helsinki, 1967.

Vanttinen O. (ed), Itsenäinen Suomi-Puolueeton Pohjola. Poimintoja lehdistökeskustelusta Suomessa, Ruotsissa ja Norjassa [Independent Finland - neutral North. Extracts from newspaper articles in Finland, Sweden and Norway]. Helsinki, 1967.

Väyrynen, Raimo, "A Case Study of Sanctions: Finland - The Soviet Union in 1958-59", Cooperation and Conflict, 1969:3.

Väyrynen, Raimo, Conflicts in Finnish - Soviet Relations: Three Comparative Case Studies. Acta Universitatis Tamperensis, Ser A. Vol 47. Tampere, 1972.

Väyrynen, Raimo, EEC ja ulkopolitiikka [The EEC and foreign policy]. Helsinki, 1973.

4. NORWAY

A. Official Statements and Documents

Parliamentary documents on foreign economic cooperation etc.:

St. meld. nr. 11 (1951) [Report to Parliament] Norges deltakelse i Organisasjonen for europeisk samarbeid (O.E.E.C.) fra april 1948 til utgangen av 1950. [Norway's participation in the OEEC from April 1948 to the end of 1950].

St. prp. nr. 75 (1959-60) [Government bill]. Om samtykke til ratifikasjon av konvensjonen av Det Europeiske Frihandelsforbund med tilknyttet protokoll. [Concerning the ratification of EFTA, with appended protocols].

St. meld. nr. 15 (1961-62). Om Det Europeiske Økonomiske Fellesskap og de europeiske markedsproblemer [On the European Economic Communities and European market problems].

Appendixes to St. meld. nr. 15 (1961-62):

Uttalelser og utredninger vedrørende Norges stilling til de europeiske markedsproblemer, Tillegg I til St. meld. nr. 15 for 1961-62. [Speeches and reports concerning Norway's position on the European market problems. Appendix I to St. meld. nr. 15 for 1961-62].

Oversikter og utredninger vedrørende de europeiske markedsproblemer, Tillegg II til St. meld. nr. 15 for 1961-62. [Perspectives and elucidations concerning European market problems]. [Appendix II to St. meld. nr. 15 for 1961-62].

Tillegg III til St. meld. nr. 15 for 1961-62. [Appendix III to St. meld. nr. 15 for 1961-62]:
   1. *Det Europeiske Økonomiske Fellesskap og tredjeland* [The EEC and third countries.
   2. *Ministerrådets vedtak av 14. januar 1962 om overgang til annen etappe* of the Council of Ministers of 14 January 1962 regarding the transition to the second phase].
   3. *Brev av 15. februar 1962 fra Norsk Bonde- og Småbrukarlag til Stortingets og konstitusjonskomite* [Letter of 15 February 1962 from the Norwegian Farmers and Small Farmers Association to the Foreign and Constitutional Affairs Committe of Parliament].
   4. *Oversikt over forodninger og vedtak om en felles landbrukspolitikk, godkjent av Ministerrådet i Det Europeiske Økonomiske Fellesskap. 14. januar 1962* [Overview of the regulations and decisions about a common agricultural policy, accepted by the Council of Ministers of the EEC on 14 June 1962].

Viktigere avgjørelser truffet av Ministerrådet i Det Europeiske Økonomiske Felleskap, Tillegg IV til St. meld. nr. 15 for 1961-62 [The most important decisions taken by the Council of Ministers of the EEC. Appendix IV to St. meld. nr. 15 for 1961-62].

St. meld. nr. 67 (1961-62). *Om Norges stilling til Det Europeiske Økonomiske Fellesskap og de europeiske samarbeidsbestrebelser.* [Concerning Norway's position on the European Economic Communities and the European striving for Cooperation].

Stortingets behandling av forslaget til ny paragraf 93 i Grunnoven [Parliament's handling of the proposal to insert a new paragraph 93 in the Constitution]. Contains: 1. Instilling fra utenriks- og konstitusjonskomiteen om forslag til ny paragraf 93 i Grunnloven (Innst. S. nr. 100) [Recommendation from the Foreign and Constitutional Affairs Committee for a new paragraph 93 in the Constitution (Recommendation S. nr. 100)]. 2. Stortingets behandling (debatten) av Innst. S. nr. 100 den 6., 7. og 8 mars 1962 [Parliament's handling (debate) of Recommendation S. nr. 100 on 6,7 and 8 March 1962].

Stortingest behandling av spørsmålet om Norges forhold til Det Europeiske Økonomiske Fellesskap (EEC) [Parliament's handling of the matter of Norway's position on the European Economic Communities (EEC)]. Contains: 1. Instilling fra den utvidede utenriks- og konstitsjonskomite om Norges forhold til Det Europeiske Økonomiske Fellesskap (EEC), Innst. S. nr. 165 [Recommendation from the expanded Foreign and Constitutional Affairs Committee concerning Norway's position on the EEC, Inst. S. nr. 165]; 2. Stortingets behandling (debatten) av. Innst. S. nr. 165 den 25-28 april 1962 [Parliament's handling (debate) of Innst. S. nr. 165 on 25-28 April 1962].

310

St. meld. nr. 33 (1962-63). *Om Norges stilling til Det Europeiske Kull-og Stålfellesskap* (CECA). [Concerning Norway's position on the European Coal and Steel Community (CECA)].

St. meld. nr. 61 (1962-63). *Om utbyggningen av samarbeidet i Det Europeiske Frihandelsforbund* (EFTA). [Concerning the development of cooperation in EFTA].

St. meld. nr. 6 (1963-64). *Om den fortsatte utbyggning av samarbeidet i Det Europeiske Frihandelsforbund* (EFTA). [Concerning further development of cooperation in the EFTA].

St. meld. nr. 47 (1965-66). *Om Norges deltakelse i Organisasjonen for Økonomisk Samarbeid og Utvikling* (OECD). [Concerning Norway's participation in OECD].

St. meld. nr. 33 (1966-67). *Om samarbeidet i Det Europeiske Frihandelsforbund* (EFTA). [Concerning cooperation in EFTA].

St. meld, nr. 86 (1966-67). *Om Norges forhold til de europeiske felless-kap* [Concerning Norway's position on the European Communities].

Innst. S. nr. 289 (1967-67). *Instilling fra utenriks- og konstitusjonskomiteen om Norges forhold til de europeiske fellesskap* (St. meld. nr. 86). [Recommendation from the Foreign and Constitutional Affairs Committee concerning Norway's position on the European Communities.

St. meld. nr. 92 (1969-70). *Om Norges forhold til de nordiske og europeiske mardedsdannelser.* [Concerning Norway's position on the formation of the Nordic and European markets].

Instilling fra utenriks- og konstitusjonskomiteen om Norges forhold til de nordiske og europeiske markedsdannelser (St. meld. nr. 92) [Recommendation from the Foreign and Constitutional Affairs Committee concerning Norway's position on the formation of the Nordic and European markets (St. meld. nr. 92)].

St. meld. nr. 90 (1970-71). *Om Norges forhold til De Europeiske Felless-kap* [Concerning Norway's position on the European Communities].

St. prp. nr. 101 (1970-71). *Om samtykke til ratifikasjon av Avtale om endring av samarbeidsavtalen av 23. mars 1962 mellom Norge, Danmark, Finland, Island og Sverige, undertegnet i København 13 February 1971.* [Concerning ratification of the Treaty to amend the Treaty of Cooperation of 23 March 1962 among Norway, Denmark, Finland, Iceland and Sweden, signed in Copenhagen on 13 February 1971].

St. prp. nr. 113. *Om samtykke til ratifikasjon av en avtal av 15 mars 1971 mellom Norge, Danmark, Finland, Island og Sverige om kulturelt samarbeid.* [Concerning ratification of the treaty of 15 March 1971 among Norway, Denmark, Finland, Iceland and Sweden regarding cultural cooperation].

Ot. prp. nr. 35 (1971-72). *Om lov om folkeavstemning over spørsmålet om Norge bør bli medlem av De Europeiske Fellesskap.* [Concerning the law authorizing a referendum on whether Norway should become a member of the European Communities].

Innst. O. XIV (1971-72). *Instilling fra utenriks- og konstitusjonskomiteen om lov om folkeavstemning over spørsmålet om Norge bør bli medlem av De Europeiske Fellesskap* (Ot. prp. nr. 35) [Recommendation from the Foreign and Constitutional Affairs Committee on the law to authorize the referendum on whether Norway should become a member of the European Countries (Ot. prp. nr. 35)].

Innstilling fra utenriks- og konstitusjonskomiteen om Norges tilslutning til De Europeiske Fellesskap (St. meld. nr. 50) [Recommendation from the Foreign and Constitutional Affairs Committee on Norway's accession to the European Communities].

St. meld. nr. 50 (1971-72). *Om Norges tilslutining til De Europeiske Fellesskap* [Concerning Norway's accession to the European Communities].

Traktat og Beslutning vedrørende Norges, Danmarks, Irlands og Storbritannias tiltredelse til De Europeiske Fellesskap. [Treaty and Regulations concerning Norway's, Denmark's, Iceland's and Great Britain's accession to the European Communities]. Special appendix nr. 1 to St. meld. nr. 50 for 1971-72.

Traktat om opprettelse av Det Europeiske Atomenergifellesskap (EURATOM). [Treaty establishing the European Nuclear Energy Community (EURATOM)]. Special appendix nr. 3 to St. meld. nr. 60 for 1971-72.

Traktat om opprettelse av Det Europeiske Kull- og Stålfellesskap [Treaty establishing the European Coal and Steel Community]. Special appendix nr. 1 to St. meld. nr. 50 for 1971-72.

Traktat om opprettelse av ett felles Råd og en felles Kommisjon for De Europeiske Fellesskap. [Treaty establishing a common Council and Commission for the European Communities]. Special appendix nr. 5 to St. meld. nr. 50 for 1971-72.

Traktat om endring av visse budsjettbestemmelser i traktatene om opprettelse av De Europeiske Fellesskap. [Treaty amending some budget regulations in the treaties establishing the European Communities]. Special appendix nr. 6 to St. meld. nr. 50 for 1971-72.

St. prp. nr. 126 (1972-73). *Om samtykke til ratifikasjon av Avtale mellom Norge og Det Europeiske Økonomiske Fellesskap og Avtale mellom Norge og medlemsstatene i Det Europeiske Kull- og Stålfellesskap* [Concerning the ratification of the Treaty between Norway and the European Economic Community and the Treaty between Norway and the member states of the European Coal and Steel Community].

Avtaler mellom Norge og De Europeiske Fellesskap. [Agreements between Norway and the EEC]. Special appendix 1 to St. prp. nr. 126 for 1972-73.

Uttalelser vedrørende Norges avtaler med De Europeiske Fellesskap. [Statements concerning Norway's agreements with the EEC]. Special appendix 2 to St. prp. nr. 126 for 1972-73.

Traktat om opprettelse av organisasjonen for nordisk økonomisk samarbeid [Treaty concerning establishment of an organization for Nordic cooperation]. No date.

Other government documents:

Angerman, Havard, *The Fishing Industry in Norway.* Oslo, Royal Ministry of Foreign Affairs, Press Dept., 1971.

312

Ekeland, Sigurd, *Norway in Europe: An economic Survey*. Oslo, Royal Ministry of Foreign Affairs, 1970.

Royal Norwegian Ministry of Finance, *The National Budget of Norway*, (an English summary), annual.

Norges Offisielle Statistikk. *Folke-Avstemningen Om Ef* [The Advisory Referendum On Norway's Accession to the EEC].
Vol I - 1972
Vol II - 1973
Oslo, Central Bureau of Statistics.

Central Bureau of Statistics, *Norges Økonomi etter krigen*: The Norwegian post-war economy. *Samfunnsøkonomiske studier*, Vol 12, 1965.

Central Bureau of Statistics, *Foreign Ownership in Norwegian Enterprises* (by Arthur Stonehill). *Samfunnsøkonomiske studier*, No. 13, 1965.

Central Bureau of Statistics, *Langstidslinjer i Norsk økonomi 1865-1966: Trends in Norwegian economy 1865-1960*. *Samfunnsøkonomiske studier*, No. 16, 1966.

Central Bureau of Statistics, *To Artikler om Norsk Industri -Two Articles on Norwegian Manufacturing Industries*: Bela Balassa, "Industrial Development in an Open Economy: the Case of Norway"; and Odd Ankrust, "Industriens plass i det økonomiske totalbilde" [The role of manufacturing industry in the Norwegian economy]. *Artikler fra Statistisk Sentralbyrå*, Nr. 30, 1969.

Norges Offisielle Statistikk, *Økonomisk Utsyn over Året*; [Economic survey over the year --], annual.

Utenriksdepartementet. *Norge og E.F. Sammendrag av Stortingsmelding nr. 90, 1970-71*. [Norway and the EEC. Resume of Report to Parliament No. 90 for 1970-71].

Royal Ministry of Foreign Affairs, *Norway's National Report to the United Nations Conference on the Human Environment*. Oslo, 1972.

Utenriksdepartementet, *De Europeiske Fellesskap* [The European Communities] 15 pamphlets publicizing different aspects of the EEC. Oslo, 1971-72.

Utenriksdepartementet, Markedsuvalget [The Market Commission] *Rapport om det europeiske fellesskap* [Report on the European Communities]
Vol I   Feb   1967
    II   June   1967
    III April   1968
    IV   June   1969
    V   April   1970
    VI   April   1971
    VII May   1972.

B. Books and Articles

Alstad, Bjørn (ed), *Norske meninger* [Norwegian public opinion].
Vol I: *Norge, nordmenn og verden* [Norway, Norwegians, and the world].
Vol 2: *Politikk og samfunn* [Politics and society].
Vol 3: *Velferds-samfunnet* [The Welfare society]. Oslo, 1969.

Angell, Valter and Johan Jørgen Holst (ed), *EF - Norges vei?* [The EEC - Norway's destiny?]. Oslo, 1972.

Arnstad, Per M. (ed) *Foran Folke-avstemningen.* Fakta og vurderinger om Norge og EF [Before the referendum. Facts and evaluations about Norway and the EEC]. 1972.

Berg, Arthur (ed), *Nei til EEC* [No to the EEC]. Oslo, 1971.

Burgess, Philip M., *Elite images and foreign policy outcomes: a study of Norway.* Columbus, 1967.

Bøstrup, Bjørn A., *The Foreign Policy of Norway.* Royal Ministry of Foreign Affairs, Oslo, 1968.

Dorfman, Herbert, *Labour Relations in Norway.* The Norwegian Joint Committee on Internation Social Policy, in collaboration with the Office of Cultural Relations, Ministry of Foreign Affairs, Oslo, 1966.

Eckstein, Harry, *Division and cohesion in democracy: a study of Norway.* Princeton, N.J., 1966.

Eikestøl, Oddbjørn (ed), *Vil Norge overleve i EEC?* [Will Norway survive in the EEC?]. Oslo, 1971.

Folkebevegelsen mot norsk medlemskap i Fellesmarkedet [The People's Movement against Membership in the Common Market], Folkebevegelsens melding om Norges forhold til De Europeiske Fellesskap (EF). [The People's Movements White Paper on Norway's position in the European Communities (EEC)]. Oslo, 1972.

Frydenlund, Knut, *Norsk utenrikspolitikk i etterkrigstidens internasjonale samarbeid* [Norwegian foreign policy and postwar international cooperation]. Oslo, 1966.

Gleditsch, Nils and Sverre Lodgaard, *Krigsstaten Norge* [The war state Norway]. Oslo, 1970.

Greve, Tim, *Norway and NATO.* Oslo, 1959.

Gundersen, Fridtjof Frank, *EEC-handbøker* [EEC-handbooks].
Vol 1 *Romatraktatens virkefelt* [The operational field of the Rome treaty].
Vol 2 *Rettslig og økonomisk system* [The legal and economic system]. Oslo, 1971.

Holst, Johan Jørgen, *Nordflanken i europeisk sikkerhetspolitikk* [The northern flank in European security policy]. Oslo, 1972.

Holst, Johan Jørgen and John Sanness, *Huvorfor JA til EF* [Why "yes" to the EEC]. JA til EF -aksjonen [Yes to the EEC Movement], Oslo, 1972.

Holst, Johan Jørgen and Svein Otto Løvås, *Norge og EF: Utfordringer satt i perspektiv* [Norway and the EEC: The challenges in perspective]. Europabevegelsen i Norge [The Europe Movement in Norway], Oslo, 1973.

Hveem, Helge, *International Relations and World Images: A Study of Norwegian Foreign Policy Elites.* Oslo, 1972.

Høivik, Susan (ed), *10 inlegg om EEC* [10 contributions about the EEC]. Oslo, 1971.

Høivik, Susan and Sverre Lodgaard (eds), *6 nye innlegg om EF* [6 new contributions about the EEC]. Oslo, 1972.

Lange, Halvard M., *Norsk utenrikspolitikk siden 1945* [Norwegian foreign policy since 1945]. Oslo, 1952.

Lange, Halvard M., *Norges vei til NATO* [Norway's road to NATO]. Oslo, 1966.

Løchen, Einar, *Norway in European and Atlantic Cooperation*. Oslo, 1964.

Løchen, Einar, *Felles-markedet og Norge* [The Common Market and Norway]. Oslo, 1971.

Norden-Norge -EF. Supplement to *Internasjonal Politikk*, 1972: 4B.

Norges Industriforbund [Federation of Norwegian Industries], *Industrien, Norges største naering* [Industry, Norway's greatest support]. Oslo, 1970.

Norges utviklingshjelp - principper og retningslinjer [Norway's developmental assistance -- principles and directions]. Specially issued by the Directorate for Development, Oslo, 1972.

La Norvège et le Marché Commun, Revue de *Marché Commun*, No. 150, Jan. 1972.

Ørvik, Nils, *Europe's Northern Cap and the Soviet Union*. Cambridge, Mass., 1963.

Ørvik, Nils, *Trends in Norwegian Foreign Policy*. Oslo, 1962.

Ørvik, Nils (ed), *Departmental Decision Making*. Oslo, 1972.

Ørvik, Nils (ed), *Fears and Expectations: Norwegian Attitudes toward European Integration*. Oslo, 1972.

Siesby, Erik and Johan Wilhjelm (eds), *EF og Kapitalen*, Kapital liberalisering og økonomisk dominans [The EEC and capital. Capital liberalization and economic domination]. Albertslund, 1972.

Skodvin, Magne, *Norden eller NATO?* [The Nordic area or NATO?]. Oslo, 1971.

Skogan, John Kristen, "Sikkerhetssituasjonen i Nord-Europa" [The security situation in northern Europe], *Internasjonal Politikk*, 1971: 2-3.

Storing, James A., *Norwegian Democracy*. Boston, Mass., 1963.

Udgaard, Nils Morten, *Great power politics and Norwegian foreign policy*. Oslo, 1973.

Ulstein, Egil, *Nordic Security*. Adelphi Papers, No. 81. International Institute for Strategic Studies, London, 1971.

5. SWEDEN

A. Government Publications

Den Framtida jordbrukspolitiken [The future agricultural policy]. 1960 Commission on Agriculture report. SOU 1966: 30-31.

Ministry of Finance, *The Swedish Budget.* English summary, annual.

Finansdepartementet [Ministry of Finance], *Svensk ekonomi 1960-1965* [The Swedish economy 1960-65]. Report by the Secretariat of Economic Planning. SOU 1962:10.

Svensk Ekonomi 1966-1970 med utblick mot 1980. [The Swedish Economy 1966-1970 with a view to 1980]. Report by the Secretariat for Economic Planning. SOU 1966:1.

Ministry of Finance, Secretariat for Economic Planning, *The Swedish Economy, 1971-1975.* Stockholm, 1971.

Åberg, C.J., *Plan och Prognos.* En studie av de Svenska Långtidsutredningarnas metodik [Plans and Prognoses. Study of the methods used by Swedish commissions studying long term planning]. Appendix 9 to the 1970 Long Term Planning Commission. SOU 1971:70.

Publications relating to foreign economic cooperation etc.:

Handelsdepartementet, *Aktuellt i Handelspolitiken,* monthly.

Kungl. Maj:ts propostition 1960:25 till riksdagen angående godkännande av Sveriges anslutning till konventionen angående upprättandet av Europeiska frihandels - samanslutningen, mm: [Government bill 1960:25 concerning ratification of Sweden's accession to the convention of the European Free Trade Association, etc.,]. Stockholm, 1960.

Svensk industri och europamaknaden [Swedish industry and the European market]. Overview of different studies and aspects by various industry groups, compiled by the Swedish Federation of Industry and the Board of Trade. Stockholm, 1962.

Europeiska ekonomiska gemenskapen [European Economic Communities]. Volumes I-VII. Stockholm 1962-1970.

Svensk utrikeshandel och den europeiska integrationen [Swedish foreign trade and European integration]. Stockholm, 1963.

Utevecklingen av den svenska exporten på EEC - marknaden [The Development of Swedish exports in the EEC market]. Stockholm, 1967.

Sverige och EEC. Romfördraget ur svensk synvikel [Sweden and the EEC. The Rome Treaty from a Swedish viewpoint]. Stockholm, 1968.

Industriella utvecklings-tendenser i Europa [Tendencies of industrial development in Europe]. Stockholm, 1970.

Davignon-rapporten; Werner-rapporten (Davignon report; Werner report). Stockholm, 1970.

EEC:s handelspolitik [The trade policy of the EEC]. Stockholm, 1971.

Sveriges utrikeshandel under 1960-talet [Sweden's foreign trade during the 1960's]. Stockholm, 1971.

Inför Sveriges EEC Förhandlingar-Fakta och övervagünden [Before Sweden's EEC negotiations - facts and considerations]. Stockholm, 1971.

Ekström, J.A., Larsson, O., Sundström, and L. Thalin, *Sverige och EEC* [Sweden and the EEC]. Ministry of Commerce, Stockholm, 1971.

316

En Ekonomisk och Monetär Union [An economic and monetary union]. Stockholm, 1972.

Sveriges avtal med EEC och CECA [Sweden's treaty with the EEC and the CECA]. Stockholm, 1972.

Publications of the Ministry of Foreign Affairs:

Utrikesdepartementet [Ministry for Foreign Affairs]. *Utrikesfrågor, Offentliga document mm. rörande viktigare svenska utrikespolitiska frågor* (also published in English as *Documents on Swedish Foreign Policy*), 1950:51, 1952 et seq., annual.

Royal Ministry for Foreign Affairs, *Sweden in Europe, 1971*. Swedish Institute, 1971.

[SOU: Statens Offentliga Utredningar- Official State Reports].

B. Books, pamphlets and articles

Abrahamsen, S., *Sweden's Foreign Policy*. Washington, 1957.

Andrén, N., *Modern Swedish Government*. Stockholm, 1961.

Andrén, N. and Å. Landqvist, *Svensk utrikespolitik efter 1945* [Swedish foreign policy after 1945]. Stockholm, 1965.

Andrén, N., *Power-Balance and Non-aligment*. Uppsala, 1967.

Andrén, N., *National Security and International Solidarity: Sweden in the Sixties*. Uppsala, 1967.

Andrén, N., "In Search of Security", *Cooperation and Conflict*, 1968:4.

Andrén, N., "Neutralität - aktiver? Schweden", *Schweizer Monatshefte*, 49, 1969:1.

Andrén, N., *Den total säkerhetspolitiken* [Total security policy]. Ystad, 1971; revised ed. Stockholm, 1972.

Back, Pär-Erik, *Det svenska partiväsendet* [The Swedish party system]. Stockholm, 1967.

Bergquist, M., *Sverige och EEC* [Sweden and the EEC]. Stockholm, 1970.

Bergquist, M., "Sweden and the European Economic Community", *Cooperation and Conflict*, 1969:1.

Bergström, V., and O. Svenning, *Fackföreningsrörelsen och EEC* [The trades union movement and the EEC]. Stockholm, 1971.

Birnbaum K.E., "The Formation of Swedish Foreign Policy: Some points of departure for an inquiry", *Cooperation and Conflict* 1965:1.

Björkman, Bo, *Sverige och Sossarna* [Sweden and the Social Democrats]. Askill and Karnekull, 1973.

Board, Joseph B. Jr., *The Government and Politics of Sweden*. Boston, Mass., 1970.

Boman, R., *Nedrustningsfrågor och Sveriges framtida säkerhet* [The question of disarmament and Sweden's future security]. Södertalje, 1970.

Braunerhielm, E., *Sverige och den gemensamma marknaden* [Sweden and the Common Market]. Stockholm, 1962.

Brodin, K., "The Undén Proposal", *Cooperation and Conflict*, 1966:2.

Brodin K., K. Goldmann and C. Lange, "The Policy of Neutrality: Official Doctrines of Finland and Sweden", *Cooperation and Conflict*, 1968:1.

Danckwardt, J.-C., and S. Hellman, *Svensk säkerhetspolitik, Förutsättningar och inriktningar* [Swedish security policy, conditions and directions]. Stockholm, 1966.

Eek, H., *Sveriges utrikespolitik och FN som internationell organisation* [Sweden's foreign policy and the UN as an international organization]. Stockholm, 1955.

Ekström, T., G. Myrdal, and R. Pålsson, *Vi och Västeuropa* [We and West Europe]. Stockholm, 1962.

Ekström, T., G. Myrdal and R. Pålsson, *Vi och Västeuropa: Andra ronden* [We and West Europe: the second round]. Stockholm, 1971.

Engman, I., *Säkerhets- och försvarspolitikens grunder* [The foundations of security and defence policy]. *Försvar i nutid*, 1972:1.

Erlander, T., *Sveriges utrikespolitik* [The foreign policy of Sweden]. Stockholm, 1959.

Fahlen, Olle, *Företagstillväxt och Internationalisering* [The growth of private enterprise and internationalization]. Sveriges Industriförbund, Stockholm, 1972.

Fox, A.B., "Sweden: armed neutral", in A.B. Fox, *The Power of Small States*, Diplomacy in WW II. Chicago, 1959.

Goldmann, K., "An 'Isolated' attack against Sweden and its world political preconditions", *Cooperation and Conflict*, 1965:2.

Goldmann, K. and C. Lange, "A Nordic Defence Alliance 1949-1965-197?", *Cooperation and Conflict*, 1966:1.

Grape, L. and B.-C.. Ysander, *Säkerhetspolitik och försvarsplanering* [Security policy and defence planning]. Stockholm, 1967.

Heckscher, G., *The Role of Small Nations*. London, 1966.

Håstad E., *Den svenska utrikesdebatten om FN och alliansfriket* [The Swedish foreign policy debate on the UN and non-alignment]. Stockholm, 1955.

Iveroth, Axel, *om EEC-läget: Vart Tog Sverige Vägen?* [About the EEC situation: What happened to Sweden?]. Sveriges Industriförbund, Stockholm, 1971.

Landergren, N., *Krigsmaktens perspektiv- och programplaner* [The perspective and programme plans of the armed forces]. *Försvar i nutid*, 1971:6.

Levin, O. (ed), *Metallindustrin och europamarknaden* [The metals industry and the European market]. Stockholm, 1959.

Lindbeck, Assar, *Svensk ekonomisk politik* [Swedish economic policy]. Stockholm, 1971.

318

Lundberg, S., *Trovärdigt ekonomiskt försvar i en integrerad väld?* [Is there a credible economic defence in an integrated world?]. *Kungl. Krigsvetenskapsakademiens Handlingar och Tidskrift,* 176, 1972:5.

Moberg, E. "The effect of security measures: a discussion related to Sweden's security policy", *Cooperation and Conflict,* 1967:2.

Odhner, C.-E., *Sverige i Europa* [Sweden in Europe]. Stockholm, 1962.

Paues, Wilhelm, *Företaget och EEC-Avtalet* [Private enterprise and the EEC agreement]. Falun, 1972.

Paues, Wilhelm, *Varför Umeåstudenterna lurades säga Nej til EEC.* En granskning av studentkårens skrift. [Why the students at Umeå were enticed to say no to the EEC. An overview of the student press]. Sveriges Industribörbund, Stockholm, n.d.

Paues, Wilhelm, *EG och Företaget* [The EEC and private enterprise]. Stockholm, 1973.

De Politiska partiernas program [The party programmes of the political parties]. Bokförlaget Prisma, Stockholm, 1968.

Samuelsson, H.-F., *Foreign Direct Investment in Sweden 1965-1970.* Industriens Utredningsinstitut, Stockholm 1973.

SIFO/SAFO skriftserie [Swedish Institute for Opinion Research Publications Series],
Nr. 1 1970 - *Structural Base of Swedish Politics.*
Nr. 1 1971 - *On the Management of Expectations in the Welfare State: Durkheim's Theory of Anomie Revisited.*

Swedish Banks Association and Federation of Swedish Industries, *Sweden Partner in Europe.* Stockholm, n.d.

Ørvik, N. and N. Andrén, "Dialog om svensk säkerhet" [Dialogue about Swedish security], *Strategisk bulletin,* 1970:3-4.

Prawitz, J., "A nuclear doctrine for Sweden", *Cooperation and Conflict,* 1968:3.

Sweden and the United Nations. New York, 1956.

Tingsten, H., "Issues in Swedish Foreign Policy", *Foreign Affairs 37,* 1959.

Undén, O., *Tankar om utrikespolitik* [Thoughts about foreign policy]. Stockholm, 1963.

INDEX OF PERSONS

SUBJECT INDEX